Lacanian Ethics and the Assumption of Subjectivity

Lacanian Ethics and the Assumption of Subjectivity

Calum Neill
Edinburgh Napier University, Scotland

palgrave
macmillan

First published 2011 by
PALGRAVE MACMILLAN

Palgrave Macmillan in the UK is an imprint of Macmillan Publishers Limited, registered in England, company number 785998, of Houndmills, Basingstoke, Hampshire RG21 6XS.

Palgrave Macmillan in the US is a division of St Martin's Press LLC, 175 Fifth Avenue, New York, NY 10010.

Palgrave Macmillan is the global academic imprint of the above companies and has companies and representatives throughout the world.

Palgrave® and Macmillan® are registered trademarks in the United States, the United Kingdom, Europe and other countries

ISBN 978-0-230-29409-7   hardback

This book is printed on paper suitable for recycling and made from fully managed and sustained forest sources. Logging, pulping and manufacturing processes are expected to conform to the environmental regulations of the country of origin.

A catalogue record for this book is available from the British Library.

Library of Congress Cataloging-in-Publication Data

Neill, Calum, 1968–
    Lacanian ethics and the assumption of subjectivity / Calum Neill.
        p. cm.
    Includes bibliographical references (p.   ) and index.
    ISBN 978-0-230-29409-7 (alk. paper)
    1. Ethics–Psychological aspects. 2. Lacan, Jacques, 1901–1981.
    3. Subjectivity. 4. Desire. I. Title.
    BJ45.N38 2011
    171'.2–dc22   2011012072

Printed and bound in the United States of America

For Claire

Contents

List of Figures and Graphs

Figures

The Graph of Desire

Note: All graphs reproduced from *Écrits: A Selection* with kind permission from Routledge.

Acknowledgements

I would like to express my gratitude to all those who helped to make this project possible; to the late Antony Easthope who introduced me to Lacan and set me on this path; to Ian Parker for his friendship, generosity, belief and inspiration; to Derek Hook, for his inimitable friendship, for long walks and chats over wine, dissecting Lacan and what it might all mean; to Lisa Baraitser and Stephen Frosh for their friendship and the joy and challenge of shared reading; to Carol Owens for friendship, support and an uncanny ability to say it as it is; to Dany Nobus for inestimable support; to Yannis Stavrakakis for friendship and support; to Joanna Hodge for valuable time and support; to my family for being there unquestioningly; to all my colleagues, past and present, especially Hilary Tait for support beyond the call of duty; to all my students who pushed me to be clearer and questioned my thinking; and to Miles Davis who unknowingly provided the soundtrack to much of the writing of this book. Finally, but primarily, to Claire who encouraged and inspired in immeasurable and ineffable ways.

Earlier versions of four chapters have appeared as journal articles. An earlier version of Chapter 3 appears as Neill, C. (2006) 'Choang-tsu's Butterfly: Objects and the Subjective Function of Fantasy', *Objects: Material, Psychic, Aesthetic*, a special issue of *Gramma: Journal of Theory and Criticism*, Vol. 14. An earlier version of Chapter 6 appeared as Neill, C. (2005) 'The Locus of Judgment in Lacan's Ethics', *The Journal of Lacanian Studies*, Vol. 3, No. 1. An earlier version of Chapter 11 appeared as Neill, C. (2006) 'An Idiotic Act: On the Non-example of Antigone', *The Letter*, Issue 34. An earlier version of Chapter 12 appeared as Neill, C. (2010) 'Eating the Book: On the Centrality of Sublimation and Knowledge in Lacan's Ethics', *Journal of the Centre for Freudian Analysis and Research*, Issue No. 20. I am grateful to the editors and publishers for allowing these to be used here.

Introduction – A Brief History of Ethics

The question of ethics is one which persists. On a personal level, on a social, on a global level, what is it we *should* do? And why? Why should we adopt this or that stance, this or that perspective on what is right and what is wrong? How can we know the good that we would wish? If there is available some clear cut notion of the good then this would surely be the good for all and would surely be available to us all. Such a conception of a sovereign good, a singular good above all other instances of or interpretations of good in particular circumstances, is tempting insofar as it promises to settle questions of ethics or at least suggests that there might be a possibility of them being settled. Such a notion, the persistence of some higher moral authority which would somehow guarantee any particular human conception of morality, is perhaps best exemplified in Plato's notion of the good (*to agathon*) which 'persists' beyond being (*epekeina tēs ousias*).

For Plato, the question of the good is already a question of epistemology. Rather, however, than it being a question of how we might know the good which would preside over our (potentially) moral actions and judgements, it is the good itself which would be the condition of all knowledge. In Book 6 of the *Republic*, Plato, through the character of Socrates, explains this by means of an analogy with the sun. Just as the sun, in Plato's understanding, is the source of all seeing and thus the condition of possibility of the realm of the visible, the good is the source of all knowing and thus the condition of possibility of all knowledge.

So what gives truth to the things known and the power to know to the knower is the form of the good. And though it is the cause of knowledge and truth it is also an object of knowledge. Both knowledge and truth are beautiful things, but the good is other and more beautiful than they. In the visible realm, light and sight are rightly considered sunlike, but it is wrong to think that they are the sun, so here it is right to think of knowledge and truth as goodlike but wrong to think that either of them is the good – for the good is yet more prized. ... Therefore, you should also say that not only do the objects of knowledge owe their being known to the good, but their being is also due to it, although the good is not being, but superior to it in rank and power.

(Plato, *Republic*: 182; para.509a)

The location of the good beyond being has the advantage of providing a consistent source for or ground upon which moral edicts and actions can be based. What renders an action or judgement right or just would be its resemblance to or 'participation' in the (Form of) the Good itself. What such a conception does not, and by definition cannot, answer is the question of how we might know this good by which we would judge all other instances of goods. Aristotle, following Plato himself, refutes this formulation on precisely this point through what has come to be known as the Third Man Argument (Aristotle, *Ethics*: 8–9). Put simply, if the good in any good action can be understood to be good due to its resemblance to the form of good, then the form of good would itself have to appeal to another, third good, in order itself to be understood as good ... and so on and on *ad infinitum*. Despite this argument against the general logic of the theory of forms, Aristotle retains a notion of the good as sovereign and necessary. For Aristotle, all pursuits necessarily have an end and this end would be the good of the pursuit in question. It is, for Aristotle, therefore logical to assert that there must be some ultimate good which would be the end of all other goods, despite the fact that we may not know this good in itself.

Every art and every investigation, and likewise every practical pursuit or undertaking, seems to aim at some good: hence it has been well said that the good is that at which all things aim. ... Now in cases where several such pursuits are subordinate to some single faculty ... in all these cases, I say, the ends of the master arts are things more to be desired than all those of the other arts subordinate to them; since the latter ends are only pursued for the sake of the former. ... If therefore among the ends at which our actions aim there be one which we wish for its own sake, while we wish the others only for the sake of this, and if we do not chose everything for the sake of something else (which would obviously result in a process *ad infinitum*, so that all desire would be futile and vain), it is clear that this one ultimate end must be the good, indeed the supreme good.

(Ibid.: 3)

Aristotle's view or supposition of the good is clearly based on a conception of nature and the cosmos as ordered and, somehow, already ethically motivated. Which is to say that the assumption of the good as telos, as the logical culmination of all other goods, rests upon the prior assumption that the universe is so ordered and would have such a good. Without such an assumption, there remains little reason for supposing an ultimate good which would be the end of all others. In Aristotle's own terms, there would remain little reason to assume that all desires were not in fact futile and vain. The ultimate end and only imposes as a necessity within a conception of a system of order which posits determinate ends to all processes.

The notion of a sovereign guarantor for our earthly conceptions of morality can clearly be found at work in the Abrahamic tradition too. Here the name of the good beyond being, the good which must exist as the end and guarantor of all earthly pursuits and knowledge, would be God. It is as such, to take one example, that Nietzsche characterises Christianity as 'Platonism for the "people"' (Nietzsche, 2001: 4). The *reductio ad infinitum* is halted, as it was for Plato and Aristotle, only now that which halts it becomes God, the *prima causa* of the universe (Aquinas, 1988: 30–1). The certainty which would ensure our knowledge is again posited beyond our knowledge itself. The ground of the good is posited in a beyond beyond question.

Enlightenment thinking seeks to displace this assumption of an otherworldly guarantor of certainty, seeking instead to found knowledge on rational premises. The quintessential example here would be that of Descartes. In his *Meditations on First Philosophy*, Descartes engages in a programme of systematic doubt with the aim of adducing that 'something certain' (Descartes, 1993: 17), even if it is 'just one thing, however slight, that is certain and unshaken' (Ibid.). Descartes' method entails bracketing all those things about which he cannot be absolutely certain. He rejects, however, the notion that the one thing of which he can be certain is that there is nothing of which he can be certain, insisting that the very fact that he is engaged in a search for something certain posits a certainty outside of this rejected, contradictory, conclusion. That is to say, he can at the very least be certain that there are thoughts occurring to him. Such thoughts, for Descartes, would be indicative of some agency or, at the very least, some receptacle. The thoughts which occur may be authored by some higher entity or may be authored by Descartes himself, but, either way, they would appear to indicate that he exists in order to be the receptacle of the thoughts in question.

Is there not some God, or by whatever name I might call him, who instils these very thoughts in me? But why would I think that, since I myself could perhaps be the author of these thoughts? Am I not then at least something? But I have already denied that I have any senses and any body. Still I hesitate; for what follows from this? Am I so tied to a body and to the senses that I cannot exist without them? But I have persuaded myself that there is absolutely nothing in the world: no sky, no earth, no minds, no bodies. Is it then the case that I too do not exist? But doubtless I did exist, if I persuaded myself of something. But there is some deceiver or other who is supremely powerful and supremely sly and who is always deliber-ately deceiving me. Then too there is no doubt that I exist, if he is deceiving me. And let him do his best at deception, he will never bring it about that I am nothing so long as I shall think that I am something. Thus, after everything has been most carefully weighed, it must finally be established that this pronouncement 'I am, I exist' is necessarily true every time I utter it or conceive it in my mind.

(Ibid.: 17–18)

From this initial certainty in his existence, at least at the moment of thought, Descartes proceeds to add mental states and perceptions.

But what then am I? A thing that thinks. What is that? A thing that doubts, understands, affirms, denies, wills, refuses, and that also imagines and senses.

(Ibid.: 20)

Even given that he may not be conscious, Descartes affirms that the reception of these thoughts is undeniable. Though this may not certify the existence of a world beyond thought, it does at the very least certify thought itself.

For although perhaps, as I supposed before, absolutely nothing that I had imagined is true, still the very power of imagining really does exist, and constitutes a part of my thought. Finally, it is the same 'I' who senses or who is cognizant of bodily things as if through the senses. For example, I now see a light, I hear a noise, I feel heat. These things are false, since I am asleep. Yet I certainly do seem to see, hear, and feel warmth. This cannot be false. Properly speaking, this is what in me is called 'sensing.' But this, precisely so taken, is nothing other than thinking.

(Ibid.)

Descartes proceeds to derive from this certainty of thought a whole series of claims he asserts as necessary, if not immediately self-evident. Certainty, then, spreads out from this initial singular certainty in thought to encompass such things as the necessary existence of his body, God, material things and the external world.

In this way, we might understand that modernity succeeds in shoring up the vacuum left in the wake of the dissipation of the certainty of ancient thought. One way of perceiving this movement would be in terms of the displacement of religion by science. Where once it was religion which provided the answers, now it is science. Certainty, in a sense, has a new messenger, a new voice piece, but remains no less certain for it. This is not, of course, to say that religion is entirely vanquished. As Descartes 'return' to and reliance on God in his third mediation would indicate, God is still very much assumed as the final guarantor of thought and knowledge. What the shift does do is at least bring into question the certainty of that final guarantor. Which would be to say that the centrality and certainty of God is, to an extent, displaced and reason assumes the mantle of the guarantor or provider of truth. The moment of doubt is passed over and a new authority is instituted.

The problem which ensues here for modern 'objectivity' and science is that it is still susceptible to the same critique that would be leveled against pre-modern religiosity or mysticism. While consistency may be seen to guarantee the 'correctness' or adequacy of manoeuvres within a particular system, that same consistency cannot be assumed to apply outwith the system in question. That is to say, while modern science may well provide certain scientific answers, it is still a limited discourse, one which cannot claim to provide solutions outside its own confines. Key among such limitations is the question of ethics. There is, quite simply, no science of ethics. For example, progress in the field of genetic research and technology may well provide the means to produce human clones. Within this field or discourse it is possible to argue or even prove what would constitute more effective and successful techniques of producing such clones. What the field itself cannot do, however, is provide any answer as to why or when this might be the right thing to do. The certainty science would claim pertains only to the limits of its field. Expand as this field might and, with this, its claims to explanation would no doubt expand too, it is of necessity defined by limits. It cannot encompass all. This is not to point to a particular weakness in science but rather to acknowledge that human knowledge is necessarily structurally limited. Where, then, does this leave the field of ethics? If certainty itself is problematic, if all knowledge is now accepted as limited in its scope, then what of knowledge of the good? If the certainty of the good is not something which can be known, whether through immutable forms, deities or science, is this to conclude that the good is simply unknowable, uncertain, malleable? That is to say, are ethics a question then of conformity and consensus, dependent on culture, era or fashion? Such a conclusion, if it does not render the field of ethics meaningless, at least reduces its import and specificity and effectively renders it a variant of law.

Immanuel Kant believed that the answer to this lies precisely in our understanding of rationality. In his *Critique of Pure Reason*, he posits the possibility of rational certainty, arguing that that which would guarantee our knowledge is not to be found either in something like a substantial entity beyond being nor in the coherence of the objects of our experience. Rather, he argues, it is necessary to reverse the suppositions of such a search for certainty and consider our experience of knowing itself. Through so doing, Kant arrives at the idea that it is our 'rules' of perception themselves which provide the *a priori* foundation for the possibility of knowledge.

> If intuition must conform to the constitution of the objects, I do not see how we could know anything of the latter *a priori*; but if the object (as object of the senses) must conform to the constitution of our faculty of intuition, I have no difficulty in conceiving such a possibility.
>
> (Kant, 1965: 23)

That is to say, the very possibility of our mental experience is conditioned by certain *a priori* rules. It is such rules which would give form to what would otherwise be but the formless matter of the senses. Only by uncovering these rules which consistently give form to our experience can we arrive at certain knowledge or knowledge of that which would guarantee certainty.

In terms of the good, Kant can be understood to have displaced the notion of a transcendental guarantor and 'replaced' it with what he terms the moral law; a rational principle available to all rational beings.

Where previous theories of morality or ethics had assumed the notion of
a substantial good from which principles of morality could be derived,
Kant argues instead that it is necessary to identify that law or principle to
which anyone would rationally submit and only then might we define
the good, as the object of the will, on the basis of such an antecedent law.
That is to say, for Kant, it is 'the moral law that first determines and
makes possible the concept of the good, insofar as it deserves this name
absolutely' (Kant, 1997: 55). To do otherwise would be to 'assume as
already decided the foremost question to be decided' (Ibid.). To posit a
concept of the good as the ultimate basis for moral principles would be,
that is, to defeat in advance the possibility of deriving moral precepts
at all, insofar as it would afford no insight into how one might apply
the correlation between the ultimate good and the objects of the will
in experience. In this sense, the traditional conception of the good as the
ultimate guarantor of morality leaves open the question of what determines the good as good in the first place and effectively renders the
rational will subject to an external authority. In so doing, such a conception cannot account for the necessity of moral requirements. It is
simply a case of the good *is*, therefore we *must*.

It is important to understand then that for Kant the moral law is not
something which would be given as such. Clearly, were it so, then it
would be subject to the same critique he levels at the traditional
assumption of a substantive good. Rather, the moral law is necessary
insofar as our possibility of cognising the world of experience requires
a frame of systematicity. By showing that, rather than being derived
from an antecedent conception of the good, moral precepts can and
indeed must logically precede any determinate conception of the good
as ultimate object, Kant can be understood to have provided a ground
for morality which neither presupposes what the good must be nor
reduces morality to a force to which one would be subject absolutely,
without choice, which would be to render morality little more than the
slavish pursuit of inclination.

> Autonomy of the will is the sole principle of all moral laws and of
> duties in keeping with them; heteronomy of choice, on the other
> hand, not only does not ground any obligation at all but is instead
> opposed to the principle of obligation and to the morality of the
> will.
>
> (Ibid.: 30)

Thus the moral law which would serve as the basis of a rational morality must be purely formal, in that it is not subsequent to any prior

object, and non-pathological, in that it is not the mere slavish pursuit of desire. Such a fundamental law is formulated by Kant as the categorical imperative;

> So act that the maxim of your will could always hold at the same time as a principle in a giving of universal law.
>
> (Ibid: 28)

Importantly for Kant, the necessity of freedom with regard to the moral law means that it is not sufficient that one's actions coincide with the moral law but, rather, one would, in order to act morally, have to act such that one acts in accordance with the moral law purely because it is one's duty to do so. Adherence to the law for reason other than duty would render the law non-formal and thus eradicate its very founding principle;

> It is of great importance in all moral appraisals to attend with the utmost exactness to the subjective principle of all maxims, so that all the morality of actions is placed in their necessity *from duty* and from respect for the moral law, not from love and liking for what the actions are to produce.
>
> (Ibid.: 70)

That is to say, for Kant, those actions which happen to be in conformity with what the moral law prescribes, but are undertaken for pathological or personal reasons and not out of respect for the moral law and reverence for one's duty, would not in fact be moral. Morality is not a matter simply of conforming, but is crucially a matter of motivation. The form of the moral law demands that one freely choose it and that one freely choose it purely in virtue of its being the moral law. In this sense it is not enough, to use one of Kant's well known examples, to tell the truth out of fear of being caught lying, nor because one genuinely wants one's interlocutor to know the truth, nor because one has been brought up not to lie. Rather, one must tell the truth exclusively because it is one's duty to tell the truth. The difference here between telling the truth because one has been so raised and telling the truth because one recognises it as one's duty is crucial. In the first there is no choice as such. One is simply conditioned to respond in this way. In order for one's truth telling to be understood as a proper moral action, one must make the choice and one must make the choice in a certain way for no reason other than it is one's duty to so choose.

This also then means that one ought not to tell the truth because of any specific outcome. Consequences, for Kant are not relevant to the moral law. One has a duty to tell the moral law despite the consequences. We might ask of Kant's theory whether it is in fact ever possible to sufficiently expunge our pathological inclinations such that we might become the purely rational beings that his ethics requires. Kant's own answer to this is that we cannot – at least not here, in this world – which, importantly, is to characterise Kantian ethics, in its Earthly variant, as not tethered to the possible. Impossibility is not an excuse for non-adherence. To become the purely rational being required of Kantian ethics, that is, to attain the highest good which would be the pure rationality of moral duty, would require an infinite progression or moral refinement and would thus only be possible beyond this world. This necessitates that Kant postulate the existence of an immortal soul and, conjoined with this, God, as that which would have attained pure rational morality. This is not to say that God would exist as a pure given, a prior ground for the rational moral law. It is rather that God arises as a pure and necessary concept, one which would be, logically, subordinate to the pure rationality of the highest good itself. God here is subordinate to the rational moral law in the sense that, were the law derived from a pre-given conception of God, we would have returned to the assumption of the sovereign good and morality would have become once again a matter of pure faith. That is to say, there would still be lacking the reason for assuming God as morally perfect. As Kant argues in his earlier *Grounding for the Metaphysics of Morals*;

> every example of morality presented to me must itself first be judged according to principles of morality in order to see whether it is fit to serve as an original example, i.e., as a model. But in no way can it authoritatively furnish the concept of morality. Even the Holy One of the gospel must be first compared with our ideal of moral perfection before he is recognized as such.
>
> (Kant, 1993: 20–1)

If pathological motives are expunged from any commitment to the moral law, if, that is, the moral law must be adhered to for reason of pure duty, then this still leaves the question as to what the nature of the will to duty itself would be? Kant's initial answer to this question is that this is 'for human reason an insoluble problem' (Kant, 1997: 62). He does, however, go on to argue that although it cannot be shown *how* such a situation is possible, it can be shown *that* it is possible. That is to say, we do feel respect for the moral law, despite the fact that we cannot rationally account for the origin of such a 'feeling'. Kant's argument here is that pathological motives, such as self-love or self-conceit, are experienced as lesser with regard to the 'weightiness of the moral law' (Ibid.: 65). That is, it is the effective removal of pathological motives which allows the incentive to duty towards the moral law to rise as an *a priori* non-pathological incentive. Kant here appeals to the image of a scale wherein it is the removal of pathological motives from one side which causes the scale to rise in favour of the moral law on the other. Such an image conveys a notion of the moral law as always already there. What it necessarily fails to account for, though, is what it would be that would allow us to know this moral law as good. Effectively Kant has argued that we feel inclined towards the moral law because we are subject to a certain feeling, a moral feeling, when we consider our actions. This peculiar feeling to which we are subject might be understood as consubstantial with what we would more commonly term conscience, that sense or voice inside which allows us to know what is right. What, following Freud, we would now term the superego.

Undoubtedly, Kant has taken us a significant distance from the sovereign good of the Greeks and the Abrahamics, but he appears to leave us here with two intertwined problems. Firstly, in arguing that the moral law is purely formal, Kant might be understood to have, in a sense, argued himself into a corner. A purely formal moral law whose only condition is that it be followed for reasons of duty alone, with no pathological or personal weight attached, is a moral law without content which would then be to say that it is one in which, formally speaking, good and evil would be indistinguishable. That is to say, were one to adopt a Sadean stance and assume as one's duty the pursuance of diabolical evil, bracketing pathological inclinations or squeamishness, how would this be any different from someone following the moral law for reasons of pure duty. If there is no content and only duty, then the direction and outcome of one's duty must remain irrelevant. The very terms good and evil here become rather meaningless. There is nothing to say they are not the same without slipping some appeal to an innate morality back in on another level. Such, arguably, is Kant's solution of the idea that we somehow know the moral law. This solution appears to rely on a subjective experience which appears rather similar to guilt, and not only might we understand guilt as indicative of pathology but, moreover, there remains the question of from where this feeling arises, what conditions it? In order to distinguish one dutiful following of the inner experience of the moral law, which coincides with what we might conventionally term evil, from another, which we would conventionally term good, we would need to already have a notion of good and evil. We would need, that is, to appeal to some other measure. It is perhaps useful to introduce a terminological distinction here. On the one hand we have firm notions of what constitutes right or wrong, ideas of a substantial and knowable good, particular edicts or prescriptions, often taking the form of traditions and often inscribed – in the Judeo-Christian tradition, quite literally – in stone. For the sake of clarity, we will term this morality. This leaves the term ethics to describe that which exceeds or cannot be reduced to any particular conception of the good, any code, prescription or tradition.

In rejecting the notion of what we are here terming morality as ultimately unfounded, as reducible to tradition or faith, Kant can be understood to have ushered in and posited the core ethical problem of modernity. Without enslavement to an exterior or prior morality, a morality which is ultimately posited as abstract from human will, what is there to stop ethics being reduced to subjective whim? The argument made in the following pages is that the answer lies in how we conceive of who or what we are. That is to say that the answer lies in our conception of subjectivity, that thinking subjectivity and thinking ethics become inseparably entwined. Ethics itself entails an assumption of subjectivity. Assuming a subjective position is already an ethical venture. Such an understanding of ethical subjectivity is provided in the work of Jacques Lacan.

Part I
The Subject

1
Lacan's Return to Descartes

Modern conceptions of ethics tend to suggest a conception of a subject. Without a sense of that which would enact what might be considered to be ethical and without a conception of that towards or for which a particular action might be considered ethical, it is difficult to see what meaning would be left in the term other than as an abstract morality. If events are understood such that they simply occur or if events affect no one, then we would not generally now consider them in ethical terms. Commonplace conceptions of ethics would tend assume something like a self-adequate, essential and substantial agent, an agent certain of its own self and its own thoughts, such as the Cartesian *cogito*, the subject which can be certain of its existence because of the fact of its thinking. Such a conception of the subject can be understood to be flawed for a number of reasons. Focusing on the Cartesian subject in particular, there appears here to be a gap which insists between the 'I' of the 'I think' and the 'I' of the 'I am' which follows as a logical conclusion from the 'I think'. That is to say, either these two 'I's are not the same thing or the second is already assumed in the positing of the first. 'I think' already entails the subject 'I' and, thus, the conclusion 'I am' is strictly superfluous. Descartes has not really proved or substantiated anything beyond what he had already pre-supposed. On the basis of such criticism, it might appear necessary, or, at least, valid, to dismiss Descartes and his notion of subjectivity. Given, however, the impact Descartes' thought has had on the manner in which we do consider subjectivity, it might seem somewhat hasty to dismiss it out of hand. As Lacan puts it;

> The type of people that we shall define, using a conventional notation, as *dentists* are very confident about the order of the universe because they think that Mr Descartes made manifest the laws and procedures of limpid reason in the *Discourse on Method*. His *I think,*

therefore, I am, so essential to the new subjectivity, is not as simple, however, as it would appear to these dentists, and some even think they detect in it a pure and simple sleight of hand. If it is in fact true that consciousness is transparent to itself, and grasps itself as such, it does seem that the *I* is not on that account transparent to it. It is not given to it as different from an object. The apprehension of an object by consciousness does not by the same token reveal to it its properties. The same is true for the *I.*

(Lacan, 1988b: 6)

Utilising Descartes' errors, in such a manner that he can at one and the same time oppose his direction while maintaining the often hidden kernel of his findings, Lacan situates the subject (and 'cogito') as *of* the unconscious. For Lacan the subject is always (being) constituted in relation to the Other and, in particular, in relation to the desire of/for the Other.

Given the non-definitional character of Lacan's theorising of the subject, it may make some sense to begin by saying what the subject is not. By indicating a subject of the unconscious, Lacan clearly rejects the notion that the subject is in any way commensurate with the conscious individual. The traditional notion of the conscious, atomised individual is generally run seamlessly into a notion of self-governing agency. In delimiting the subject of doubt as a certainty in 'I', Descartes can be understood to have glided over this crucial issue of agency. The 'I' which is certainly thinking insofar as it is doubting is posited as the master of its own perception. What is productive in Lacan's reading of Descartes is that, rather than dismiss *The Meditations* on the grounds that they simply occlude the complexities of subjectivity in favour of positing that which they set out to discover, Lacan fathoms in Descartes' text an indication of something beyond the contained subject. When Descartes asserts his desire for certainty, Lacan reads not only the 'rational' and empirical surface or aim of Descartes' text but also, and especially, the very desire attested to there.

What is Descartes looking for? He is looking for certainty. *I have,* he says, *an extreme desire to learn to distinguish the true from the false* – note the word *desire* – *in order to see clearly* – in what? – *in my actions, and to walk with assurance in this life.*

(Lacan, 1977b: 222)

In placing all certainty in doubt and yet maintaining unquestioningly the desire for certainty, Descartes not only introduces the modern concept of the subject but does so at the expense of noticing the subject *behind* the modern concept of the subject. Put simply, the subject of the unconscious is at work all along in *The Meditations* and is consequently overlooked. Lacan's reading of Descartes not only indicates the unconscious subject but indicates its primacy. The subject of the unconscious is evident but unacknowledged in Descartes. What Lacan reads into Descartes' *Meditations* is the unwitting discovery of the unconscious primacy of subjectivity and consequently – given this primacy is read through a secondary manifestation – the intractable split in the subject. In announcing the 'I' as both premise – *I think* or *I doubt* – and conclusion – *therefore I am* – Descartes indicates a significant doubling, one that Lacan will come to theorise under the terms *énoncé* and *énonciation.*

Lacan characterises the Cartesian cogito as *homunculus*, or 'little man', as a positing of something inside which retains a certain mastery. The image of the matryoshka doll is perhaps useful here in picturing Lacan's critique. In the matryoshka, each doll contains within itself another, smaller, but structurally identical, doll. The homunculus Lacan suggests in Descartes' theory works in the same way. If the cogito is but a little man within each individual, or within Descartes himself (as that is the example we have to go on), then the cogito has *proved* or adduced nothing. If the certainty of our existence is in a homunculus within, then the whole process of adducing certainty simply has to begin again – a reduction *ad infinitum.*

Against this homunculus, Lacan posits the barred subject; $. The bar here indicates something of the relation of the subject to language. Where the Cartesian *cogito* is brought about in ignorance of the functioning of language in its very formulation ('words often impede me', as Descartes himself declares (1993: 8)), Lacan's subject is first and foremost the subject of language. In the *cogito,* when Descartes believes he has uncovered the certainty of his own existence through the pursuance of doubt to its, for him, logical extreme, what he has actually done is to represent 'himself' to 'himself' or, phrased otherwise, he imagines himself but such imagining can only come about on the basis of him *symbolising* himself. Lacan illustrates this point by invoking the notch an imaginary primitive man might have made to indicate his kill in the hunt. This signifying appears to begin, then, with a pragmatic movement. The notch is made to indicate a kill in order that the hunter will be able to differentiate this kill from subsequent kills. It is counting. But, already, for Lacan, it is more than mere counting. Lacan points out that in this first mark the subject has already marked himself. The notch or stroke does not only indicate the animal but indicates the animal *killed*. That is, it indicates the subject in relation to the hunt and indicates this for the subject.

The subject himself is marked off by the single stroke, and first he marks himself as a tattoo, the first of the signifiers.

(Ibid.: 141)

In so marking the stroke as a representation to and of himself, the primal subject has already encountered 'himself' in a division. The one marked is not simply one but *'one* one' (Ibid.) (as opposed to *two* ones or *three* ones). Lacan's point here would be that the one marked operates on two levels. In marking *one*, one always necessarily brings about a division insofar as the one marked, as it signifies something, appears to the subject as *one mark meaning one*. It is at the level of calculation, of meaning making or signification that the subject constitutes himself.

In this respect, the two ones are already distinguished. Thus is marked the first split that makes the subject as such distinguish himself from the sign in relation to which, at first, he has been able to constitute himself as subject.

(Ibid.)

The logic in operation here is that of the impossibility of the 'private' language. Any attempt to communicate, albeit to *one*self, necessarily and already marks and describes a division. A similar point may be made with regard to the example of the man on the desert island who devises a complex of signs to more easily manage his life there. A series of coloured stains are used to indicate the various routes to different foods; a blue stain indicates fruit, a red stain indicates hunting ground for meat etc. Taken superficially, one might surmise that this man has indeed constructed a truly private language. There is no one else on the island who could be the recipient of the communiqués, there is not even anyone else who could immediately decipher what the complex of signs might mean or whether, in fact, they might mean anything at all. But the point is that the man on the island does in fact (endeavour to) communicate with someone; himself. The very need to devise a system of communication for delivering messages to himself indicates a certain splitting. The man who 'sends' the message is not the same man who 'receives' the message. Were he, there would be no need to construct or sense in constructing the 'language' in the first place.

The logic apparent in this example of a 'private' language not only illustrates the, *stricto senso*, impossibility of a private language as such, but allows us to grasp the radical divisionary function of language even when described on such a restricted level. The man who has to devise a system of communication in order to communicate his own survival to and for himself, just as the man who marks himself as one within the order of ones implicated in the hunt, necessarily draws attention to the non-unitary status of what might in common parlance be termed him*self*.

Similarly, Descartes, in positing 'I think' and concluding 'I am', has invoked a splitting or division. The 'I' which is said to think is already marked off from the 'I' which says that there is thinking. The subject here posits itself, but not in the sense that the subject creates itself in a pure becoming. Rather, what Lacan demonstrates is that the Cartesian subject posits itself as disunified, as duplicated, as, in a sense, impossible, insofar as, in positing itself, it presents, and only presents, itself as an image of itself for itself.

> [The subject] sees himself as constituted by the reflected, momentary, precarious image of mastery, imagines himself to be a man merely by virtue of the fact that he imagines himself.
>
> (Ibid.: 142)

This occlusion of the unconscious mechanisms and prioritisation of conscious mastery is also evident in James Strachey's translation of Freud's *Wo Es war, soll Ich werden*; 'Where id was, there ego shall be' (Freud, 1973: 112). In Strachey's version the ego can easily be read as the (desired) supersession of the id. Lacan, in 'The Freudian Thing, or The Meaning of the Return to Freud in Psychoanalysis' (1977a(iv)), questions the validity of such a translation. Lacan brings our attention to the lack of article in Freud's original. Lacan maintains that this lack of an article indicates that *Es* here – insofar as it is not objectified with any article as Freud was prone to do when referring to either *the* id or *the* ego (i.e. *das Es* and *das Ich*) – does not refer to the *Id* but rather to the unconscious subject. Hence, Lacan gives us his new translation;

> *Wo* (Where) *Es* (the subject – devoid of any das or other objectifying article) *war* (was – it is a locus of being that is referred to here, and that in this locus) *soll* (must – that is, a duty in thc moral sense, as is confirmed by the single sentence that follows and brings the chapter to a close) *Ich* (I, there must I – just as one declared. 'this am

I' before saying, 'it is I'), *werden* (must become – that is to say, not occur (survenir), or even happen (advenir), but emerge (venir au jour) from this very locus in so far as it is a locus of being).

(Lacan, 1977a(iv): 128)

Where the subject was, there must I come into being.

or

There where it was, it is my duty to come into being.

Lacan's re-translation not only avoids the prioritisation of the ego implicit in Strachey's translation – where one can easily read the ego as supplanting the id – it also draws out of Freud's sentence an ethicality. At the heart of Lacanian subjectivity is an ethical calling. In Strachey's translation there is an indication of development where a temporal progress supplants the primacy of the id with the primacy of the ego. This might be understood in the fashion in which ego-psychology has often interpreted Freud, as advocating the goal of analysis as the strengthening of the ego. In Lacan's re-translation, on the contrary, the ego is not mentioned and the id is not supplanted. Rather, the 'it' and the 'I' here can both be understood to stand for the subject. The 'it' indicates the unconscious mechanisms or that which arises in the unconscious without the appearance of any conscious agency or agencies author(is)ing it. The 'I' indicates the position to be assumed wherein the subject assumes responsibility for that which has arisen in the unconscious without the appearance of any conscious agency or agencies author(is)ing it. This is not, however, to suggest that in assuming responsibility one somehow attains one's proper position and the unity of subjectivity. There is none. The ethical invocation of *Wo Es war, soll Ich werden* is not something than can be responded to once and for all in an attainment of subjective security. Rather it is momentary and perpetual. It is momentary insofar as it manifests in conscious life only fleetingly. It is perpetual insofar as it is indicative of the unconscious processes which necessarily continue unobserved.

If, for Descartes, *I am thinking* proves that *I am*, the question remains, what happens to *I* after the thought? If *I am thinking* can be understood as a representation which posits, and thus proves, the (existence of the) subject, then this might suggest that when the subject is not being represented in the thought *I am thinking*, it does not exist. That is to say, not only is Descartes' formulation of the *I* temporal and temporary, but it also conjoins the notions of thinking and being in this temporariness. If *I am* so long as and only so long as *I am thinking*, then the being adduced by Descartes is necessarily a punctual one. What Descartes does not adequately answer here, but what is nonetheless raised in his text, is the question of what is going on when *I am not thinking*, i.e. when 'I' is not (re)presented in thought. Such questioning necessary raises a question over Descartes hasty conjunction of *being* and *thought*, a question which will become central to Lacan's reformulation of the subject.

As in the example of Descartes, the subject, in order to present itself, necessarily relies upon some form of language or signifying system, whether this be the notch on the cave wall, Descartes' *cogito* or a proper name etc. In so representing itself for itself or, more accurately, as represented, the subject comes into play and experiences itself in the Other (as language) and consequently as other (to or from itself). The signifier of the subject comes to take the place of the subject and, as such, constitutes the subject as extinguishable.

Language, in the sense of a natural language, is other insofar as it precedes any given subject. We do not invent the language we speak, read, write or think and, consequently, the words we use, even the most 'personal' of words, are always already something alien to us. Language precedes us and succeeds us.

We are fundamentally and radically in a world that is beyond us. In one sense this world is the *actual* world around us, the paraphernalia of our lives, including the objects with which we surround ourselves and the people by whom we are surrounded. In another sense, this is the language with which we attempt to communicate and understand both ourselves and the world around us, including the language or languages we are immersed in. To conceive of a thought, or even a feeling, requires us to utilise and, therefore, rely upon language. To assign meaning to anything is to necessarily rely upon language. When, therefore, Descartes endeavours to ascertain the certainty of his own existence, he not only relies upon the languages he already 'knows' but he unwittingly falls back on and falls into the trap of the grammar of those languages.

In the sense that we are represented in language both by ourselves and by other people and both for ourselves and for other people, we can understand language to be constitutive of our own self perceptions and formative of the ego.

Through reading Descartes, we can understand, then, that the subject is split. For Descartes, as exemplified in the claim *I am thinking, therefore*

I am, being and thought are expressed as isolatable concepts. That they are again conjoined into one moment, while testifying to Descartes conception of them as unified or unifiable, nevertheless testifies to their 'initial' separation. For Descartes the *I* can be located in this conjunction, thus rendering, as we have seen, the punctual conjunction of being and thought as the point at which the *I* can, momentarily, arise; 'this limits me to being there in my being only in so far as I think that I am in my thoughts' (Lacan, 1977a(v): 165). Lacan here radicalises Descartes by inverting his, implicit at least, conclusion. For Lacan, there is no conjunction of being and thought as such. The subject, *I*, must 'choose' between the two. Hence Lacan's reformulations of the cogito as 'I think where I am not, therefore I am where I do not think' and, subsequently, 'I am not wherever I am the plaything of my thought; I think of what I am where I do not think to think' (Ibid.: 166).

Lacan here would appear to indicate that where the Cartesian formulation posits an immediacy between thought and being – and thus language, which would be explicit in the former and which would encapsulate both in expression – there is, in fact, none. For Lacan, the subject, *I*, arises in the disunity of being and thought and is rendered both possible and impossible through the functioning of language. As such, the place in which Descartes would locate the subject is, for Lacan, no place. One might understand Lacan here as criticising humanity's tendency to place itself in a central or axial position between not only being and thought but between signifier and signified.

> the S [signifier] and the s [signified] of the Saussuarian algorithm are not on the same level, and man only deludes himself when he believes his true place is at their axis, which is nowhere.
>
> (Ibid.)

Lacan's reformulation of the cogito here indicates the disunity of the subject. Either *I am not thinking* or *I am not*. Being and thought are mutually exclusive. One reason for such a reformulation is the notion of the unconscious. Thinking, for Lacan, would connote unconscious thought, as opposed to the (desired) conscious thought attested to in Descartes. This would then suggest that the *I am* in Lacan's 'I am where I do not think' (Ibid.) indicates an illusory or fantasmic being insofar as it is a pure assumption; i.e. the ego. The split here between the unconscious which refuses being and the ego which refuses unconscious thought does not indicate a true choice of positions between which some atavistic *I* must or even can choose. Rather, for Lacan, the split is constitutive of subjectivity itself.[1]

Insofar as the cogito is indicative of a representation of the subject, albeit a fantasmic representation, in as much as it (re)presents a false or desired (re)presentation, it indicates something of the subject's relation to and dependence on language. By marking *himself* with *cogito ergo sum*, Descartes can be understood to exemplify the logic at work in the relation between the subject and language. Such a relation should not be understood as one of easily identifiable separation. The subject, in a sense, is nothing but language while, at the same time, the subject is nothing because of language. It is only through being represented that the subject can be said to exist at all and yet, at the same time, in being so represented, the subject is strictly not there. The signifier is there.

> The signifier, producing itself in the field of the Other, makes manifest the subject of its signification. But it functions as a signifier, to petrify the subject in the same movement in which it calls the subject to function, to speak, as subject. There, strictly speaking, is the temporal pulsation in which is established that which is the characteristic of the departure of the unconscious as such – the closing.
>
> (Lacan, 1977b: 207)

Lacan's particular use of the logical concept of the *vel* is useful here. *Vel* conventionally signifies an *either/or* choice of the type *either A or B*. Lacan, however, uses it to express a somewhat different type of choice;

---

[1]The precise manner in which the subject would be divided as it is constituted in relation to language, its emergence in the field of the Other, the symbolic order, would determine the clinical structure of the subject in question. That is, whether the subject is neurotic (obsessional or hysteric), psychotic or perverse. Lacan's discussion of the subject in relation to the Cartesian *cogito* and the subsequent definition of the formula of fantasy as the subject in relation to *objet petit a*, ($\lozenge$a), strictly speaking describes the obsessional subject. While aspects of the different manners in which hysteric and obsessional subjects would figure in the relation of fantasy are discussed in Part III below, it is beyond the scope of this work to engage in a full discussion of the differences between the two structures. It remains the case, however, that both hysteric-female and obsessional-male positions are characterised by the division of the subject in relation to the symbolic order and, thus, the lack constitutive of the subject persists for both hysterics and obsessionals, albeit the relation to this lack is not the same.

either A and not B or not A and not B. His formulation has often been described as a forced choice or no real choice at all (see, for example; Zupančič, 2000: 215). However 'forced' it may be, it is clear in his own formulation that there is very much a choice to be made; 'The choice then is a matter of knowing whether one wishes to preserve one of the parts, the other disappearing in any case' (Lacan, 1977b: 211). What disappears in this case is the subject.

> If we choose being, the subject disappears, it eludes us, it falls into non-meaning. If we choose meaning, the meaning survives only deprived of that part of non-meaning that is, strictly speaking, that which constitutes in the realization of the subject, the unconscious. In other words, it is of the nature of this meaning, as it emerges in the field of the Other, to be in a large part of its field, eclipsed by the disappearance of being, induced by the very function of the signifier.
>
> (Ibid.)

The overlapping of the two circles in Figure 1.1 does not indicate here a conjunction, a joining together wherein the parts of one set are coupled to the parts of the other set. On the contrary, the overlap indicates that there are parts which logically belong to both sets (being and meaning). The choice which the subject faces is not, then, meaning and the exclusion of that part of being which is not also enclosed in meaning *or* being and the exclusion of that part of meaning which is not also enclosed in being. Such a choice would always leave the subject, in this

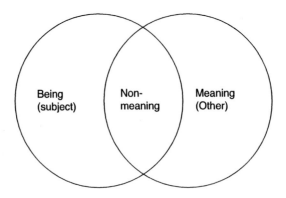

Figure 1.1

instance, with a complete circle, a complete set. The choice Lacan extrapolates is rather that between the remainder of one circle when the overlap is subtracted or the remainder of the other circle when the overlap is subtracted. Complicating this choice further, the left-hand side, *Being*, is, strictly speaking, from the perspective of subjectivity, an impossible choice. This is not to say, however, that it cannot be chosen. Lacan himself provides us with the example of the highwayman to illustrate and clarify this choice (Ibid.: 212). In the traditional cry of the highwayman, the victim is offered a choice; *your money or your life*. Clearly here there is a choice to be made but it is not as straightforward as it might first appear. The highwayman is not, presumably, suggesting that if one would rather not relinquish one's money, one is free to keep it only on condition that one lays down one's life instead. The choice is rather that one can surrender one's money and, hopefully, walk away at least still alive *or* one can die there and then and one's money will be taken anyway. It is a lose-lose situation in which there is still very much a choice to be made. The impossibility of one side does not negate the fact of choice. *Being* in the *vel* of alienation is akin to money in the example of the highwayman. If the subject chooses *meaning*, it loses *being*. If the subject chooses *being*, it loses both meaning and subjectivity and consequently results in an absence of subjectivity; as non-being.

Contra the Cartesian proclamation that *I am thinking, therefore I am*, Lacan offers an exclusionary choice which, in effect, not only inverts the cogito but inverts it with the emphasis on the renunciation; either *I am not thinking* or *I am not*. That is to say, *I* can renounce being or *I* can renounce meaning (thinking).

The poles of the choice here can be understood to signify the poles *unconscious/conscious*. The *thinking* alluded to would indicate the unconscious; the (false) *being*, consciousness. Such a split helps us to understand the problem Lacan discovers in Descartes' formulation. In the Lacanian reading, the Cartesian *I think, therefore I am* attests to conscious thought. In Lacan's understanding, such conscious thought is only ever illusory. It is as such that he can designate it as false being. The *I* here would be akin to the ego. The affirmation that *I am* is, for Lacan, an affirmation of a false self at the expense of the unconscious seat of subjectivity.

Recalling that knowledge only ever surfaces in language and that, consequently, 'self'-knowledge is ultimately oxymoronic insofar as *my* knowledge of *my*self, even were that somehow possible, would have to appear in the field of the Other, i.e. language, it becomes clearer why one might characterise Descartes formulation thus. Transposing Descartes' formulation onto our Lacanian diagram illustrates the extent of the Cartesian discovery:

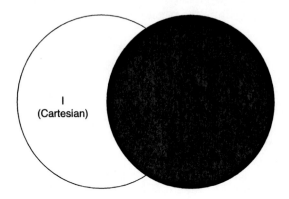

Figure 1.2

The Lacanian-Freudian *I* is quite different from this Cartesian *I*. It is neither the *I* of *I think,* insofar as it is formulated by Descartes with all its philosophical ramifications, nor is it the *I* of *I think* in any everyday sense, with all its grammatical dependency. The former *I* is but an illusion. The latter, a shifter; a signifier which assumes a different referent depending on who is uttering it. The Lacanian *I*, the *I* of '*Wo Es war, soll Ich werden*' is a becoming, an assumption.

There where it was, *I* must come into being.

As Nietzsche has pointed out, that the occurrence of thoughts implies an agency is by no means a certain assumption, never mind Descartes' assumption that they imply a human agency which can then be ascertained as *I*.

A thought comes when 'it' wants, and not when 'I' want. It is, therefore, a *falsification* of the facts to say that the subject 'I' is the condition of the predicate 'think'. It thinks: but to say the 'it' is just that famous old 'I' – well that is just an assumption or opinion, to put it mildly, and by no means an 'immediate certainty.' In fact, there is already too much packed into the 'it thinks': even the 'it' contains an *interpretation* of the process, and does not belong to the process itself. People are following grammatical habits here in drawing conclusions, reasoning that 'thinking is an activity, behind every activity something is active, therefore -.'

(Nietzsche, 2001: 17–18)

Lacan's *I* then comes from another place. It is by no means central and it is not the root of thoughts. Lacan's *I* is rather a position taken in response.

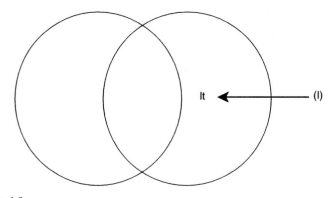

Figure 1.3

For Lacan, the *I*, the subject of the unconscious, is not commensurate with a concept of agency, nor is it even a permanent fixture. The *I*, as subject of the unconscious, is not commensurate with the unconscious. One might do well to emphasise the preposition here; subject *of* the unconscious. The *I* or subject is an effect. Just as the unconscious can be understood to manifest in conscious discourse through such effects as slips of the tongue, so the subject can be understood to manifest in the assuming of responsibility for its own ex-sistence; 'one is always responsible for one's position as subject' (Lacan, 1989: 7).

This impermanence is one suspected by Descartes himself in his *Third Meditation* when he questions what it is that guarantees the subsistence of the *I* from moment to moment.

Therefore I must now ask myself whether I possess some power by which I can bring it about that I myself, who now exist, will also exist a little later on. For since I am nothing but a thinking thing – or at least since I am now dealing simply and precisely with that part of me which is a thinking thing – if such a power were in me, then I would certainly be aware of it. But I observe that there is no such power; and from this very fact I know most clearly that I depend upon some being other than myself.

(Descartes, 1993: 33)

If Descartes' *I* can be understood to be coterminous with the ego, or with that in which conscious thoughts arise, then his argument here would point to the necessity of something beyond conscious thought, or beyond that field in which conscious thoughts arise. Leaving aside Descartes' somewhat spurious assertion that such a beyond must be termed *God*, with all the preconceived attributes that a Seventeenth Century thinker would ascribe to *Him*, we can understand Descartes to have posited that consciousness itself cannot exist or arise in isolation, that it can only exist or arise against a background which is other than itself. The 'being other than myself' to which Descartes alludes might be something akin to the unconscious of Lacan. This is not to suggest that there is any unquestionable certainty at work here. That something like conscious thought, the ego or the *cogito* requires something other than itself to sustain it appears as little more than a presumption. That some field of permanence must subsist 'beneath' it is by no means proven. However, combining Descartes' insights with those of Freud and Lacan, it can perhaps be understood that there 'is' an unknown, whether this unknown exists or not. That is to say, what both Cartesian philosophy and psychoanalysis point to is the incompleteness of conscious thought. Whether or not one concurs with Descartes' conclusion that such an incompleteness then proves the existence of a completeness elsewhere, the conclusion that the cogito itself, conscious thought, is incomplete remains. Transposing such a conclusion onto psychoanalysis, it would then be over-hasty to suggest that the unconscious is in fact a permanent, continuous substratum of consciousness which occasionally manifests in or arises in the conscious field. All that can be concluded is that it does arise.

I should define unconscious cause, neither as an existent, nor as a οὐκὄν, a non-existent – as, I believe Henri Ey does, a non-existent of possibility. It is a μὴὄν of the prohibition that brings to being an existent in spite of its non-advent, it is a function of the impossible on which a certainty is based.

(Lacan, 1977b: 128)

Such uncertainty of the unconscious as cause allows a better understanding of the notion of the *I* as Lacan uses it in this context. This *I*, which is neither Cartesian nor a grammatical function, can be under-stood as that which is purely assumed. It is the very uncertainty of thought, of what might otherwise ground thought, of any substantial, albeit unknown, kernel of subjectivity in anything approaching a tradi-tional conception of *I*, that gives rise to the Lacanian *I*. The *I* here is posited as purely contingent and this contingency, in turn, necessitates a certain responsibility. Faced with the 'forced' and impossible choice between meaning and being, the *I* arises in response to the *vel*, in response to the uncertainty of its own (non-)existence and arises as that which assumes responsibility for the 'decision' (*de-caedere*; cutting away) taken. The Lacanian *I* is a response to the unknown and as such, insofar as it is assumed, it entails a responsibility for its own assumption.

That one is always, then, responsible for one's position as a subject is not to suggest that the subject is some independent self-creating thing. The subject properly understood in the Lacanian sense is not a *thing* at all.

> The unconscious is the sum of the effects of speech on a subject, at the level at which the subject constitutes himself out of the effects of the signifier. This makes it clear that, in the term *subject* ... I am not designating the living substratum needed by this phenomenon of the subject, nor any sort of substance, nor any being possessing knowledge in his *pathos*, his suffering, whether primal or secondary, nor even some incarnated logos, but the Cartesian subject, who appears at the moment when doubt is recognised as certainty – except that, through my approach, the bases of the subject prove to be wider, but, at the same time much more amenable to the certainty that eludes it. This is what the unconscious is.
>
> (Ibid.: 126)

This impermanency of the subject of the unconscious suggests a subject in motion, a subject which is neither ever secure nor securable; a subject which arises in becoming without ever assuming to be as such. This movement of subjectivity is brought further to light when one considers the other ethical injunction which Lacan gives us: 'the one thing one can be guilty of is giving ground relative to one's desire' (Lacan, 1992: 321).

2
The Graph of Desire

The structure and functioning of subjectivity, and particularly its relationship to desire, can be further illustrated with reference to Lacan's development of what he calls the Graph of Desire. What is usually referred to in the singular, as the graph, actually comprises of four graphs. Importantly, the various forms of the graph do not represent any chronological development as might pertain to the formation of the subject. Their development is rather pedagogical, unveiling the complexities of the subject as Lacan envisaged it through the four stages of the graph.

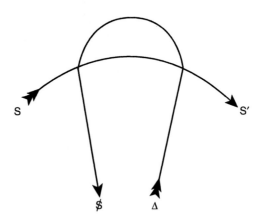

Graph I

Beginning at the lower right hand point on Graph I, we have Δ, what Žižek has termed 'some mystical, pre-symbolic intention' (Žižek, 1989: 101). The presymbolic factor here indicates the illusory nature of this

Δ. The triangle marks the impossible pre-subjective point from whence the subject might have intended something before or outwith the symbolic order. As such, this Δ is always only retrospectively posited. Δ is the conjectured position of the subject before it becomes subject or, to put it in the terms used in the previous chapter, Δ is a retrospectively posited position before the *I* assumes a position in response to the unknown.

Following the arc of the graph, this Δ results in $, the subject. The score through the S of the subject indicates that it is barred, impossible, incomplete, divided. Through the impossible choice of the *vel* of alienation, the subject comes to be as divided from itself. In coming to be in and through the order of the symbolic, that is, the field of the Other, the subject can never be in its own place; it has no place of its own. In terms of the first Graph, the subject is nothing before crossing the wider arc between S and S', all that can be said to be before this point is a retroactively posited supposition, a feeble 'must have been'. The division in the subject is also evident in the fact that the subject is always replaced by a signifier. For the subject to 'mean' anything at all, or for the subject to be meant, it relies upon a system of signification which is always beyond itself. In this sense the subject necessarily is replaced or effaced by a signifier. Put simply, one can only conceive of oneself, (re)present oneself, and one is only ever conceived or represented by others, through the medium of signification. To say 'I am this', or 'My name is X', 'I like this' or in fact any instance of speech – even when one might believe one is absent from the content of the speech, one is still (re)presented in it, albeit implicitly, as speaker – is to mis-present oneself. Such mis-representation, however, should not suggest that some true representation could somehow occur. The division and thus impossibility of the subject is the very condition of its possibility at all. Moreover, any such split of the subject is redoubled in the division between consciousness and unconsciousness. It is thus that it can be said that, not only is the subject divided, but the subject is this very divide itself (Fink, 1995: 47).

The wider arc in the Graph, from S to S', indicates the signifying chain, an instance or example of the symbolic order in operation. The signifying chain and the point being made of it here can be elaborated on two levels; that of its paradigmatic function and its syntagmatic function. The syntagmatic function is exemplified in the unravelling of any sentence. Natural languages, being structures of rules purporting to convey meanings, always allow the possibility of a certain limited and yet unstable anticipation of meaning to come. Indeed, for Lacan, such anticipation is not only possible but intrinsic.

> For the signifier, by its very nature, always anticipates meaning by unfolding its dimension before it. As is seen at the level of the sentence when it is interrupted before the significant term: 'I shall never ...', 'All the same it is ...', 'And yet there may be ...'. Such sentences are not without meaning. A meaning all the more oppressive in that it is content to make us wait for it.
>
> (Lacan, 1977a(v): 153)

The logic here is that in the production of any utterance, prior to the production of each signifier which would retrospectively be understood to have comprised that utterance, it is obviously uncertain what is going to be said. In the place of such uncertainty, a variety of alternative possibilities can be imagined, each possibility inflecting upon the previous components of the utterance. The battery of signifiers, any one of which might come to occupy the place still left open, is what would be termed the paradigmatic dimension; the entire network of available signification. At the point at which the gap of anticipation is filled, meaning, and consequently the significance of the other words in the sentence, is momentarily secured (without, however, ever erasing the other possibilities which might have been previously entertained). This is the point at the left-hand intersection of the two arcs of the Graph (which appears in the second Graph as A, *Autre* or the place of Other), what Lacan terms the *point de capiton* or anchoring point.

> The diachronic function of this anchoring point is to be found in the sentence, even if the sentence completes its signification only with its last term, each term being anticipated in the construction of the others, and, inversely, sealing their meaning by its retroactive effect.
>
> (Lacan, 1977a(viii): 303)

Importantly here, the *point de capiton* is no guarantee, it does not fix meaning and offer up an unambiguous reading of the sentence. It is not a 'full stop'. Rather, it holds meaning in place for a moment, for an instant; it is a 'rhythm, rather than a duration' (Ibid.: 304). With this in mind, it is clear then that the *point de capiton*, the possibility of the intersection of the syntagmatic and paradigmatic scales, occurs potentially at every point in any utterance, sentence, or even word. A series of *points de capiton* then occurs as meaning unfolds at junctures at which meaning is taken to be *more* secure, only for that security to vanish again as the utterance continues, as other meanings unfold and on and on. The first Graph thus illustrates the retroactive constitution of the (barred) subject in relation to the symbolic order, the field of the Other. That is to say that it is only in relation to the Other and through the mediating effects of the Other that the subject, albeit as barred, can be understood to have come about.

> The Other as previous site of the pure subject of the signifier holds the master position, even before coming into existence, to use Hegel's term against him, as absolute Master. For what is omitted in the platitude of modern information theory is that fact that one can speak of code only if it is already the code of the Other, and that is something quite different from what is in question in the message, since it is from this code that the subject is constituted, which means that it is from the Other that the subject receives even the message that he emits.
>
> (Ibid.: 305)

The intention with which one might assume to begin, for Lacan, must properly be placed on the right of the graph, where, in French and English at least, we would conventionally end. The constitution of the subject runs 'backwards' from this point, through the field of the Other, the utterance, language. It is thus that it can be understood that, not only is language prior to the subject in the mundane sense that other people have spoken the language we come to speak before we come to speak it, the sense in which Bruce Fink speaks of a child being born 'into a pre-established place in its parents' linguistic universe' (Fink, 1995: 5), language is also prior to the subject in the stricter sense that without language there is no subject as such. The subject is not some*thing* which exists independently of language only to come to be supplemented by language, to learn to negotiate a pre-existing language to better express oneself or more easily attain one's needs and wants, the subject as such only ever comes to be anything at all in the field of signification. This 'anything at all', as we have seen, is the erased subject, the subject which can emerge only as split, as barred, as impossible.

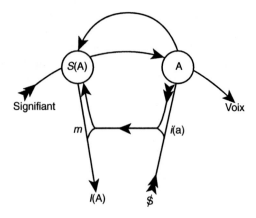

Graph II

In the second graph, the barred subject moves over to occupy the position previously held by the Δ, the retrospectively posited intention. It
is important to hold in mind here that, as already stated, Lacan's series
of graphs is not indicative of any subjective development wherein the
subject, in the point in case, would come to supersede the mythical
intentionality. Rather the series offers a conceptual complicating of
Lacan's theorising of subjectivity which cannot properly be reduced to
any temporal plane. Each graph builds on and simultaneously unsettles the graph before it. Where in the first graph the notion of retrospection is symbolised with the anti-clockwise arc which runs counter
to the wider clockwise arc of the signifying chain, in the second graph,
this retrospection is indicated by the shift of $ from the left-side to the
right-side of the graph.

> This is a retroversion effect by which the subject becomes at each
> stage what he was before and announces himself – he will have been
> – only in the future perfect tense.
>
> (Lacan, 1977a(viii): 306)

$ is displaced from its former position on the left-side, (logically)
posterior to the movement through the signifying chain, by *I(A)*, the
ego ideal or symbolic identification.[2]

---

[2]I have here and throughout retained the symbolisation as used by Lacan, thus
retaining, for example, *S(A)*, rather than rendering it *S(O)*.

The speech marked in Graph II by the trajectory 'signifier → voice' indicates a relation with Truth, insofar as Truth might be understood to entail a 'fictional structure' (Ibid.). That is to say, speech, and the Truth implied therein, is indicative of a conventional structure which seeks to provide a certain guarantee. The Truth of speech is not then concerned with an external, pre-existing reality, but rather, it is speech which endeavours to create, or author, a certain 'reality';

> it is from somewhere other than the Reality that it concerns that Truth derives its guarantee: it is from speech ... The first words spoken (*le dit premier*) stand as a decree, a law, an aphorism, an oracle; they confer their obscure authority upon the real other.
>
> (Ibid.)

It is only in speech, in an involvement in a pre-existent language, that the subject can come to be constituted. However, such a constitution through the mediation of the signifying field results in a certain division wherein the subject, in coming to be anything at all, is rendered other than itself. The ego ideal here is one aspect of this effect. Insofar as the subject is only constituted as subject ($) through the mediating effects of the symbolic order, that which comes to be within the subject, that without which the subject could not be anything at all, is necessarily alien to the subject insofar as it is a part of the Other. This ego ideal, in terms of its function within the subject, is 'an agency which speaks, that is to say a symbolic agency' (Lacan, 1988a: 135). It is 'the other as speaking, the other in so far as he has a relation to me [*moi*]' (Ibid.: 142). This would appear then to relate the ego ideal not only to the function of speech as it manifests in and is manifest of the subject and to the other as social other but also to the function of law.

The ego ideal might then be understood as that within the subject which carries out the function of the Other, the subject as function of the Other. This would be to stand it in contradistinction to both the ego proper (*moi*) and the ideal ego (*i(a)*).

The movement described in the second graph is now figured as entailing a 'short-circuiting' from $ to I(A) marked on either side by *m* (*moi* or ego) and *i(a)*. This 'short-circuiting' indicates what Lacan terms a 'double articulation', wherein the vector which could be seen in the first graph to pass from Δ, through the symbolic plane, to $, now passes from $, through the symbolic plane, to *I(A) and* short-circuits underneath at the point marked *i(a)* to the point marked *m.*

This would suggest that there is something pertaining to the subject which does not fall entirely within the realm of the symbolic, which escapes to an extent, the full mediation of language. This *something* which escapes is that of the subject which is of the imaginary realm.

Lacan explains in his essay 'The Mirror Stage as Formative of the Function of the I' (1977a(ii)) how the subject's sense of self is constituted in relation to a misrecognition of unity and mastery engendered in the encounter with an external image (the specific example Lacan gives is of the mirror image of one's own body, but there is no real reason to suggest that this misrecognised and formative image could not be something else entirely). The fixation or 'formal stagnation' (Lacan, 1977a(i): 17) of this image marks the point of separation between ideal ego and ego ideal. The ideal ego, as an internalised image based on a fundamental misrecognition, is a function of the imaginary order; it is imaginary (mis-)identification. The graphic representation then suggests that there is an at least partial separation between the functions of the imaginary and the functions of the symbolic, insofar as the 'short-circuit' occurs beneath the signifying chain, that is, not having entirely passed through the mediation of the symbolic order. This might also suggest that the imaginary is always subordinated to, placed under, the symbolic.

This separation indicates a separation between subject and object, a separation which is both constitutive of and forbidding of the subject, rendering it an aphanisic point of its own constitution. That the ego ideal, *I(A)*, comes to figure on the left-hand side of the graph where, previously, the barred subject had been placed, indicates that it, the ego ideal, is what one might call a properly subjective function. The ideal ego on the other hand, like the ego to which it is conjoined, is an object; 'the ego is an object – an object which fills a certain function which we here call the imaginary function' (Lacan, 1988a: 44).

This distinction between the ego ideal and the ideal ego can be further clarified by turning to Lacan's *Freud's Paper on Technique: The Seminar on Jacques Lacan, Book 1, 1953–1954.* Here Serge Leclaire, in reference to Freud's *On Narcissism*, points out that ideal ego is constituted as an ideal which would come to supplant the function of the true or 'real ego' as 'the target of the self-love' (Ibid.: 133). Leclaire brings our attention to the fact that Freud, in his text, having for the first time introduced the term 'ideal ego', then goes on to introduce the other term, 'ego ideal'. It is Lacan who proffers an explanation here,

> Freud makes use there of the *Ichideal* [ego ideal], which is precisely symmetrical and opposed to the *Idealich* [ideal ego]. It's the sign that Freud is here designating two different functions.
>
> (Ibid.)

The opposition referred to here is clarified as that between the imaginary and symbolic planes because, according to Lacan, 'the *Ichideal* [ego ideal] takes up its place within the totality of the law' (Ibid.: 134). This would then suggest, as Leclaire interprets it, that the ego ideal is 'imposed from without' (Ibid.: 136).

> it's the symbolic relation which defines the position of the subject as seeing. It is speech, the symbolic relation, which determines the greater or lesser degree of perfection, of completeness, of approximation, of the imaginary. This representation [schema of two mirrors] allows us to draw the distinction between the *Idealich* and *Ichideal*, between the ideal ego and the ego ideal. The ego-ideal governs the interplay of relations on which all relations with others depend. And on this relation to others depends the more or less satisfying character of the imaginary structuration.
>
> (Ibid.: 141)

The ideal ego, then, is figured as the idealised image which is internalised in one, that towards which one's desire is necessarily directed. In terms of relations to the world, desire is projected onto those objects which appear to coincide with or 'become[s] confused with' (Ibid.), however fleetingly, this idealised image. The ego ideal, on the other hand is that which allows one a passage beyond this coincidence or confusion of images ('real' and 'imagined'). It is that of the symbolic which interferes and facilitates an exchange on the level of the symbolic plane.

The *Ichideal*, the ego-ideal, is the other as speaking, the other in so far as he has a symbolic relation to me [*moi*], which, within the terms of our dynamic manipulation, is both similar to and different from the imaginary libido. Symbolic exchange is what links human beings to each other, that is it is speech, and it makes it possible to identify the subject.

(Ibid.: 142)

This identification of the subject, then, is at the level or in the realm of the Other. It is symbolic identification or, in Jacques-Alain Miller's interpretation, it is 'a social and ideological function' (Miller, J.A. (1987) *Aspects du malaise dans la civilisation*, quoted in Žižek, 1989: 110). The retroactive movement from $ to *I(A)*, passing through the signifying chain from the point of the A, the place of the Other, the point at which the Other pins meaning, to S(A), the signifier as it functions as part of the Other, 'results' in the subject identified as an effect of the symbolic, *I(A)*. Within this trajectory, we find the necessary short-circuit of imaginary identification which will account for the formation of the ego and helps us to understand the double identification in action; the image of the (non)self, *i(a)*, and the symbolisation of the (non)self, *I(A)*.

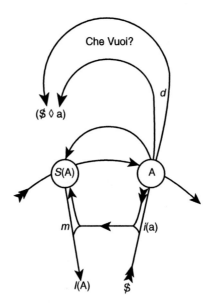

Graph III

The lower segment of the third Graph is a duplication of the second graph, however, there is now added a double curve emanating from the *point de capiton*, A. Both lines of this curve lead to the same destination, ($◊a), the formula of fantasy. En route, they appear to encapsulate *d*, desire, and the question, 'Che voi?', *what do you want?*

The double curve extending from *A* takes a graphic form indicative of a question-mark, stressing the questioning addressed both to and from the Other. Lacan delineates desire from three other, conceptually related, notions; need, demand and drive. Need, for Lacan, would be that which would be (or would have been) necessary outwith language. Here we are in something akin to the Δ, the mythical pre-symbolic intention marked on the first graph. If the human being is grounded in a certain biological necessity, this necessity must still be marked and experienced through the mediation of language. As we have seen above, the human being as speaking being would know nothing of such necessity, and could thus not be said to have experienced this necessity as such, were it not for the intervention of language. Need, then, this biological necessity, is always only ever posited or conjectured retrospectively from the standpoint of having come to 'be' in language. The human being's 'dependence is maintained by a world of language' (Lacan, 1977a(viii): 309). This maintenance in and by language has the effect of reducing and diversifying needs 'to a point where their scope appears to be of quite a different order' (Ibid.) from the basic biological necessity we retroactively suppose. Where need would be supposed to be a need for some*thing* in particular (food, warmth, etc.), as it is taken over into the realm of the symbolic, it becomes generalised through its attachment to the Other who provides it. As such, what perhaps began as need becomes detached from any biological necessity and comes to figure as the demand for subjugation in the willingness to satisfy those needs; love.

> In this way, demand annuls (*aufhebt*) the particularity of everything that can be granted by transmuting it into a proof of love, and the very satisfactions that it obtains for need are reduced (*sich erniedrigt*) to the level of being no more than the crushing demand for love.
>
> (Lacan, 1977a(vi): 286)

The particularity abolished, as need is transmuted into demand, resurfaces at the level of desire. It is thus that Lacan can say,

> desire is neither the appetite for satisfaction, nor the demand for love, but the difference that results from the subtraction of the first from the second, the phenomena of their splitting.
>
> (Ibid.: 287)

Need would arise as an appetite for this or that particular satisfaction. Demand would emanate as the demand for proof of love carried through the asking for the satisfaction of each need. In removing the necessity of satisfaction which would thus be entailed in the articulation of demand, one is left with a pure desiringness. However, where need would be the need for a concrete satisfaction and demand would be the asking for proof of (unconditional) love, desire is always desire for something else. As demand arises out of need in response to a reliance on the (M)Other, desire, as the remainder of the subtraction of need from demand, remains radically attached to the Other. It is as such that Lacan formulates desire as always being 'the desire of the Other' (Lacan, 1977a(viii): 312). Here, the preposition *of* marks a rich ambiguity which allows us to understand the complexity of this relation of desire between the subject and the Other.

The subject's desire is the desire of the Other insofar as it is the desire for the Other to desire him or her. It is the subject's desire to be the object of the Other's desire. This would entail the desire to be recognised by the Other. It is perhaps primarily this sense of *desire of the Other* that we can understand in the relationship between the infant and mother. The child wants to be the object of the mother's desire, it wants the mother to desire it (Lacan, 1977b: 218). As Lacan himself puts it, the relation between child and mother is 'a relation constituted ... not by his vital dependence on her, but by his dependence on her love, that is to say, by the desire for her desire' (Lacan, 1977a(vii): 198).

In another sense, the subject's desire is the desire of the Other insofar as it is the desire *for* the Other. Here we would understand *of* in the sense of the womaniser's love of women, or the child's incestuous desire *for* the mother, the latter of which is, for Lacan and, in Lacan's reading, for Freud, 'the fundamental desire' (Lacan, 1992: 67). The subject desires the Other *qua* Other. It desires the Other in its otherness. Bound to this sense of the otherness of the Other is the fact that the Other is always elsewhere. This links to a further sense in which the subject's desire is the desire *of* the Other, that is insofar as it is a desire which is always necessarily deferred. Desire is that which cannot be satisfied. Where need could be, albeit temporarily, satisfied (the need for hunger is abated with food, the need for warmth is abated by a blanket, etc.), desire is unfulfilable. The object of desire is never quite *that* and thus desire moves on to another object which, again, once it is 'attained', will prove not be *that* which was desired. Desire is a perpetual movement in which the response to that which presents itself as that which might possibly fulfil one's desire is always, 'That's not it' (Lacan, 1998: 126). This is the logic of the *objet petit a*, the small *a* in the graph in relation to which the subject finds itself in the formula of fantasy ($\$\lozenge a$).

Additionally, the subject's desire is the desire of the Other insofar as it is the desire for that which the Other desires. What is desired is not desired because of any intrinsic qualities of its own or even any intrinsic qualities erroneously or not perceived in or of it by the subject, but, rather, it is desired because it is seen to be desired or valued by the Other. Put simply, one desires some*thing* because it is perceived as desirable and it is only perceived as desirable because one perceives it being desired by another. The quintessential example from the psychoanalytical canon here would be that of Lacan's interpretation of the Dora Case (Freud, 1977; Lacan, 1993; Lacan, 1982). Lacan interprets Dora as identifying with Herr K. and turning for her object of desire to his wife, Frau K. That is to say, Lacan interprets Dora as desiring what the other, in this instance Herr K., desires (Lacan, 1982: 66). This is perhaps the logic which underpins much of the current phenomena of celebrity endorsement – a perfectly mundane object suddenly becomes extremely (hysterically) desirable because it is presented as being desirable for some valorised other.

Finally, recalling the fact that the subject is only ever constituted as subject through the mediation of the symbolic plane, the realm of the Other, the subject's desire is the desire *of* the Other insofar as this desire must necessarily emanate in the place of the Other. The desire of which Lacan speaks is always unconscious desire and the unconscious is that which is Other in the subject.

Importantly here, these various interpretations of the function of the preposition *of* in the proclamation, *the subject's desire is always the desire of the Other*, are not mutually exclusive or competing. Though the infant desires that the mOther desire it, this desire is never accomplished, as the mOther never totally or exclusively desires the infant. That is to say, the infant, in desiring the mOther's desire, cannot ever have and hold that desire in its entirety. There is always going to be something else competing for the mOther's attention and affection, something else in addition to the child that she will desire. One significant instance of this something else would be the Father. The figure of the Father also bears on what Lacan has termed 'the fundamental desire' (Lacan, 1992: 67), the desire for the mOther herself. The child, then, wants the mOther in and of herself, a desire which is intricately bound up with wanting the mOther to exclusively desire it. This desire of the mOther is already inflected as a reflection of the desire perceived to be focused on the mOther by the Father, a desire, or complex of desire, arising in the place of the Other.

Such allusions to the child/mother relationship should not serve to suggest that this complex of desire is something which is encountered and surpassed in one's formative years. The various instances of the *of* in *desire of the Other*, just as they are inseparable from each other, are also unalleviable. Just as desire itself is continuous, so the various inflections and emphases placed on the phrase by Lacan are continuous.

Returning to the Graph, as we have seen, the subject is only ever constituted as subject through the mediating effects of language, that is, through the intervention of the Other. Such an effect is not, however, reducible to an absorption or incorporation. The very fact that the subject is constituted in relation to the Other should suggest that it is other than the Other. In passing through the symbolic chain, in encountering itself and the Other in the field of the Other, the subject is necessarily left in perplexity. This perplexity is formulised by Lacan in the question *Che Vuoi?* or *What do you want?* The question here is doubly directed in that it is the question addressed by the subject to the Other – what does it want from me? – but also in that it is the question assumed by the subject to be addressed to him – what do *you* want? what is it that you desire?

The 'answer' to this question is provided in the form of fantasy ($\$\Diamond a$). As we have seen, the subject is necessarily constituted as incomplete. The subject, in its coming to 'be' through the mediating effects of the Other can only come to 'be' as lacking in itself. Conjoined with this notion, the Other itself is also seen to be lacking insofar as the desire which the subject does experience is, in all its complexity, the desire of the Other, thus indicating that both sides in this relation – the subject and the Other – are necessarily incomplete. Were either complete, they would not desire, lack being that which gives rise to the movement of desire. Put simply, if one truly had everything, one would necessarily not want for anything else. A certain space or lack must exist in order for the movement of desire to function.

Although this incompleteness cannot be completed, fantasy serves as a veil, a safeguard against facing this incompleteness. *Objet petit a*, as the imaginary cause of desire, allows a fantasmic sense of wholeness otherwise denied to the subject. The sense of wholeness gives rise to a certain *pleasure* which comes to operate, through the mode of fantasy, as surrogate for the being lost in the movement into meaning, the *vel* of alienation. The sense of wholeness which would have been experienced in being (were that not strictly impossible) or the sense of wholeness that the infant mistakes in the mirror stage is (re-)enacted on the level of fantasy. This is not to suggest, however, that the subject's desire is in any way satisfied by this *pleasure*. *Objet petit a* in the fantasy, or the imagined relation of the subject ($) to *objet petit a*, is never achieved as such but rather functions as the imaginary cause of desire.

As we have seen in Chapter 1, in Lacan's appropriation of Freud's *Wo Es war, soll Ich werden*, 'Where It was, there must I come into being', there is an implication of a movement from the impersonal it, the unconscious, to the purely assumed position of subjectivity. That which arises in and from the unconscious does so in a pulsating moment and does so in the mode of the Other. The 'I' of the subject is the pure assumption of responsibility for this arising. As we have seen, the language one has at one's disposal to express 'oneself' is always the language of the Other and as such is radically other to, although also constitutive of, the subject. For Lacan, the fantasy is the '"stuff" of the "I" that is originally repressed, because it can be indicated only in the "fading" of the enunciation' (Lacan, 1977a(viii): 314). That is to say, it is in and through the fantasy that the mythic 'I' supposed to have preceded the advent of the subject ($) as an effect of the Other is relived. This being the case, it is clear that the subject who comes to 'be' (*soll Ich werden*) in the place where 'it' was (*Wo Es war*) must be radically incommensurate with the subject sustained in relation to the *objet petit a*, that is, with the subject in fantasy.

Fantasy, then, is at one and the same time a veil sustaining the subject against the *Che vuoi?* – against the radical unknowingness inherent in the symbolic order – and the very structuration which allows desire to operate, which allows us to experience desire. One way of understanding this dual function would be to recall that the subject's desire is always *the desire of the Other*. This formula, not unproblematically, suggests that desire is never simply one. Desire, as experienced by the subject, is always desire in response to the desire of the Other, in response to anOther desire. Fantasy supports the subject's desire and defends the subject against the threatening approach and call of the Other's desire. A desire which can only arise in the Other insofar as the Other is itself incomplete. This allows us to more easy understand the top half of the completed graph of desire.

Where on the lower half of the graph, the graph as represented in its second formulation, we have on the left-hand side the symbol S(A), the signifier as a function of the Other, in the upper half of the completed graph we have what might be understood as the (partial) negation of this symbol, S(Ⱥ), here set to mark the 'signifier of a lack in the Other'

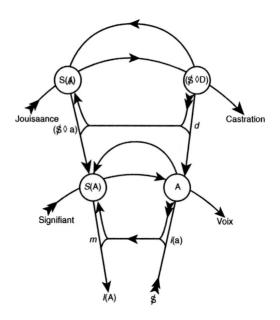

Graph IV

(Ibid.: 316). This is the notion that the Other in order to be desiring must also be lacking. For Lacan, this signifier, S(Å), functions as that 'signifier for which all the other signifiers represent the subject' (Ibid.). As we have seen, the subject in Lacan's understanding is not some being which can exist outside language, utilising the armoury of words available for its own, independent, caprice.

> The signifier, producing itself in the field of the Other, makes manifest the subject of its signification. But it functions as a signifier only to reduce the subject in question to being no more than a signifier, to petrify the subject in the same movement in which it calls the subject to function, to speak, as subject. There, strictly speaking, is the temporal pulsation in which is established that which is the characteristic of the departure of the unconscious as such – the closing.
>
> (Lacan, 1977b: 207)

Against what one might characterise as the 'common-sense' notion that language (pre)exists as a tool to be utilised by a subject (or person) in the expression of their (pre-linguistic) needs, wants, beliefs etc., the notion of subjectivity in Lacan's work posits a subject who only ever comes to be anything at all because of the signifying chain of language, because of the (pre)existence of a symbolic order in which it comes to operate. What is crucial here is that, if it is the order of signifiers which takes logical precedence, then signifiers are not arsenal to be deployed between subjects, or, to oversimplify, words are not carriers of meaning between people, but, rather, it is the subject which is constituted in the movement of *signifiance* between signifiers. It is in this sense that Lacan borrows Hegel's dictum that 'the symbol manifests itself first of all as the murder of the thing' (Lacan, 1977a(iii): 104) and adds that 'this death constitutes in the subject the eternalization of his desire' (Ibid.).

An example of this notion of the signifier representing the subject for another signifier is already apparent in Freud when he writes, in *A Project for a Scientific Psychology*, of a soldier's willingness to sacrifice himself for his country's flag or, as Freud emphasises it, for 'a many coloured scrap of stuff' (Freud, 1966: 349). Here, the soldier is clearly not concerned with the *thing* of the flag, the flag as material object. The flag only assumes its significance in relation to another signifier, in this instance, the 'fatherland' (Ibid.). The soldier, the subject, is *given* his subjectivity through the mediating representation between one signifier, 'the flag', and another, 'the fatherland'.

For Lacan signifiers operate as representations of drives. To the formula of a signifier being 'that which represents a subject for another signifier' (Lacan, 1977a(viii): 316), Lacan adds that the matheme S($\cancel{A}$) indicates that 'signifier for which all the other signifiers represent the subject: that is to say, in the absence of this signifier, all the other signifiers represent nothing, since nothing is represented only *for* something else' (Ibid.). This signifier of the lack in the Other thus stands quite apart from other, 'normal' signifiers. The collection of signifiers available in any given language or indeed the collection of signifiers available to any given individual is necessarily, by definition, complete. This obviously does not mean that it cannot be added to, as new words are coined and adopted into a natural language or new words are acquired by a speaker of a language. The collection of signifiers is complete in its synchronic dimension, insofar as the collection at any one point is what it is. It is, however, by definition, both complete, in itself, and non-totalising, insofar as it can, at the very least in theory, be added to or changed (simply, new words are coined, people do acquire new words). S($\cancel{A}$) can thus be conceived as the outer limit of the set of all available signifiers; it is neither a part of the array of available signifiers nor is the array of available signifiers conceivable without it. Were it recuperated to the array of available signifiers, another outer limit would necessarily emerge to take its place. Were there no outer limit, the existent array of signifiers would slide into non-meaning, that is, they would cease to signify, as there would no longer be any*thing* for which or to which they would represent the subject.

And since the battery of signifiers, as such, is by that very fact complete, this signifier can only be a line (*trait*) that is drawn from its circle without being able to be counted part of it. It can be symbolized by the inherence of a (–I) in the whole set of signifiers.

As such it is inexpressible, but its operation is not inexpressible, for it is that which is produced whenever a proper noun is spoken. Its statement equals its signification.

(Ibid.: 316–17)

What Lacan terms the 'battery of signifiers' is, by the very fact of being a battery, complete. This then necessitates that S($\cancel{A}$) is both conditioned by and outwith the battery. This Lacan indicates with the matheme (–I). The signifier of the lack in the Other, S($\cancel{A}$), is indicative of a negative moment of the *I*, an absence of or inconsistency of *I* (that 'I' is still inscribed in the inscription (–I) suggests that this is not meant to indicate an absolute non-existence of *I*). This, then, points again to a strict co-relation between the lack in the Other and a lack in the subject. The symbol (–I) is inherent in the sense that it indicates a nonpart which takes part, that its existence and maintenance is supervenient on that from which it is necessarily excluded. As (–I) and its inherence clearly have a subjective feature as well, as this describes a feature not only of signifiers but also a feature of the subject, it might also be explained in terms of the concept of 'extimacy' – a term coined by Lacan in his Seminar VII and developed by Jacques-Alain Miller in his essay 'Extimité' (1994). The term extimacy (extimité) combines the prefix ex- with the term 'intimacy' (intimité) to convey the notion that that which is most intimate or interior has, at the same time, an external quality. The term extimacy might be used to clarify the relation of subject and Other insofar as the Other can be characterised as that which is *in me more than myself*, that 'something strange to me ... at the heart of me' (Lacan, 1992: 71). In the current context, S($\cancel{A}$) is extimate to and for the whole set of signifiers, indicating also that (–I) is extimate to the whole set of signifiers. The shift from the signifier of the lack in the Other to a lack of 'I', in turn suggests a polyvalent extimation wherein the S(A̸) is extimate to the collection of available signifiers, the (–I) is extimate to the subject, the Other is extimate to the subject and the subject is extimate to the Other. These latter two instances of extimation should not, however, be understood to imply an equivalence or symbiosis. That the Other and the subject are both extimate to each other is not in any way to suggest that they somehow perform the same function for each other, that the subject is the Other of the Other. Strictly speaking, the Other has no Other; 'there is no Other of the Other' (Lacan, 1998: 81). Thus, while the subject and Other are in some senses codependent (without the subject the battery of signifiers would not be representing anything, without the Other the subject would not be represented), this mutual implication must be regarded as radically asymmetrical. In another formulation, Lacan describes the Other as non-existent but functional (see Miller, 1994: 81), suggesting that the Other is an inessential illusion but one which is nonetheless essential (necessary) for the maintenance of subjectivity. As Miller illustrates with the example of a bomb-scare, something does not need to exist in order for it to effectively carry out its function.

One function which is set in play by this barring or incompleteness of the Other is, as we have seen, a certain subtraction or lacking in the subject. For Lacan this results in the subject's inability to represent itself comprehensively with a notion such as the *cogito* or, phrased otherwise, it helps us to understand why it is that the *cogito* does not go far enough in explaining the subject. The (–I) implied in S(A̸) is that which is 'unthinkable' (Lacan, 1977a(viii): 317) for the subject. This suggests that the subject is radically incapable of surmising the aetiology of his own existence and thus short-circuits any attempt to prove its own existence in any way comparable to the attempt made by Descartes. It is perhaps thus that, for Lacan, we are led 'to oppose any philosophy directly issuing from the *Cogito*' (Lacan, 1977a(ii): 1). It is not, as shown in Chapter 1, that Lacan opposes everything *about* Descartes' deduction. Here the emphasis should be placed on the adverbial 'directly'. The suppositions of the *Meditations* lead to (and emanate from) a conceptualisation of the subject as complete in itself, though necessarily supplemented by the existence of something other to it; i.e. Descartes' God. This dualism, in Descartes, is, as would befit the Christian tradition from within which he writes, strictly hierarchical. For Lacan, on the other hand, the failure of the *cogito* itself points towards a subjectivity which is not only essentially lacking but which is also deficient in terms of knowing this lack. One might understand Lacan here as, rather than rejecting Descartes' findings *per se*, pointing to the underlying logic of the *Meditations*, suggesting that the hierarchical schema of complete subject supplemented by God is in fact a foreclosure of the inherent incompleteness of the subject and thus pointing to a realm of unknowability. That is to say, the essential hierarchical supplementation of impossibly complete subject with unattainable God effectively serves to cover over the disavowed lack in the subject itself.

> [the subject] lacks everything needed to know the answer [to the question of its own origin], since if this subject 'I' was dead, he would not, as I said, earlier, know it. He does not know therefore, that I am alive. How, therefore, will 'I' prove to myself that I am?

> For I can only just prove to the Other that he exists, not, of course, with the proofs for the existence of God, with which over the centuries he has been killed off, but by loving him, a solution introduced by the Christian *kerygma* [preaching]. Indeed, it is too precarious a solution for me even to think of using it as a means of circumventing our problem, namely: 'What am 'I'?'
>
> (Lacan, 1977a(viii): 317)

Here Lacan might be understood to be claiming that the only possibility of an engaged relation towards the Other, the only mode in which 'I' might be understood to have asserted the Other's existence, would be through the assumption of an act of love. Such a movement might be seen to be symptomatic of a 'circumventing' of the problem of ascertaining a proof of the existence of the subject itself. 'Circumventing' here should be understood in all its weight as the movement of enclosing as well as the idea of outwitting or avoiding. To circumvent the problem would be to encircle it, divesting it of its necessarily open status. The subject which is radically unable to conceive of its own self, and thus its own origin, is consequently a subject which is, at the very least on an epistemological level, non-finite. But circumventing would also entail avoiding or denying the problem as such. In these entwined senses, invoking the potential love of the Other (or other) effectively reinforces and restages the question of the subject; 'What am 'I'?' (Ibid.) The attempt to circumvent is circular. This is not to suggest however that the assumption of an act of love, of loving the Other, is something to be rejected. Rather, it is to suggest that it is necessarily not an answer to the subjective question of the existence of the subject. An act of love would be that in which the subject *stricto sensu* loses itself or *is not*.

The term *jouissance*, used in the graph, is a term which alters in its significance through the course of Lacan's work. Where in its common-place French usage the term denotes pleasure or enjoyment, often being used to denote sexual pleasure in particular, from 1960 onwards Lacan opposes *jouissance* to pleasure, with the effect of emphasising the location of *jouissance* as 'beyond the pleasure principle'. The term continues to develop in its significance when, for example, in *Seminar XX*, Lacan distinguishes between male (phallic) *jouissance* and specifically female *jouissance*. The sense of *jouissance* as it is used here will refer primarily to the usage circa *Seminar VII*, the seminar on ethics, where the emphasis is on *jouissance* as posited lost wholeness, the impossible 'pleasure/pain' supposed to 'be' beyond the split which constitutes the subject. This conception of *jouissance*, as will be shown, is bound to desire and allows us to understand desire as directed towards the 'inaccessibility of the object as object of *jouissance*' (Lacan, 1992: 203).

In the enunciation of the question, 'What am I?' (Lacan, 1977a(viii): 317), the 'I', according to Lacan, speaks from the location of this *jouissance*. This is marked on the graph on the upper-left parabola, evocative of the parabola of signification on the lower half of the graph. Here, *jouissance*, the place from which the 'I' speaks, like the significance on the lower part of this graph and in earlier graphs, can only be 'known' or 'suspected' retrospectively. At the other end of the parabola we find castration and it is, thus, only through the mediating effects of this castration that the *jouissance* that might be taken to have preceded it, the *jouissance* which might be assumed to be that which is lost in the process of castration, can be posited at all. That is to say, in a manner similar to the mythical intentionality, Δ, which could only be imagined to have been after the advent of the subject for which it is the retroactive starting point, *jouissance* can only be posited retroactively as the mythic starting point of completion or wholeness which is assumed to have been annulled as an effect of castration. That the 'I' is said to speak from this impossible position indicates again the necessity of the assumption of 'I' outlined earlier in terms of *Wo Es war, soll Ich werden*; there where it was, 'I' must come to be. *Jouissance* can be understood to be (one name for) that (impossible) location from whence the 'I' which does not exist emerges and assumes its own place.

'I' am in a place from which a voice is heard clamouring 'the universe is a defect in the purity of Non-Being'.

And not without reason, for by protecting itself this place makes Being itself languish. This place is called *Jouissance*, and it is the absence of this that makes the universe vain.

Am I responsible for it, then? Yes, probably. Is this *Jouissance*, the lack of which makes the Other insubstantial, mine, then? Experience proves that it is usually forbidden me, not only as certain fools believe, because of a bad arrangement of society, but rather because of the fault (*faute*) of the Other if he existed: and since the Other does not exist, all that remains to me is to assume the fault upon 'I', that is to say, to believe in that to which experience leads us all, Freud in the vanguard, namely, to original sin.

(Ibid.)

Jouissance is always perceived – whether as a retroactive positing of the subject's 'own' *jouissance* or the detection of the *jouissance* of the Other – that is, *jouissance* is always potential and never actual, in the sense that, though mediated through the symbolic network and the mechanisms of the subject's desiring, it is never experienced directly in its entirety. This might suggest that *jouissance* is an imaginary function. Why might it be then that Lacan insists that *jouissance* ex-sists in the Real? *Jouissance* as perceived *is* an imaginary function but, as such, it necessarily points to a facet of the Real. This complex and undividable relation is clarified by the mathematical phenomenon of the Borromean Knot wherein each circle is maintained *only* with the support of all the other circles. Were one circle to be broken or removed, the remaining circles would fall apart.

The impossible and retroactively posited *jouissance* is, then, not something which might be considered to be *at home* in the subject, but neither is it something which is at home in the Other. The *jouissance* retroactively construed in and through the process of castration, the *jouissance* implied by the imposition of the signifier of the lack in the Other, $S(\cancel{A})$, the *jouissance* implied in the effects of the subject in relation to Demand, ($\cancel{S} \Diamond D$), at the other end of the graph, might be taken as a summation of and indication of the lack in both the subject and the Other. It is as such and only as such that that which is necessarily denied of the subject is also that for and towards which the subject can assume a certain responsibility. That it is through castration, and through the force of law that is implied in this moment, that the notion of *jouissance* arises should not be understood to imply an erroneous social structuring, or the imposition of the 'wrong' law. Such an interpretation would deny *jouissance* the necessity of its function. *Jouissance* is not indicative of an error in cohabitation or an effect emerging from an erroneous point in human social development which could be surpassed with the institution of a more efficacious social system or the 'correct' body of laws. Rather, *jouissance* is a structural necessity arising from the manner in which 'we' as speaking beings relate to 'our' world in and through language and the multifarious effects that this wreaks on our constitution. Thus, while *jouissance* is not a social accident, neither is it a 'natural' fact. It is rather, as Lacan states, an assumed place from which and in relation to which the 'I' might emerge. While *jouissance* might be perceived to be (in) the place of the Other, as the Other, strictly speaking, does not exist, the 'I' must (in the same imperative sense as 'there where it was, I *must* come to be'), as *jouissance* has already been posited, as its effects have (always already) been felt, assume responsibility for it. Like the Catholic notion of original sin, there is no one else to 'put it on'.

How the subject 'copes' with (its) *jouissance* returns us to the formula of fantasy which occupied the end of the questioning top arc in the previous version of the graph. The four mathemes which delineate the upper half of the graph – *d*, ($◊D), S($) and ($◊a) – respectively represent, in short, desire, the formula of the drive, the signifier of the lack in the Other, and the formula of fantasy. The short circuit from *d* to ($◊a), like its mirror on the lower part of the graph, from *i(a)* to *m*, indicates both a support and a *not-all*. That is to say, the subject's enjoyment (*jouissance*) is maintained by the movement of desire and its correspondence in fantasy and, because of this latter, it is never entirely subsumed by the intervention of the Other. The *points de capiton* on the upper part of the graph, ($◊D) and S($), like their mirrors on the lower part, S(A) and A, indicate those moments of anchoring in and by the realm of the Other. As A and S(A) represent respectively the place of the Other and the signifier as a function of the Other, so too do ($◊D) and S($) represent functions of the Other as they operate on the subject. But the very fact of the lack in the Other (S($)) opens the way for another route, a short circuit which defends against the Other and allows the subject a certain and necessary 'respite'.

The subject, it is clear, is constituted in relation to the Other but there is always some remainder which cannot be entirely subsumed within the Other without this resulting in the disappearance of the subject, which would in turn result in the disappearance of the Other as the two stand in a symbiotic relation of mutual dependence. This is not, of course, to suggest that were one person to 'disappear' the entire edifice of language and social organisation would irrevocably collapse. What is crucial here is that the Other, as such, does not exist. The Other is necessarily constituted *idiotically* in relation to each subject. It is also, crucially, not to suggest that the relation between subject and Other is in any way reciprocal or equal. While subject and Other can be understood to be, in a sense, codependent, this must be understood to be a radically dissymmetrical codependence.

The remainder here, that which cannot be recuperated entirely to the Other, is what constitutes the short-circuit of the upper part of the graph; *d* and (𝄳◇a), and the passage between them. As we have seen, desire (*d*) is that which remains when the particularity inherent in need is expulsed with the intercession of demand. This process can be further clarified with reference to (𝄳◇D), the right-hand *point de capiton.*

When the demand of the Other intercedes on need this effectively bars need from ever being a properly subjective function insofar as it is only with the advent of the demand and its barring effect on need that the subject properly is constituted. The demand, as the intervention of language, is coterminous with the emergence of the subject in the field of the Other, the symbolic realm. Through this intervention two other 'effects' are apparent; the drives and desire. This might be pictured something as follows (Figure 2.1).

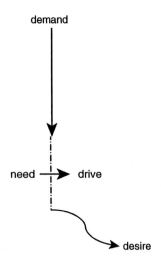

Figure 2.1

If demand can be understood as the moment of intervention by language, that is, as the splitting or aphanisis of the subject in its alienation between being and meaning, then the drive would have to be situated on the side of the symbolic. It is as such that the drive can be understood as 'that which proceeds from demand when the subject disappears in it' (Ibid.: 314). The drive, then, as a symbolic function or product of the intervention of the symbolic, is necessarily differentiated from the organic functions of need, though it still maintains a relationship to something of the organism to which need is retrospectively perceived to have been attached. This remainder is signalled, according to Lacan, in what he terms 'the cut', suggesting the non-place of a border or boundary. This cut is the effect of the symbolic dimension of demand, the fact that it arises in signification from the place of the Other (A). One effect of this is that the drives come to be conjoined with certain aspects of the body, as the body can be understood as the site of needs. This is not, however, to suggest that drives are in any sense an organic function, rather they can be understood as that which 'inhabits' (Ibid.) an organic function, that is, maintains a relation with a limit point of the organism which might have served as the receptacle for an organic function. It is in this sense that Lacan describes the drives and their concomitant objects as partial. It is not that the drives attend to parts of the body which could together comprise an organic whole, for their relation with the body is at most arbitrary. Rather, as symbolic functionaries they 'represent only partially the function which produces them' (Ibid.). That is to say, although the drive is separated from the organic functions of need, each drive remains associated with an organic function through the mediation of the very cut which separates them. The drive can then be said to have its source in certain aspects of the body (such as 'lips, "the enclosure of the teeth", the rim of the anus, the tip of the penis, the vagina, the slit formed by the eyelids, even the horn-shaped aperture of the ear' (Ibid.)) but its object is always dissociated from the organic function of this source. Its object, in Freud's terms, is 'a matter of total indifference' (Lacan, 1977b: 168), an indifference Lacan interprets as signifying that, while the object may retain a certain specificity to the source and the drive (such as the breast being the object of the oral drive), it does so in a symbolic manner, thus reducing the object from its organic function and necessitating that the object's relation to the drive, as opposed to its organic function, be reconfigured.

As far as the oral drive is concerned, for example, it is obvious that it is not a question of food, nor the echo of food, nor the mother's

> care, but of something that is called the breast, and which seems to go of its own accord because it belongs to the same series. If Freud makes a remark to the effect that the object in the drive is of no importance, it is probably because the breast, in its function as object, is to be revised in its entirety.
>
> (Ibid.)

In short, that which is to be the object of the drive, although it maintains a certain link with some aspect of the organic body, it does so with a different significance, rendering it essentially not the same at all. The real breast has been taken over into the realm of the symbolic where it is imbued with other significations. Lacan explains this characteristic of the drive in terms of its *fixation*.

> primal repression, a first phase of repression, ... consists in the psychical (ideational) representative of the drive, being denied entrance into the consciousness. With this a *fixation* is established; the representative in question persists unaltered from then onwards and the drive remains attached to it.
>
> (Lacan, 1966–67, *La Logique du Fantasme* (Unpublished),
> quoted in Fink, 1995: 74)

Primal repression is thus the consignment to the unconscious of the representatives of the drive. An example of such a representative would be the above example of the breast. The permanent status of the relation between the representative (here the signifier 'breast' or breast as signifier) and the drive attached to it renders the drives as essentially unchanging. This then allows us to understand that the drive is not concerned precisely with the attainment of its object as such and the corresponding satisfaction that might be expected to result from this, insofar as a satisfaction, in the strict sense, would insist upon at least some modification. Instead, the drive circles around its object and is thus concerned less with the goal, in the sense of that final point which would render its course complete, than it is with the aim, in the sense of the path it takes. The drive's movement is then perpetual, circling its object and returning to its source but always, as it is insatiable, persisting to traverse the object again. In this way, the drive can be understood as repetition, or as having as its ultimate goal its own repetition. The satisfaction proper to the drive is that attained through the repetition of the route and not the attainment of the object. The function, then, of the object of the drive is, in Lacan's formula, '*la pulsion en fait le tour'* (Lacan, 1977b: 168), where *tour* signifies both a movement around and a deception; i.e. 'the drive moves around the object and "the drive tricks the object"' (Ibid.; translator's note). It moves around it insofar as its circuit is conditioned by the object but its 'aim' is not to attain that object but rather to return to its source and, again, continue its course. In so doing, it 'tricks' the object in two senses; first, in that it does not treat the object as a proper object, as such, one which would constitute the goal of its movement, and, secondly, in the sense that it renders the object a signifier.

To recapitulate, the intercession of demand on need can be understood as coterminous with the advent of language and, thus, as the constitution of the subject as barred ($). This process gives rise to the primal repression which can be understood as formative of the unconscious. The result is both the expulsion of need to the realm of being and the creation of the subject as disunified. What is retroactively supposed to have been in the form of need is 'translated', and thus irrevocably altered, emerging in part as the drives. The drives, however, are fixated on those objects which would have been the objects of need and, as they are fixated, persist in perpetual motion around those objects, achieving their satisfaction through repetition and never aiming to attain the objects themselves. What this does not account for, however, is the particularity and wholeness inherent in need. A need is strictly a need for something. It is not concerned with anything additional, supplementary or adjacent. This particularity, lost in the intercession of demand, as it does not re-emerge in the functioning of the drive, escapes as a remainder. This remainder is desire. This is seen on the graph in the fact that the drives are presented in the relation between the subject and the demand of the Other, ($◇D), while it is desire which 'slips out', returning in the short circuit to ($◇a), the formula of fantasy.

3
Objet petit a and Fantasy

What is both crucial and confusing in trying to understand Lacan's theorisation of drive and desire is how, exactly, the two relate to each other and their individual relations to their objects.

> the object of desire is the cause of desire, and this object that is the cause of desire is the object of drive – that is to say, the object around which the drive turns. ... It is not that desire clings to the object of the drive – desire moves around it, in so far as it is agitated in the drive. But all desire is not necessarily agitated in the drive. There are empty desires or mad desires that are based on nothing more than the fact that the thing in question has been forbidden you. By virtue of the very fact that it has been forbidden you, you cannot do otherwise, for a time, than think about it. That too is desire. But whenever you are dealing with a good object, we designate it – it is question of terminology, but a justified terminology – as an object of love.
>
> (Lacan, 1977b: 243)

While the drives and desire are both constituted in relation to demand and, in a sense, both are constituted in relation to the same object, they are not the same function.

One differentiation between them is the crucial fact that while drives are always partial, in the sense that they attain to an object which only ever partially represents the *jouissance* to which they aspire, desire, due to its defining particularity, is always necessarily unitary. That this distinction can be maintained while upholding that it is in relation to the same object, *objet petit a*, that they are both configured is explained by the different mode of relating each has towards *objet petit a*. While the drives relate to the object as a partial representative of an unattainable pleasure or *jouissance,* and thus constitute their satisfaction (although this is never satisfaction in the strong sense of completion or fulfilment) through repetitive circumvention of the partial object, desire pertains to the object as a cause.

As discussed in Chapter 2, the subject's desire is in essence the desire of the Other with all the ambiguity carried in the preposition *of.* What each of the available meanings of this phrase maintain is that the subject's desire is *caused* by something in the Other. In summary, then, we could say that the subject's desire or desiringness arises in the field of the Other. *Objet petit a* would then stand in for that in or of the Other which gives rise to such desire in or of the subject. As divided, ꟼ, the subject aspires to a(n imaginary) lost unity which was supposed to have been before the subject's constitution as divided in the process of alienation; something akin to Δ, the mythical intention supposed to have been before the advent of the subject.

Similar to the manner in which the object functions in the drive, this is not to suggest that *objet petit a* as cause of desire can be reduced to a strictly non-subjective function or a function which is exclusively proper to the Other. *Objet petit a* must be understood as being both of the Other and of the subject and neither of the subject nor of the Other. *Objet petit a* is the lack around which the subject is constituted, that 'small part of the subject that detaches itself from him while remaining his, still retained' (Ibid.: 62). In this sense *objet petit a* can be characterised as *extimate* to the subject in a manner similar to the relation of extimacy inherent in S(Ⱥ). It is at one and the same time that which is most central to the subject and that which is always beyond the subject. This points to the fact that *objet petit a* is not an object, as such, in any usual sense of the term.

> To designate the *petit a* by the term object is, as you see, a metaphor-ical usage, since it is borrowed precisely from this subject-object rela-tionship from which the term object is constituted, which no doubt is suitable for designating the general function of objectivity; and this object, of which we have to speak under the term *a,* is precisely an object which is outside any possible definition of objectivity.
>
> (Lacan, 1962–63, *Seminar X: L'Angoisse* (Unpublished),
> quoted in Boothby, 2001: 262)

Here we should understand the refusal of 'definition' in the entwined senses of escaping the conventional understanding we would have of what constitutes an object and in that it, *objet petit a*, refuses the limitations which might be imposed by such an understanding. That is to say, *objet petit a* is indefinite, both insofar as it cannot be (re)presented in itself and insofar as it cannot be ascribed with any finitude. This infinitude may be understood as adhering to the lacking status of the object or the relation the object has with the concept of lack.

> The *objet a* is something from which the subject, in order to constitute itself, has separated itself off as organ. This serves as a symbol of the lack, that is to say, of the phallus, not as such, but in so far as it is lacking. It must, therefore, be an object that is, firstly separable and, secondly, that has some relation to the lack.
>
> (Lacan, 1977b: 103)

Objet petit a is then that unattainable (non-)object which is simultaneously impossible and necessary in order for the subject to come to, and to continue to, be constituted as a subject. It is impossible insofar as, strictly speaking, it does not exist and necessary insofar as the locus of its non-existence, its very lack, is that towards which desire aims. The fact that *objet petit a* does not exist as such does not mean that it does not have very real effects. It may in some sense be understood as a pure effect insofar as it functions to produce or give rise to desire without it being that which would or could quell desire. Against what might be understood as the common sense notion that there must exist something which desires or is at least capable of desiring which can then be attenuated with an object which is desirable or capable of being desired, a notion which would suggest an at least potential appeasement of (that) desire when the object in question is attained, Lacan's formulation posits a conception of the relation between desiring subject and object in which it is the object itself, or, properly, its lack, which not only gives rise to or causes desire, but also gives rise to or causes the subject itself.

The movement of desire can then be understood to take the form of a perpetual slippage from one object, thing or aspect of a thing, to the next; a perpetual search for that which caused the desire in the first place but which, as it does not exist as such, can never be (re)found.

This lack which would constitute the movement of desire proper to the subject is also crucially a lack in the Other. As the subject's desire, as we have seen, is always the desire of the Other, the Other is also always lacking. S($\cancel{A}$), the signifier of the lack in the Other, can thus be understood as both constitutive of the subject's desire – insofar as without lack the Other would not desire and the subject would not come to be as subject of desire and, thus, would not come to be as a divorced entity – and as that against which the subject must defend itself.

This conception of *objet petit a*, the object cause of desire, as, simultaneously, the stand in for the lack in the Other, S(Ⱥ), and the lack in the subject can be understood as symptomatic of or corresponsive with the lack of being (*manque-à-être*) experienced by the subject. Through the machinations of desire, the subject necessarily experiences both the Other and itself as lacking. This lack is inherent in the alienating constitution of the subject as effect of language, in the forced *vel* between meaning and being, and is also coextensive with that which is experienced retroactively as that which causes desire; *objet petit a*.

Desire is produced in the beyond of the demand, in that, in articulating the life of the subject according to its conditions, demand cuts off the need from that life. But desire is also hollowed within the demand, in that, as an unconditional demand of presence and absence, demand evokes a want-to-be under the three figures of the nothing that constitutes the basis of the demand for love, of the hate that even denies the other's being, and of the unspeakable element in that which is ignored in its request. In this embodied aporia, of which one might say that it borrows, as it were, its heavy soul from the hardy shoots of the wounded drive, and its subtle body from the death actualised in the signifying sequence, desire is affirmed as the absolute condition.

Even less than the nothing that passes into the round of significations that act upon men, desire is the furrow inscribed in the course; it is, as it were, the mark of the iron of the signifier on the shoulder of the speaking subject. It is not so much a pure passion of the signified as a pure action of the signifier that stops at the moment when the living being becomes sign, rendering it insignificant.

This moment of cut is haunted by the form of a bloody scrap – the pound of flesh that life pays in order to turn it into the signifier of the signifiers, which it is impossible to restore, as such, to the imaginary body; it is the lost phallus of the embalmed Osiris.

(Lacan, 1977a(ix): 265)

Desire is manifest through the experience of a *manque-à-être* – where the ambiguity of the French conveys the experience of lacking, the lack which is experienced and the wish to rectify this lack. As we have seen, this lack is not, however, something which can be rectified as it is precisely constitutive of the subject that encounters it.

> Desire is a relation of being to lack. This lack is the lack of being properly speaking. It isn't the lack of this or that, but the lack of being whereby being exists. ... Being comes into existence as an exact function of this lack. ... Being attains a sense of self in relation to being as a function of this lack, in the experience of desire.
>
> (Lacan, 1988b: 225)

The lack experienced by the subject (*manque-à-être*) is obviously not, however, something which can be embraced in itself. *Objet petit a*, therefore, must be understood at one and the same time as indicative of the lack in the subject and the Other and as that which can guard against the traumatic effects of this lackingness.

It is thus that we can understand why *objet petit a* stands at the conjunction of the three Lacanian realms – the symbolic, the imaginary and the Real – without properly speaking being situated in any one of them. *Objet petit a* is the symbolic representative of the lack experienced by the subject (the subject's lack, the Other's lack), it is the imaginary *thing* which would rectify the lack and it is the kernel of the Real which cannot be gathered into the symbolic world.

Returning to the final permutation of the Graph discussed in Chapter 2, we can then understand the upper part as representing this complex movement of demand, drive and desire in conjunction with *objet petit a* and the lack that it simultaneously covers and marks. Through the intercession of demand, the *Che Vuoi?* of the previous graph, the drive begins its perpetual circuit around the transmuted object. The remainder which is experienced as emerging from this transmutation is desire, which is experienced as being caused by and points towards that mythical object which would have provided and embodied the impossible wholeness of *jouissance*. Desire here is symptomatic of a lack in the Other which is also indicative of a lack in the subject itself. However, in order for this lack not to be experienced as the impossible encounter with the Real, that is, in order to protect the subject from the trauma of the lack of being (*manque-à-être*), the subject maintains an impossible relation with that which marks the place of this lack; *objet petit a*. This impossible relation is represented by the formula of fantasy, ($\$\lozenge a$).

If *objet petit a* is conceived as the remainder produced in the splitting of the subject ($\$$), the reminder of the hypothetical lost unity inherent in the notion of *jouissance*, then the formula of fantasy, the subject in the impossible relation with this object, ($\lozenge a$), can be understood as the protective function wherein the subject guards against the terror of facing this splitting and the encounter with the Real which that would imply. Fantasy could then be understood as the subject's illusory but necessary staging of its own completeness.

Clearly, then, there is an intimate relation between desire and the fantasy. Fantasy at one and the same time represents for the subject how they desire to be positioned in relation to the desire of the Other and, inseparable from this double articulation of desire, how they defend their imaginary self (*m*, the *moi* or ego, and *i(a)*, the ideal ego), their sense of self, against the desire of the Other in all its complexity. It is for this reason that Lacan emphasises that it is fantasy, not *objet petit a*, that supports the subject's desire.

> The phantasy is the support of desire; it is not the object that is the support of desire. The subject sustains himself as desiring in relation to an ever more complex signifying ensemble. This is apparent enough in the form of the scenario it assumes, in which the subject, more or less recognisable, is somewhere, split, divided, generally double, in his relation to the object, which usually does not show its true face either.
>
> (Lacan, 1977b: 185)

Embedded in the fantasy is the path to *jouissance*, that unbearable excitement or enjoyment which blurs the distinction between what might in common parlance be understood as pleasure and pain. As Bruce Fink suggests in his *The Lacanian Subject*, there are two notions of *jouissance* at work here (1995: 60). Fink dubs these *jouissance* before and after the letter. The former would denote that purely presumed *jouissance* of wholeness which could never actually have been experienced by the subject in itself, as it could only have been before the subject is constituted in its own division, and yet, paradoxically, it is experienced in terms of its own absence. The latter would denote the surrogate *jouissance* facilitated by fantasy, a second order *jouissance* which stands in place of and, in so doing, marks the (impossible) place of (the lack of) original *jouissance*.

Fantasy functions to obscure or defend the subject against an encounter with the Real. This Real is implied in the functions of demand, drive and desire, inherent in the impossibility and insistence of the Other's question, *Che Vuoi? Objet petit a*, that elusive object with which the subject conjoins itself in fantasy, can be understood as that which conceals the lack in the symbolic order which is indicative of the Real as that which cannot be symbolised.

> The function of the *tuché*, of the real as encounter – the encounter in so far as it is essentially the missed encounter – first presented itself in the ... form ... of the trauma. ... The trauma reappears, in effect, frequently unveiled. How can the dream, the bearer of the subject's desire, produce that which makes trauma emerge repeatedly – if not its very face, at least the screen that shows us that it is still there behind? ... the reality system, however far it is developed, leaves an essential part of what belongs to the real a prisoner in the toils of the pleasure principle.
>
> The place of the real, which stretches from the trauma to the phantasy – in so far as the phantasy is never anything more than the screen that conceals something quite primary, something determinant in the function of repetition – this is what we must now explain. This, indeed, is what, for us, explains both the ambiguity of the function of awakening and of the function of the real in awakening. The real may be represented by the accident, the noise, the small element of reality, which is evidence that we are not dreaming. But, on the other hand, the reality is not so small, for what wakes us is the other reality hidden behind the lack of that which takes the place of representation [*Vorstellungsreprasentanz*] – this, Freud says, is the *Trieb*.
>
> But be careful! We have not yet said what this *Trieb* is – and if, for lack of representation, it is not there, what is this *Trieb*? We may have to consider it as being only *Trieb* to come [*Trieb avenir*]. ... The real has to be sought beyond the dream – in what the dream has enveloped, hidden from us, behind the lack of representation of which there is only one representative. This is the real that governs our activities more than any other
>
> (Lacan, 1977b: 55–60)

That which sustains the fantasy or necessitates that the fantasy is sustained, is the unrepresentable Real which is the lack of the drive. As any absolute encounter with the Real would result in the trauma of an unbearable *jouissance,* the subject maintains itself against this in the 'security' of the fantasy. But as this *Trieb* is, strictly speaking, not there, it can only be maintained in the fantasy itself as '*Trieb* to come'. Phrased otherwise, behind or enveloped in the fantasy which the subject structures for itself in its unconscious resides the Real which the subject cannot directly encounter. *Objet petit a* functions here as the unitary representative which masks and, thus, (impossibly) represents this abyss of the Real.

As remainder, as that which exceeds the demand of the Other, as that which is not properly contained within the symbolic, *objet petit a* can be understood as that which it is not possible to symbolise. This is not to suggest that *objet petit a* is beyond the symbolic network in any absolute sense of being without relation to it. Rather, it is beyond the symbolic network insofar as it cannot be brought to reign by it. By this we should understand that *objet petit a* is that which cannot be represented in itself or, more precisely, it is the mark of that which cannot be represented. Its effects are felt, its place is marked, it insists on the field of signification, but, insofar as it stands in opposition to this field, it is indicative of its limit point and, consequently, the impossibility of totalisation that the absence of such a limit point would entail.

It is in this sense that *objet petit a* cannot properly be conceived as an object. It is also, clearly, here that we can see that *objet petit a* escapes the domain of the Other and thus marks the place of the impossible encounter with that which is beyond the Other, the Real. The subject's desire is that which is set in motion by the insistence of *objet petit a* and it is in relation with *objet petit a* that the subject both regains the possibility of some, incomplete, experience of the *jouissance* which would be found in this impossible encounter with the Real and sustains itself against the overwhelming effects of such an impossible encounter.

The properly subjective function of the fantasy can be elaborated with reference to Lacan's treatment of Choang-tsu's famous paradox of the dream of the butterfly. Waking from a dream in which he experienced himself as a butterfly, Choang-tsu poses himself the question of how he can be certain that he is now himself, Choang-tsu, and not the butterfly dreaming that he is Choang-tsu. Put simply, Choang-tsu's dilemma can be phrased as that of how we can know which self is the 'real' or authentic self and which self is an illusory, 'invented', dream version. This should also, perhaps, remind us of Descartes quandary as to how he knows he is not dreaming when he is 'in fact' awake (Descartes, 1993: 14). Where Descartes, to an extent, circumvents this problem, leading to the conclusion that, even if he is the dream version, this in itself is indicative of a real Descartes beyond the dream, insofar as the dream 'copy' necessitates an original from which it is abstracted (Ibid.: 15), Lacan's treatment is a little more involved. For Lacan, Choang-tsu is correct to pose himself this question for two reasons. First, taking such a question seriously indicates that one has not fallen so under the sway of the master signifier as to have foreclosed one's own division; that is, one does not assume that one is adequate to one's perceptions of oneself. In fact, one does not assume one is one.

> When Choang-tsu wakes up, he may ask himself whether it is not the butterfly who dreams that he is Choang-tsu. Indeed he is right, and doubly so, first because it proves he is not mad, he does not regard himself as absolutely identical with Choang-tsu.
>
> > (Lacan, 1977b: 76)

In addition to this, the question Choang-tsu poses to himself holds within it a certain truth of Choang-tsu. In a sense, he is the butterfly. The butterfly, in Lacan's reading, cannot be reduced to some mere chimera, an arbitrary construct of Choang-tsu's dream-state. On the contrary, it is as dream butterfly that Choang-tsu was able to grasp something of his own identity, namely;

> that he was, and is, in his essence, that butterfly who paints himself with his own colours.
>
> > (Ibid.)

For Lacan, it is through this penetration of the unconscious that something of Choang-tsu can emerge, as opposed to some social construct or status known as Choang-tsu. This can be reformulated in terms of the relation of subject to signifier. What we have in the parable of Choang-tsu are two signifiers, 'Choang-tsu' and 'butterfly'. The subject, in the proper Lacanian sense, of the parable is that which is represented between these two signifiers. Phrased otherwise, the subject of the parable is placed under these two signifiers:

$$\frac{\text{Choang-tsu}}{\$} \quad \rightarrow \quad \frac{\text{butterfly}}{\$}$$

It is, however, actually only in the movement between them that the subject proper emerges.

The difference here, for Lacan, between the dream and 'reality' is attested to by the mechanism of representation. In the dream the subject is represented as a butterfly, thus confirming something of his subjective apperception. Outside the dream, the subject is represented as Choang-tsu but feels it necessary to question this representation. This logic of uncertainty is in itself what points towards the subjective truth of the situation. As a butterfly, the subject does not pose the same question as when he is awake; 'when I am not this dream butterfly, when I am awake, am I actually this dream butterfly?' Lacan's explanation here, and thus his conclusion, is that, as dream butterfly, the subject is but his own representation whereas as Choang-tsu, he is a social representation.

> when he is the butterfly, the idea does not occur to him to wonder whether, when he is Choang-tsu awake, he is not the butterfly that he is dreaming of being. This is because, when dreaming of being the butterfly, he will no doubt have to bear witness later that he represented himself as a butterfly. But this does not mean that he is captivated by the butterfly – he is a captive butterfly, but captured by nothing, for, in the dream, he is a butterfly for nobody. It is when he is awake that he is Choang-tsu for others, and is caught in their butterfly net.
>
> (Ibid.)

The point we can extract from Lacan's reading of this parable is that the subject, $, cannot be reduced to either instance; neither butterfly nor Choang-tsu. Neither, however, is the subject properly some entity outwith the two instances. The subject is neither the property of, a pure effect of, the symbolic order – here that which is fixed under the signifier Choang-tsu – nor can the subject be reduced to a pure effect of itself (beyond or outwith the signifying realm).

In this sense, following Žižek (1989: 46), we could understand the dream (and its content) as the fantasy of the subject wherein the butterfly constitutes the (representative of the) object: ($◇ *butterfly*). For Žižek;

> In the symbolic reality he was Zhuang Zi [Choang-tsu], but in the real of his desire he was a butterfly. Being a butterfly was the whole of his positive being outside the symbolic network.
>
> (Ibid.)

What Žižek's interpretation occludes is the fact that, despite the impossibility of inverting the terms of the dream/fantasy to which he correctly attests, the parable does contain two instances of fantasy. While only one instance can, as Lacan confirms, be understood as a dream, fantasy is not reducible to dream states – we fantasise when awake and the unconscious continues to pulsate when awake. While clearly, in accordance with Žižek's reading, the butterfly is a fantasised representation of the subject such that it can be represented as $\$\Diamond butterfly$, the parable also contains the fantasy of being Choang-tsu; $\$\Diamond$ *Choang-tsu*.

What is significant in the parable, in terms of the light it casts on the notion of fantasy, is that by raising and posing the question of his own identity and, in Lacan's words, in 'not fully understand[ing] how right he is' (Lacan, 1977b: 76), Choang-tsu points us towards the impossibility of the subject in either position. The subject is the aphanisic point of its own departure, the subject is nothing but its own division.

In this sense the fantasy embodies a relation to some *thing* or image which functions as the *objet petit a* and thus protects the subject from the (im)possibility of the traumatic encounter with the Real by masking or obfuscating the site of the lack in the symbolic order. At the same time, and in a sense it is but a different perspective on the same function, the fantasy serves to protect the subject from the *jouissance* of the Real by providing a surrogate, fantasised, sense of unity.

Through the mode of fantasy we can perceive the mechanism of desire at work. The *objet petit a*, as that which causes desire, can be understood to stand-in for the unity we would wish to achieve. In both scenarios posed in the parable, as we have seen, there is something of an imagined sense of unity at work; I *am* the butterfly or I *am* Choang-tsu. In a sense, the psychoanalytic 'reality' is both attested to and negated in both versions – I am neither the butterfly nor Choang-tsu but I am positioned in response to my conceptualisation of myself as the butterfly and Choang-tsu. The truth of the subject is the mark of desire inscribed in both fantasies. The Lacanian point here would thus not be that the dream can be equated to fantasy and the waking state could not. Rather the point would be that both dream and waking state attest to the same fundamental fantasy albeit in necessarily different modes.

$S(\cancel{A})$, the signifier of the lack in the Other, points also to the impossibility of wholeness for the subject. In the face of this encounter, not with the void of the Real, but with the point on the signifying chain which is indicative of the ex-sistence of this void, the subject resorts to or finds support in fantasy. The fantasy thus constitutes a veil for this lacking both in the Other, the symbolic field, and in the subject. It is as such that the object of fantasy, that in relation to which the subject places itself in fantasy, constitutes the cause of subjective desire and thus constitutes the subject proper as subject of desire. Without the function of fantasy the subject would fail to mobilise itself. That is to say, it would not properly be (a) subject;

> in its fundamental use the phantasy is that by which the subject sustains himself at the level of his vanishing desire, vanishing in so far as the very satisfaction of demand hides his object from him.
>
> (Lacan, 1977a(ix): 272)

The castration of the subject, the dividing and alienating effect of the symbolic order as it functions at one and the same time to allow the possibility of the subject and to deny the subject the coherence it might (impossibly) have otherwise enjoyed, is attested to in the intercession of demand. The desire which then arises as one effect of this intercession is caused, set in motion, by the object of fantasy. But this object, attesting as it does to the state before castration, before the intercession of demand, is never actually available to be attained. Fantasy is thus the mode whereby the subject can 'flirt' with the (semblance of the) object in a relatively secure manner. In this sense, fantasy can be understood as the provision of a surrogate *jouissance* which, as surrogate, serves to guard the subject against Real *jouissance* by masking the lacking point in the symbolic network which is indicative of the (possibility) of the emergence of the Real.

The relation of the function of fantasy to the symbolic field, that the fantasy is that which covers over the lack in the symbolic and thus functions as a support for the symbolic, insofar as the subject relates to it, indicates that fantasy not only offers a certain (illusory) coherence for the subject, in terms of his own self-identity, but it also confers an equally illusory coherence on 'reality' (as it is mediated in terms of the Other). Properly, these should not be understood as two distinct moments. The subject's identity is always symbolically effected and the symbolic reality to which the fantasy lends some coherence is always a subjective representation. The identity thus secured in the mode of fantasy is, then, both indicative of the desire to identify oneself, to 'find' or construct one's identity, and to do so in relation to something of the 'outside' world, that which is mediated and structured by the symbolic network. It is in this identificatory sense that fantasy can be understood as the subjective response to the *Che Vuoi?* or to the demand.

Recalling the ambiguity of *Che Vuoi?*, the fact that it signals both the question addressed to the subject from the (place of the) Other and the question addressed to the subject by itself, that it is both 'what do you, the subject, want?' and 'what is it that the Other wants of me, the subject?', we can see that fantasy, insofar as it functions as a response to this questioning, provides a double answer. The fantasy in this sense encapsulates what it is that the subject wants, albeit in a surrogate form. That is, the object standing in for *objet petit a* is never *it* and, thus, fantasy can and will necessarily move onto another object which will also not be *it*. It also provides some answer to what it is that the Other wants, in the sense that it offers the possibility of an explanation of what it is that the Other is lacking and why it is that the Other is lacking. Again, this is not to suggest that *the* answer is found, that we can actually solve the lack in the Other, but that this lack is obfuscated by *an* (impossible and) illusory answer (Stavrakakis, 1999: 47 and 150–2). It is in this sense, again, that Lacan can assert that it is fantasy which is the support of the desire, not the object (Lacan, 1977b: 185).

Fantasy is thus that within the subject which attempts to shore up both its own constitutive lack and the lack in the Other. This operation is made possible by *objet petit a*, that remainder of the Real which insists on the subject, both indicating and serving to mask and protect against the trauma of the Real. Crucial to the logic of fantasy and desire however is the impossibility inherent in its operation. Were *objet petit a*, the object of fantasy, to be attained, the subject would be faced with the very trauma from which the fantasy serves to protect it. It is thus that desire must be understood as a perpetual movement, not in the sense of the drive, whose aim is its ultimate goal, but in the sense that the object which causes it would, if attained, negate its very own function.

Perhaps the quintessential example of the fantasy would be that of love as original unity. The myth, as presented by Aristophenes in *The Symposium* (Plato, 1994), tells of how humanity once consisted of three genders – male, female and hermaphrodite – and how each individual, of whichever gender, was complete in itself though combining what we would now understand as the attributes of two people; four hands, four legs, two faces etc. Due to these creatures' ambition and power, they were considered a threat to the Gods who decided to split each one in two. Because, however, each creature had previously formed a whole with its other half, they clung to them and, if separated, searched for them relentlessly (Plato, 1994: 25–8). The myth, as it has come to pass into popular culture, has us each in restless pursuit of our true other half, that other person who would really complete us.

This example illustrates the different functions performed in fantasy. Firstly, it proffers an identity, the answer to the question of who I *really* am; I am really the other half of my lost other half. Secondly, it does so with reference to the promise of a wholeness to come; when I find my lost other half, I will again be complete and everything will be perfect. Lastly, it offers an excuse as to why things are not (yet) perfect, why it is that both I and the world are lacking. Through each of these complementary functions, the fantasy serves to forestall any final resolution. When we do find or think we have found our lost other half, the girl or boy of our dreams, it inevitably turns out that they are not quite the magical someone we had hoped for, the world is not suddenly put to rights, nothing is really perfect and thus they cannot be *it* and the hope can continue that our real Platonic other half is still 'out there'.

For Lacan, one of the fundamental operations of, and thus lessons to be learnt from, psychoanalysis is that of 'traversing the fantasy'. As we have seen, the formula of fantasy is represented by the symbol ($\$\Diamond a$) wherein the subject is presented in relation to *objet petit a*, the object cause of desire. Traversing, crossing over the fantasy, would thus involve the assumption of responsibility for the cause of one's own desire and thus of one's own cause as subject, as without desire the subject cannot come to be. Traversing the fantasy would thus involve assuming a position of responsibility towards (the function of) one's fantasy. That is to say, assuming the role of the cause of desire and thus accepting the perpetual sliding of *objet petit a*. Put simply, accepting one's desire for what it is, accepting one's desire as interminably bound to the desire of the Other and not attaching oneself to the illusory dream of attaining impossible lost *jouissance* 'elsewhere'.

Graphically this could be represented as ($\$\overset{\longrightarrow}{\Diamond a}$); i.e. the subject assuming responsibility for the (object as) cause.[3] It must be kept in mind, however, that such an assumption can never be a permanent effect. Desire is in perpetual movement and the subject in question is the barred subject of the unconscious, not some monadic subject of pure being. Thus, the pulsative nature of the unconscious must be accounted for. The subject emerges as pulsation in and through the symbolic realm and it is only

---

[3]This should not be confused with ($a\Diamond\$$), with the subject exchanging places with the object as cause, which would be the formula of the perverse fantasy wherein the subject places itself in position of object.

thus that the operation of traversing the fantasy can be enacted, as speech.

> what's important is to teach the subject to name, to articulate, to bring this desire into existence, this desire which, quite literally, is on the side of existence, which is why it insists. If desire doesn't dare to speak its name, it's because the subject hasn't yet caused this name to come forth.
>
> That the subject should come to recognise and name his desire, that is the efficacious action of psychoanalysis. But it isn't a question of recognising something which would be entirely given, ready to be coapted. In naming it, the subject creates, brings forth, a new presence in the world.
>
> (Lacan, 1988b: 228–9)

Insofar as *objet petit a* is, as such, *not*, that which attains to the position of *objet petit a* is always necessarily a functionary of the subject. This is not, however, to suggest that there is something 'out there' chosen by the subject which would provide the lost *jouissance* implied by *objet petit a*. Rather, it is to say that the subject has, in the mode of fantasy, chosen something to function as the necessary surrogate of the object cause of desire. In so naming, and thus constituting, this desire, the subject puts itself in a position to claim responsibility for it. As desire is that which motivates and constitutes the subject, this naming and bringing forth allows the subject to assume responsibility for itself and thus assume a subjective position which is not in thrall to, though it is, clearly, still dependent upon, the Other.

Traversing the fantasy thus returns us to one interpretation of the Lacanian imperative *Wo Es war, Soll ich werden*, 'there where it was, I must come to be'. It also sheds some light on Lacan's emphasis on desire in his seminar on ethics when he asks, 'Have you acted in conformity with the desire that is in you?' (Lacan, 1992: 314) or declares that 'the only thing of which one can be guilty is of having given ground relative to one's desire' (Ibid.: 319).

Wo Es war, soll Ich werden in this context would indicate the movement, the traversing, from the subjugated subject of fantasy, wherein the subject is (perceived as) constituted by, caused as subject of desire by, the elusive *objet petit a*, to a position of subjectivity wherein it, the subject, is its own cause. We could thus reformulate the dictum 'Where It was, there must I come into being' as 'Where the object was (perceived to be the cause my desire), there shall I come to be (the cause of my own desire)'. Such a shift is a radical realtering of the subjective position from which one speaks. It is clear also, however, that such a realtering is and can only be momentary as, in enunciating and thus creating its desire, the subject necessarily does so in the mode of the Other; i.e. language. The desire the subject brings into existence through its enunciation is necessarily passed over into the realm of the Other (desire is still the desire *of* the Other) but through the process of enunciating its desire the subject can succeed in repositioning itself and thus attaining something of its own.

Here we can see that traversing the fantasy does not entail a 'getting over' or moving beyond fantasy in any absolute sense. It is not that the subject who has traversed the fantasy will no longer have any need of such a function. As we have seen, fantasy is a necessity in subjective life in order to avoid the traumatic effects of the Real and to accept castration. Rather, traversing the fantasy involves the formation or configuration of a new fantasy which allows or reflects the assumption of a 'new' subjective position in relation to the Other and the Other's desire. Such a (re)formation of the subjective position is the moment of *Wo Es war, soll Ich werden*, wherein the subject ($) assumes a position in that place previously occupied by the Other or the discourse of the Other. Such a moment, the traversing of fantasy, can then be understood to be a moment of (taking) responsibility; a retroactive assumption of responsibility for the position one will have come to occupy. Such occupation and its concomitant responsibility is indicative of a temporalisation which resists temporalisation. It is not the 'despite what has been, I will be' of ego-psychology but rather a reconfiguration of and assumption of responsibility for the very relation of cause and effect which might be taken as having, or having been seen, to have occurred.

Recalling the *vel* of alienation, it is clear that the subject who results from the choice in a barred or impossible form(lessness) cannot, meaningfully, have been that which originated the choice or that which was faced with the choice. In this sense, Lacan's formulation is one which renounces any traditional notion of or conceptualisation in chronological terms. The retroactive positing of the subject's responsibility is one which occurs within what Lacan terms logical, rather than chronological, time. This points towards an understanding of the relationship between cause and effect which unsettles traditional or received notions of what such a relationship would 'naturally' be in any given situation and emphasises the assumptive and forced qualities of this relationship. Simply put, the uninvested, received notion that A is (and always is) the cause of B in any (comparable) circumstance is put under question.

> cause is a concept that, in the last resort, is unanalysable – impossible to understand by reason – if indeed the rule of reason, the *Vernunftregel*, is always some *Vergleichung*, or equivalent – and that there remains essentially in the function of cause a certain *gap*.
>
> (Lacan, 1977b: 21)

This logic can also be detected in Lacan's statement concerning not ceding or giving ground relative to one's desire. By allowing the relation with the object to pertain in such a way that the object is Other, that is, that the subject finds its cause in something radically external to itself, the subject cannot yet bring itself to be in a properly subjective position. The assignation of cause is always a retroactive and subjective affect. By assigning the role of cause to something else, the subject denies itself and places itself under the sway of the Other, albeit in a deluded form. It is only through the subjective assumption of the cause that the subject allows its own possibility.

Part II
Lacanian Ethics

4
Guilt

Lacan's dictum that 'the only thing of which one can be guilty is of having given ground relative to one's desire' (Lacan, 1992: 319) raises a number of interpretative problems. Any considered reading of this statement would have to account not only for the precise meaning of the dual terms 'desire' and 'guilt' but, crucially, for how these two terms might interrelate, that is, what might be meant by 'having given ground relative to'.

A very simplistic reading of this statement might suggest that Lacan is advocating that it is non-ethical to renounce what one (truly) wants, to relinquish one's particular enjoyment, that the only true ethical imperative is that one ought to discover and pursue one's wishes or one's pleasure to the end and, if one does not, then one has betrayed one's ethical duty. Such a reading might seek to emphasise the groundless nature of the external authority of traditional moral systems. It might argue that there is, ultimately, no basis for or proof of the truth of grand moral systems; the Good, as such, does not exist, therefore, the only ethical perspective one could take is the pursuit of one's own 'desire', one's own (configuration of the) good. One would be guilty before oneself (as there is no other, valid, external authority) if and when one subordinates one's desire to the arbitrary dictates of an external authority, even, or particularly, when the dictates of the external authority have been internalised through the function of the super-ego. The problem with such a reading is that it disregards the theoretical complexity of the terminology with which Lacan constructs his 'imperative'. Such a reading would suppose that desire is maintained in a relatively straight-forward relation to an accessible *jouissance*. Furthermore, such a reading, while implicitly invoking the super-ego, also glides over the complexities of this function and consequently does not account for the interrelation of desire, feelings of guilt and the law. In transposing the dictum 'the only thing of which one can be guilty is of having given ground relative to one's desire' (Ibid.) into something like the imperative 'Do not give way on your *jouissance!*' (Johnston, 2001: 411), one is effectively re-inscribing the law which had previously been disregarded as groundless. If there is no exterior ground for the law, this pertains to the very functioning of the law, not to this or that content of this or that law. The imposition of any alternative imperative is no more grounded than any other. 'Do not give way on your *jouissance!*' on this reading has claim to no more justification or support than 'Renounce your *jouissance!*'

Another reading of this statement is that advanced by Adrian Johnston, which suggests that it does not in fact promote an ethics at all, but is rather a conclusion on the nature of 'guilt', that Lacan here is separating the notion of guilt from the field of ethics insofar as guilt would appear as an emanation from the 'greedy' machinations of the super-ego and, as such, actually stands in opposition to any successful furtherance of the field of human ethics. The question here might be phrased as that of whether Lacan is concerned with feelings of guilt or of being guilty (Ibid.: 420). While such a reading does help to clarify something of the complexity of Lacan's statement, it also runs the risk of oversimplifying the notion of guilt at work here. While it would seem remiss in this context to ignore the psychic resonance of guilt, the relation between feeling guilty and the work of the super-ego, there equally appears to be little justification for restricting the sense of being guilty ('être coupable' (Lacan, 1986: 368)) to a pure effect of the super-ego. Given the context of *Seminar VII*, the centrality of the concepts of law and judgement, and the situating of Lacan's discussion of ethics in relation to traditional theories of ethics, a considered reading of the use of the term 'guilt' cannot easily ignore the connotations of judgement and the related legal sense of 'being found guilty'.

Moreover, the reading in which guilt here would signify nothing but a psychic manifestation, feeling guilty, while claiming to explain what might be construed as the obstacles to a viable theory of ethics, actually denies the possibility of such a viable theory unless it chooses to slip a juridical sense of ethics in again at a later stage through the back door. A conception of ethics would require, in order for it to maintain any sense, both the idea of *being ethical* or *acting ethically* and the concomitant idea of *not being ethical* or *not acting ethically*. The possibility of the non-ethical or of a non-ethical position requires that a judgement be made. Add to this the fact that in order for something to be judged ethical something or someone must also be judged here. That is, someone or something would have to be potentially found guilty or not. By reducing the sense in which guilt is applied in Lacan's teachings on ethics to the psychic manifestation of guilt in response to the machinations of the super-ego, we effectively occlude any possibility of ethics at all. To recuperate to this reading a sense of ethics which would still be an ethics, would be to necessarily reverse this reduction to *feeling guilty* and reintroduce *being guilty* at a subsequent level. What effectively falls out of this picture is that this 'second order' use of guilt, guilt as being found guilty, is precisely at work all along in Lacan's thinking on this matter.

Lacanian theory allows us to configure an ethics in such a way that it is neither reducible to the super-ego and the concomitant feelings of guilt which would arise as a result of the working of the super-ego nor is it ignorant of the working of the law. Rather, Lacan offers us the possibility of a conception of the ethical which would account for but also move beyond the super-ego, which would acknowledge the necessary force and function of the law while indicating the necessity of a conceptual space which cannot be reduced to the law.

For Lacan, the pursuance of the good, as would typify the goal of traditional ethics, does not and cannot protect one from manifestations of guilt. That is, pursuing the good will not stop us from feeling guilty or experiencing the effects of guilt in our psychic mechanisms. It would perhaps not be going too far to say that such protection from guilt or the expunging of guilt from the subject's psychic life, were it at all possible, would in fact be disastrous. Guilt is a necessary manifestation, an essential product of the process of becoming subject. At the same time, Lacanian theory allows an understanding of the law which cannot be totalised, which necessarily maintains a gap which cannot be accounted for in the opposition of obedience/disobedience and yet is not reducible to ignorance of the law. Such a gap would be the subject's own confrontation with the law, the subject's own confrontation with the desire which would arise in them in the face of the law. It is this gap which would necessitate the assumption of responsibility on the part of the subject and this gap which invites the properly ethical moment.

While an understanding of the processes which would give rise to guilty feelings is useful in delimiting an understanding of the field of ethics and certainly in unravelling an aspect which would necessarily be encountered within a pursuance of ethics, ethics, in Lacan's formulation, would also entail a judgement which would require a conception of guilt which would be beyond the effects of the super-ego.

That is to say, without losing the significance of the guilt which would arise in response to the super-ego, a viable ethics would necessitate another sense of guilt. As such a notion of guilt cannot be reduced to a mere functionary of the law, insofar as the law itself cannot account for its own foundation, the question that needs to be addressed here would be that of the fashion in which this other guilt might arise and what might be available to ground a possible guilty verdict?

To develop an understanding of guilt as a psychic manifestation as it arises in relation to the functioning of the super-ego, it is useful to return to Freud. In *Civilization and Its Discontents* Freud delimits two theoretical stages in the formation of a sense of guilt and conscience. The first stage relates to an amorous privation wherein, fearing the aggression of an external authority which would manifest as the threat of deprivation of love, the subject renounces its pursuit of that which would have been the object of its (perceived) satisfactions (Freud, 2002: 64). In such a first stage, it might seem reasonable to suggest that the desire for those objects of satisfaction have gone largely unaltered, that the fear of being caught abates the pursuit of the object but not the desire for the object. It is in the second stage, when the external authority is in part replaced by an internal authority in the shape of the super-ego that the privation is brought to bear on the very desire for the object beyond the actualisation of any pursuit of the object. As the super-ego is internal to the subject, there can no longer be any hope of concealing one's desires from it. Thus, the prior fear of being caught, of the external authority discovering one's intentions or desires, becomes obsolete as one has always already been 'caught' by the super-ego. This serves to meld together the desire and the acting upon the desire. As Freud puts it, 'an evil deed is on a par with an evil intention' (Ibid.). This, for Freud, is clearly not to say that the super-ego merely replaces the function of an external authority. Where in the first stage, that of the external authority, the fear of amorous privation gives rise to the renunciation of acting on one's desire, in the second stage it is the very renunciation of desire which gives rise to the conscience, thus strengthening the power and effects of the super-ego. Put simply, although originally it is prohibition which inculcates renunciation, in the later stage it is renunciation which bolsters the prohibitory force of the super-ego; 'every fresh renunciation reinforces its severity and intolerance' (Freud, 2002: 65).

This shift from the (external) prohibitory force demanding and being, momentarily at least, appeased by the subject's renunciation of its desires and the (internal) prohibitory force demanding and being bolstered by the subject's renunciation of its desires results from the location and orientation of the subject's aggressivity and the relation of this aggressivity towards the prohibitory force. In the initial stage, the subject is liable to feel aggressive towards the external authority which (is perceived as being that which) deprives it of the satisfaction of its desires. In the second stage, as the prohibiting force is no longer something separable from or external to the ego, as the super-ego is, properly, a facet of the ego, the aggressivity which would have been directed against the agent of prohibition is now conjoined with its prohibitory force and directed against the ego. As the subject then 'is obliged to forgo the satisfaction of this vengeful aggression' (Ibid.) against the external authority, it instead identifies itself with and thus internalises the authority. In this process of internalisation, the super-ego becomes the site of the force of aggressivity previously felt towards the external authority. Thus, in the move from the initial to the latter stage, the force of the super-ego is not so much constituted as the assumption of the aggressivity perceived in the external authority as constituted from the existent and arising aggressivity previously felt against this authority. In this shift, the ego, not the internal authority, assumes the place of recipient of the aggressive tendencies. This then goes some way to explaining why the super-ego is bolstered and not abated by renunciation. Where, previously, the privating authority might have been appeased by renunciation, while the subject would harbour a certain aggressivity in response to this privation, now renunciation leads not to appeasement but to an intensified aggressivity as the super-ego has conjoined the function of authority with the subjective aggression previously motivated against authority.

In terms of the distinction which might be made between the feelings of guilt attenuated to an intention or a deed not enacted, which would properly be the effect of the machinations of the super-ego, and the feelings of regret associated with a deed actually enacted, Freud argues that only the former properly deserves the title of 'guilt', the latter being better titled 'remorse'. While this is not to suggest that *remorse* is not in any way associated with the conscience or a propensity for guilt, it does suggest that remorse only manifests when conscience and guilt have already been constituted.

> If one has a sense of guilt after committing a misdeed, and because one has committed it, this feeling ought rather to be called *remorse*. It relates only to a deed, although of course it presupposes that

> before the deed there was already a *conscience*, a readiness to feel
> guilty.
>
> (Ibid.: 67)

That is to say that the conditions of remorse are the anterior constitution
of the super-ego and the readiness to feel guilty which this would result
in. The myth of the primal horde recounted in *Totem and Taboo* is such a
case of remorse and serves, for Freud, to illustrate the necessary distinction here. The myth, which in the context of *Totem and Taboo* is intended
to facilitate an aetiology of morality, tells of the dominant male figure in
a primitive horde who banishes the younger subordinate males in order
to maintain all the available females for himself. At some point the exiled
males band together and kill this primordial father figure. The slaying of
the father is followed by the consumption of his body by the slayers in a
cannibal act of identification.

> The violent primal father had doubtless been the feared and envied
> model of each one of the company of brothers: and in the act of
> devouring him they accomplished their identification with him,
> and each one of them acquired a portion of his strength.
>
> (Freud, 1950: 141–3)

However, rather than then enjoying the women, as had presumably
been their avowed intention, the males now proceed to prohibit the
very enjoyment they had set out to attain. The reason Freud provides
for this is the ambiguity of feelings arising in the males after the
accomplishment of their deed.

> the tumultuous mob of brothers were filled with the same contra-
> dictory feelings which we can see at work in the ambivalent father-
> complexes of our children and of our neurotic patients. They hated
> their father, who had presented such a formidable obstacle to their
> craving for power and their sexual desires; but they loved and
> admired him too. After they got rid of him, had satisfied their
> hatred and had put into effect their wish to identify themselves
> with him, the affection which had all this time been pushed under
> was bound to make itself felt. It did so in the form of remorse. A
> sense of guilt made its appearance, which in this instance coincided
> with the remorse felt by the whole group. The dead father became
> stronger than the living one had been ... . What had up to then
> been prevented by his actual existence was thenceforward prohibited

by the sons themselves ... . They revoked their deed by forbidding the killing of the totem, the substitute for their father; and they renounced its fruits by resigning their claim to the women who had now been set free. They thus created out of their filial sense of guilt the two fundamental taboos of totemism ... . Whoever contravened those taboos became guilty of the only two crimes with which primitive society concerned itself.

(Ibid.)

The supposed events of the myth here perfectly encapsulate the hypothesis of the formation and functioning of the super-ego advanced in *Civilization and Its Discontents*. There is originally an external authority, the father, who prohibits the attainment of a certain enjoyment. This prohibition gives rise to feelings of aggression or hatred. Following an identification with and internalisation of the authority (in this case the literal consumption of the father), the force and subject of prohibition comes to be located within those previously subject to the external prohibition; the brothers forbid themselves access to the women just as the father had before they killed him. Only, now, the force of prohibition, being internalised, is strengthened.

Crucially, Freud tells us that the suppressed affection that the brothers felt towards the father manifests after the murder, making itself felt 'in the form of remorse' (Ibid.) and that a 'sense of guilt made its appearance, which in this instance coincided with the remorse felt by the whole group' (Ibid.). In *Civilization and Its Discontents* (2002), Freud clarifies this point and the coincidence of the remorse felt with, and thus the relation of the remorse felt to, the guilt experienced, contending that it is the very contradictory status of the sons' feelings towards the father which allows an understanding of the relations of remorse and guilt to accede. Having exercised their hatred and aggressivity in the act of killing the father, it was now possible for their love for him to surface, which it does in the form of remorse. As a result of the operation of identification symbolised in the cannibal act, the authority of the father is internalised as the super-ego which can then not only set about punishing the act of aggression which was his murder but also construe further prohibitions intended to ensure that such aggressivity is not outwardly manifest again. For Freud, this foundation of the super-ego is then reinforced with each subsequent generation as aggressivity and its attendant guilt rises again, and is subsumed into the increasing force of the super-ego.

It is thus that the real source of feelings of guilt, for Freud at least, is neither specifically in a 'wrongful' act or the desire to engage in such an act, nor is it purely emergent from the redirected aggressivity, the turning of that which had originally been directed towards an external authority towards the ego itself. The source of feelings of guilt, rather, resides in and arises from a conflict which manifests in the subject, namely the irreconcilable clash of love and aggressivity. This is later formulated by Freud, in the terms of the second topography, as 'the struggle between Eros and the death drive' (Freud, 2002: 75). That is, the drive for the satisfaction, the enactment of which, in the initial stage, would have been renounced in the face of the external authority and the aggressive drive which would have been directed against this authority are, in the formation of the function of the super-ego, seen to be entwined or fused (Freud, 1973: 137–41).

Set in motion, then, as the internalisation of a previously external – for example, societal or paternal – authority, the super-ego is that which supervises, assesses and censors the activities and intentions of the ego. This function of supervision, assessment and censorship, we would call conscience. Feelings of guilt emanate as a response to the austerity of the super-ego or the severity of conscience. These feelings, as located in the ego, can be accounted for in terms of the ego's own perception of the overbearing nature of the supervision and censure under which it is placed by the super-ego and its reaction to the tension between its own endeavours and the resultant demands placed upon it by the super-ego. This whole mechanism is underpinned by a sense of fear of the harsh authority of the super-ego and is coterminous with a need for punishment arising from what Freud describes as the 'inherent drive for internal destruction' (Freud, 2002: 73) which is in part directed towards the establishment of an 'erotic bond' (Ibid.) between the ego and the super-ego. That the subject will renounce its drives, at least in part, due to a desire for love or, what amounts to the same thing, a fear of deprivation of love, illustrates the entwined and conflictual nature of the base subjective inclinations. That this conflict is then internalised and heightened in the process allows us to understand the root of the sense of guilt which can be understood to be part and parcel of the very emergence of a subjective position.

Feelings of guilt, in Freud's understanding, do not issue directly and necessarily from a contravention of the law, be it moral law or otherwise. The explanation of one's feelings of guilt cannot be reduced to the question of whether or not one has acted or even desired to act in accordance with the law or with some given notion of right and wrong. Rather, one's feelings of guilt are related to the internal conflict one experiences in relation to one's own desires and the attendant expectation of gratification and aggressivity therein. This is clearly not to suggest that such feelings of guilt are not in any way related to the law. They are, but in a manner significantly more complex than that of an equation between contravening the law and guilt.

In 'Function and Field of Speech and Language' (1977a(iii)) Lacan follows Freud's aetiology of the law, positing its origins as incest prohibition and accrediting this 'primordial Law' (1977a(iii): 66) as instituting human culture. Adding clarity to Freud's assertion that the prohibition of incest can be understood as the beginnings of moral law and human culture, Lacan indicates that it must also have coincided with or given rise to nominative needs and abilities. Without the advent of language, the emergent law of prohibition could not have been instituted as an 'order of preferences and taboos that bind and weave the yarn of lineage through succeeding generations' (Ibid.). To clarify this slightly further, the condition of law, or law in its more general sense, as opposed to this or that particular law, what we might call law as the condition of law, can be understood as the institution of organising principles. Thus law, in its general and structural sense, can be understood to be commensurate with culture and language. As such, for Lacan, it is also indicative of desire.

> Freud designates the prohibition of incest as the underlying principle of the primordial law, the law of which all other cultural developments are no more than the consequences and ramifications. At the same time he identifies incest as the fundamental desire.
>
> (Lacan, 1992: 67)

As we have seen previously, desire arises as a result of the emergence of the subject in the field of the signifier. The lack upon which the movement and maintenance of desire is predicated is an effect of the division in the subject which can be understood as resulting from the *vel* of alienation. In the 'choice' to move from being to meaning the subject loses a part of itself. This choice, as we have seen, should be understood as the very possibility of the subject's emerging at all, insofar as the refusal of 'meaning' would negate the possibility of the assumption of a subjective position. Clearly, however, the paradox which reveals itself here is that this 'lost part' could never have been other than lost, as before the choice was made there was no possibility of subjectivity. The posited wholeness which would have preceded the *vel* of alienation thus becomes that mythical state towards which the subject's desire is motivated. The desire for the attainment of this impossibly lost unity can thus be understood as correlative with the law or the field of signification insofar as it is the imposition of the prohibitive organising structures which banishes some*thing* which is only later both assumed to be or to have been banished and assumed to be that which would resolve the lack apparent in the subject.

We have previously called that which would be indicative of this lost part *objet petit a*, the (impossible) object cause of the subject's desire. In *Seminar VII* Lacan describes something akin to, although not reducible to, *objet petit a* under the term *das Ding*. Lacan separates *das Ding* from *Sache*, as present in the German term, *Sachevorstellungen*, which Freud uses to denote what in English has been rendered 'thing-presentations'. Where the *Sache*, the thing, in *Sachevorstellungen* is caught up in the chain of language, where it designates the 'things' of the human experience insofar as they are 'structured by words' and dominated by 'language, the symbolic processes' (Ibid.: 45), *das Ding* designates, rather, that which escapes the realm of signification. *Das Ding* would indicate that which cannot be brought within the symbolic order, that which cannot be understood as such. In extrapolating this notion of *das Ding*, Lacan refers to a passage from Freud's *Project for a Scientific Psychology* where Freud argues that in our encounters with our fellow human-beings we can distinguish two components, one of which 'can be *understood* by the activity of memory' as it is familiar, while the other refuses such absorption, rather staying 'together as a *thing*' (Freud, 1966: 331). In Lacan's reading, this first component, that which can be understood, is that which 'can be formulated as an attribute' (Lacan, 1992: 52). That is, it is that which would already have a place in the symbolic order. *Das Ding*, on the other hand, is that which would be isolated 'as being by its very nature alien' (Ibid.). This alien nature of *das Ding*, the fact that it is beyond or outside the realm of the subject's symbolic experience, and yet does insist upon the subject, posits it as bound to the movement of desire. *Das Ding* as that which cannot be attained, cannot be grasped, comes to figure as that which would shore up the lack in the subject. It is in this sense that *das Ding* can be conceptualised as the subject's 'good'. As that which is strictly unattainable, that which is necessarily missing, *das Ding* might be figured as that which would 'be there when in the end all conditions have been fulfilled' (Ibid.), the utopic horizon or promise of the Good to come. Clearly, such a figuration as good is a figuration, the positing of an attribute to that which properly cannot be said to or known to have any attribute. It is this very unknowability of *das Ding* which would render it open to ascription as good, as promising. As such, the Good to come, *das Ding*, would insist upon the subject as that 'lost object', 'the absolute Other of the subject, that which one is supposed to find again' (Ibid.).

> *Das Ding* has, in effect, to be identified with *Wieder zu finden*, the impulse to find again that for Freud establishes the orientation of the human subject to the object. ... Moreover, since it is a matter of finding it again, we might just as well characterize this object as a lost object. But although it is essentially a question of finding it again, the object has never been lost.
>
> (Ibid.: 58)

As that which is posited as lost and thus motivates subjective desire in the impossible venture of refinding it, *das Ding* can be conceived as that which is or has been prohibited. Like the place marked by *objet petit a*, the place of the Real as the impossibility of finitude of the symbolic order, *das Ding* is symptomatic of an absence which would entail an unbearable trauma were it to be encountered. The function of the pleasure principle operates here to safeguard the subject against this traumatic encounter through the imposition of detours and the maintenance of a distance, ensuring that the place of the (non-)object is not encountered. Here we find already a correlation between *das Ding* and the law. The pleasure principle which governs the subject in relation to *das Ding*, functioning to restrict the subject's satisfactions to the polarity pleasure/unpleasure, is effectively a prohibitive force restricting the subject from an encounter with impossible *jouissance*, that 'unbearable pleasure' which would be inherent to the impossible lost unity promised by the insistence of *das Ding*. In this sense the pleasure principle can be understood as a regulative mechanism which harbours the subject within the relative safety of the symbolic order.

> The function of the pleasure principle is, in effect, to lead the subject from signifier to signifier, by generating as many signifiers as are required to maintain at as low a level as possible the tension that regulates the whole functioning of the psychic apparatus.
>
> (Ibid.: 119)

Desire, then, might be understood as the unconscious search for that mythical lost *Thing* which would accord the subject its lost unity and, thus, its access to *jouissance*. *Das Ding*, the *Thing* which is posited as lost in and through the presumed process of prohibition which would have initiated subjective emergence in the symbolic, the locus of the Other, is, thus, at one and the same time, the effect of the originary institution of law and that which is constitutive of the foundation of law. The paradox here – that *das Ding* can at one and the same time be conceptualised as the cause and the effect of the law – is explicable in terms of the retroactive positing of this entire 'episode'. The subject can only ever come to be after the advent of the law, after the loss of *das Ding* and, thus, any notion of that which might be retrospectively posited as having been prior to the subject's constitution as a divided subject in and under the aegis of the symbolic realm can only ever be a notion projected backwards from a position within the symbolic. This retroactive projection binds *das Ding* and the law in a mutually constitutive symbiosis. It is as such that Lacan can posit that;

> *Das Ding* presents itself at the level of unconscious experience as that which already makes the law
>
> (Ibid.: 73)

and

> I can only know the Thing by means of the Law
>
> (Ibid.: 83)

and

> the law and repressed desire are one and the same thing
>
> (Ibid: 68)

Any subjective awareness of the persistence of *das Ding* is dependent upon the law as it is the prohibitory force of the law which not only indicates but gives rise to that which is prohibited. At the same time, law itself would be impossible without *das Ding* as that which is prohibited and, in this sense, it can be understood that *das Ding* is that which gives rise to the law. In both instances here, which, properly, must be understood as the same instance, desire is the necessary and constitutive subjective involvement in the process. *Das Ding*, as 'that which already makes the law' (Ibid.: 73), and the law, as that which is indicative of the persistence of *das Ding*, are, thought together, that which already sets in motion the circulation of desire, the very search for the prohibited *das Ding* itself.

This helps to clarify the point that it is only through the work of prohibition that some*thing* can come to be, for the subject, desired at all. Prohibition confers the status of prohibited and, thus, the status of desired on the object of prohibition. This logic is demonstrated by St Paul in his Epistles to the Romans.

Is the law identical with sin? Of course not. But except through law I should never have become acquainted with sin. For example, I should never have known what it was to covet, if the law had not said, 'Thou shalt not covet.' Through that commandment sin found its opportunity, and produced in me all kinds of wrong desires. In the absence of law, sin is a dead thing. There was a time when, in the absence of law, I was fully alive; but when the commandment came, sin sprang to life and I died. The commandment which should have led to life proved in my experience to lead to death, because sin found its opportunity in the commandment, seduced me, and through the commandment killed me.

(*The New English Bible*, Romans, 7: 7–11)

One can read in this passage from St Paul the same relation of desire and law as suggested in Freud's comments in *Totem and Taboo* and *Civilization and Its Discontents*. Emphasising as he does an aspect of the tenth commandment, 'Thou shalt not covet', Paul draws our attention to the correlation between sin and desire. The desire to sin might here be understood as coterminous with sin itself. The tenth commandment, like Freud's super-ego, refuses any limitation to the realm of action.

As the only commandment which is explicitly concerned with 'the inner life', it serves to emphasise the very desirousness with which law would be concerned. The sin here is then that which would be desired or, what effectively, in this context, comes down to the same thing, the desire for that which would be desired. As we have seen in relation to *objet petit a*, desire is set in motion by that which might otherwise be figured as its object. Sin here is the object cause of desire. It is thus that Lacan reconfigures the above passage replacing the word 'sin' with the word 'Thing', i.e. *das Ding*.

Is the Law the Thing? Certainly not. Yet I can only know of the Thing by means of the Law. In effect, I would not have had the idea to covet it if the Law hadn't said: 'Thou shalt not covet it.' But the Thing finds a way by producing in me all kinds of covetousness thanks to the commandment, for without the Law the Thing is dead. But even without the Law, I was once alive. But when the commandment appeared, the Thing flared up, returned once again, I met my death. And for me, the commandment that was supposed to lead to life turned out to lead to death, for the Thing found a way and thanks to the commandment seduced me; through it I came to desire death.

(Lacan, 1992: 83)

This correspondence between law and desire is particularly evident in the tenth commandment to which Paul here refers. The commandment in its entirety reads:

Thou shalt not covet thy neighbour's house, thou shalt not covet thy neighbour's wife, nor his manservant, nor his maidservant, nor his ox, nor his ass, nor anything that is thy neighbour's.

(*The Holy Bible, Authorised King James Version*, Exodus, 20: 17)

When one considers that what is generally rendered 'covet' in English translations of the Bible is a translation of the Hebrew term 'chamad', meaning *desire*, one might understand the tenth commandment as prohibiting the desire of that which (it is perceived that) the neighbour desires; the desire of the Other.

You shall not *desire* your neighbour's house; you shall not *desire* your neighbour's wife, his manservant, his maidservant, his ox, his ass, or anything that he *desires*.

It is, as we have seen, 'the dialectical relationship between desire and the Law [which] causes our desire to flare up only in relation to the Law' (Lacan, 1992: 83–4). It is thus that the law simultaneously postulates *das Ding* as that which would cause desire and serves to prohibit any attainment of this Thing. As *das Ding* marks the place of the encounter with the Real, any subjective attainment of it in itself would be, strictly speaking, impossible. It is thus that desire, in the pure sense, is always necessarily desire for annihilation. The paradox here – that law introduces *das Ding* as the object cause of desire which would, if (impossibly) attained, constitute the death of the subject – is the very logic at work in this relation of law and desire. It is this impossibility which necessitates the maintenance of *das Ding* at a proper distance, thus allowing the subject's desire to maintain its course without ever coming into contact with that which would be both its object and its termination. In this sense then, all desire is ultimately desire for, in the

sense of ultimately aiming for or ultimately constituted in relation
to, death;

> the dialectical relationship between desire and the Law causes our
> desire to flare up only in relation to the Law, through which it
> becomes the desire for death.
>
> (Ibid.)

We can thus see that the pursuit of the *jouissance* which *das Ding* would
entail can only occur within relation to the law. If access to *das Ding*
and consequently *jouissance* would result in an eradication of the possibility of the subjective position, then the law might be understood
as that which allows the subject to maintain a subjective position
within the 'safety' and confines of the symbolic order, which allows
the subject the possibility of satisfaction in something other than that
which would be unbearable.

> Transgression in the direction of *jouissance* only takes place if it
> is supported by the oppositional principle, by the forms of the law.
> If the paths to *jouissance* have something in them that dies out, that
> tends to make them impassable, prohibition, if I may say so, becomes
> its all-terrain vehicle, its half-track truck, that gets it out of the
> circuitous routes that lead man back in a roundabout way towards
> the rut of a short and well-trodden satisfaction.
>
> (Ibid.: 177)

The distance that the law puts between the subject and *das Ding*, a
distance which then situates the subject within the law, as subject of
law, is that same distance which allows the possibility of subjective
emergence in language. Language, as we have seen, can be understood
as a system of rules, a signifying structure of differential relations which
can be understood, in its structure, to be commensurate with the law.

5
The Law

The law, as commensurate with the symbolic realm, necessarily can allow no access to its own founding moment. Any sensible founding moment, any history of the law, in order to function as history, in order to come to signify anything at all, would have to be located before the emergence of law. Like the pre-subjective moment of intention on the first graph of desire, Δ, the origin of law is something which simultaneously cannot be thought within the symbolic field and cannot be thought outside of the symbolic field. Were it possible to figure it within the symbolic, it would, properly, be an aspect of the symbolic and thus could not be the necessarily exterior founding moment. However, at the same time, it is logically impossible to figure it outside the symbolic field, for outside the symbolic field nothing can be figured, represented or, to phrase the tautology in all its force, outside the field of signification nothing is signifiable. This is not, however, to suggest that the origin of law can be dismissed as impossible. The origin of law, that which can neither be attained within or symbolised outwith the symbolic with which it, law, would be commensurate, still insists. Put simply, to claim that the origin of law did not occur, to deny the origin of the law, is still to make a positive claim about the origin of law. Moreover, what is at issue here cannot be reduced to the problem of a chronological event. The search for, or postulation of, the origin of law is concerned with the grounding, the *arche* of law, that which would substantiate the authority of the law. It is for these reasons that any attempted aetiology of the law can only ever, and must necessarily, postulate the origin as a myth, a retroactively posited event, the veracity of which it would be impossible to ascertain beyond its status as myth.

It is thus that the pseudo-events of the primal-horde function as, and only as, the myth of the origin of law. This is not, however, to suggest that the myth here is somehow useless or fails in its purpose of explaining the origins of law or even that, in uncovering its mythic status, we have somehow frustrated or even nullified its intent and purpose. This myth, like all myths, functions to illuminate something of the psychic apparatus of the subject. This also serves to remind us of the crucially subjective factor of any invocation of the law. The law, like the Other with which it can be understood as coterminous, only actualises in relation to the subject. In the words of the doorkeeper at the end of Kafka's parable *Before the Law*, when the countryman asks why it is, when he has been waiting for so long to be admitted to the law, that no-one else has ever come to beg admittance, 'No one else could ever be admitted here, since this gate was made only for you' (Kafka, 1992: 4). The law as it bears on the subject, bears only on that subject. Each subject encounters the law uniquely. The law is never someone else's problem. In this sense it is not only that the myth serves to obfuscate the impossible origins of the law. The mythic status of the myth is itself explicable in terms of its impossibility. In order for the 'original' events, such as Freud recounts them, *to be seen* to have originally happened, they must have, within the very logic of the myth itself, already have happened. Without the institution of the law, the events of the myth are inconceivable. The function of the myth, then, is to signify and thus add coherence to that which would otherwise be incoherent within the subject's own psychic economy.

> myth is always a signifying system or scheme, if you like, which is articulated so as to support the antinomies of certain psychic relations.
> (Lacan, 1992: 143)

The purely mythic status of Freud's aetiology should not be interpreted as suggesting that the prohibition against incest is a purely arbitrary privation which could, without disruption, be replaced with any other arbitrary privation. What makes the prohibition of maternal incest apt for the myth can be formulated in a double articulation. First, it bears on the psychic relations of the subject, insofar as it is indicative of the subjective encounter with the formation of law. The subject, as we have seen, is constituted as divided or barred, $. Read retrospectively, this division suggests a prior state of unity. This prior state of unity might, retrospectively, be envisaged as that time when the mother (figure) and child were constituted as a single entity. The *jouissance* entailed in this supposed former unity 'must be refused so that it can be reached on the inverted ladder of the Law of desire' (Lacan, 1977a(viii): 324). This necessity of refusal of (original) *jouissance* is the effect of castration. The father, as a symbolic function, the name/no of the father (in French *nom du pere*, name of the father, and *non du pere*, the 'no' of the father are homophonic, thus serving to emphasise both the intervention as prohibition and the intervention as signifier entailed here), is that which intervenes in the supposed unity of mother and child, effecting castration and the resultant renunciation of *jouissance*.

> It is in the *name of the father* that we must recognise the support of the symbolic function which, from the dawn of history, has identified his person with the figure of the law.
>
> (Lacan, 1977a(iii): 67)

It is only through this posited interjection that the subject can gain access to the symbolic realm and assume a position as subject. Secondly, the prohibition of maternal incest, as law, carries no benefit which could be recuperated to a pragmatic social function within the symbolic realm itself. It is thus that it is indicative of the pure and arbitrary force of the law. Where, for example, a prohibition on paternal incest could be explained in terms of its facilitating a system of exogamic exchange relations, the prohibition of maternal incest is indicative of nothing but the law;

> why doesn't a son sleep with his mother? There is something mysterious there. ... [F]ar from producing results involving the resurgence of a recessive gene that risks introducing degenerative effects, a form of endogamy is commonly used in all fields of breeding of domestic animals, so as to improve a strain, whether animal or vegetable. The law only operates in the realm of culture. And the result of the law is always to exclude incest in its fundamental form, son/mother incest, which is the kind Freud emphasizes.
>
> If everything else around it may find a justification, this central point nevertheless remains.
>
> (Lacan, 1992: 67–8)

This status of the prohibition against incest as what might be termed a repressed excess, insofar as it is that which is simultaneously the condition of law, the structuring necessity of law, and that which cannot be entirely recuperated to the internal logic of the law, is what renders it applicable to the myth of the origin of law. This status is exemplified in its significant absence from the ten commandments. That there is not a commandment explicitly against incest, rather than suggesting that incest is beyond the pale of the commandments, might suggest that the ten commandments can be read as a text rich with repression. That is, the fundamental desire for incest and the correlative fundamental prohibition against incest is the unspoken commandment 'behind' the ten commandments – we could 'interpret the ten commandments as something very close to that which effectively goes on in repression in the unconscious' (Ibid.: 69). It is in this sense that we can understand the prohibition of incest as that fundamental prohibition which constitutes the very condition of the possibility of law and thus the articulation of the commandments as such. That the prohibition against incest is 'missing' from or indicative of repression in the Decalogue is not for a moment to suggest that it is not prohibited. On the contrary, it is the necessary repressed of the other commandments, that which is not 'spoken'.

The foregoing discussion allows us to see the manner in which the law, *das Ding* and desire are inextricably bound together. *Das Ding* is strictly inconceivable without support in the law which would prohibit it and the law is strictly inconceivable without support in *das Ding* as that which would be prohibited. Fundamental to both aspects of this relation is the mechanism of desire as that which would have motivated the subject towards *das Ding* and as that which would be checked by the prohibitory force of the law. In this sense, it can be understood that *das Ding* and the law are not only mutually constitutive but are also, together, dependent on and constitutive of desire. This relationship is also, for Lacan, the very condition of the possibility of speech. In order for the law to function on and for the subject, for the law to have any bearing on the subject and thus to be, albeit retroactively, construed as that which is constitutive of the subject, it must be promulgated to the subject. In this sense lack, as the lack which is constitutive of law and the lack of which the law is productive, is both reliant on and is the condition of the possibility of speech. Desire, as desire of the Other, in order to be brought to bear on the subject, must be actualised for the subject. Desire, however, as desire of the Other, can only be brought to bear on the subject through its symbolic articulation. This articulation is itself inherent to and dependent on the very structure of law as differentiating force. It is in this sense that the prohibition against incest can be understood as the very condition of possibility of not only law and thus society but also of speech. Lacan emphasises this point in relation to the ten commandments.

The ten commandments may be interpreted as intended to prevent the subject from engaging in any form of incest on one condition, and on one condition only, namely, that we recognize that the prohibition of incest is nothing other than the condition sine qua non of speech.

(Lacan, 1992: 69)

Importantly here, speech, for Lacan, cannot be reduced to language. Where language would indicate the weave of rules and differential elements which would constitute the possibility of a communicative order, speech would indicate the subjective work on such an order. Language is the 'stuff' out of which speech would be made, speech is the creative act which would be performed on and with this 'stuff'. Where language constitutes a system, or the general possibility of systems, which allows the possibility of meaning to be transmitted, it is in itself without meaning. In order for meaning to be given to language, insofar as it is given through language, it is necessary that there is someone or something to convey something to someone. Language in this sense might be understood to be the system of signification before anything is signified, before any meaning is attained or imparted. This points to a necessary subjective involvement. Where, as we have seen, language would precede the subject, would be the realm in which the subject comes to be subject, speech would be the instance of this subjective emergence. Crucially, speech is not merely concerned with a 'sending out'. It necessarily and *a fortiori* entails a reception. While the construction of a message may be assumed to be the necessary initial point of speech, it is only ever such in relation to a point of reception. As we have seen in terms of the Graph of Desire, it is only from the moment of the *point de capiton* that a message can be said to or understood to have been emitted. Lacan illustrates this point in his second seminar with the story of the three scientists who arrive on Mars to discover Martians with their own Martian language which, strangely, the scientists can understand. The first two scientists understand that the Martians are speaking about their research into aspects of physical science while the third understands that they are speaking about their research into poetic conventions. The point here being that the meaning which would be integral to speech is necessarily constituted at the level of the recipient. While language is a condition of possibility of intersubjectivity, intersubjectivity is the condition of possibility of speech.

This relation between, and differentiation between, language and speech allows us to further comprehend the centrality of desire for the possibility of subjectivity. As we saw in the discussion of the Graph of Desire, the subject in confrontation with the Other is interminably faced with

the ambiguous question of its own desire, *Che Vuoi?* This *Che Vuoi?* is
the very question of desire; the subject's question of what it is that the
Other desires of it and the Other's asking of the subject what it is that
it, as subject, desires? The persistence of this questioning is indicative
of the insistence of a lacking both in the subject and in the Other. It is,
in a sense, the question of what it might be that would fill this lack.
Che Vuoi? is inherent to all speech, insofar as speech is incapable of
totalising, of saying it all and, conjoined with this, insofar as speech itself
would be unnecessary were it not for a lack of some*thing*. In this way,
every instance of speech, whether addressed to or from the subject, would
entail this *Che Vuoi?* Consequently, every instance of speech can be seen
to pertain to desire. Desire is, in this sense, the very movement of speech.
This also, however, suggests that every instance of speech is a lie insofar
as it is always 'not all'. Whatever is said, insofar as it is understood in
terms of desire, fails to articulate desire as such. There is a 'fundamental
incompatibility between desire and speech' (Lacan, 1977a(ix): 275) evident in the fact that it is the law, of which the possibility of speech is
a facet, which places a distance between the language in which speech
would emerge and the desire it would seek to articulate;

> I always speak the truth. Not the whole truth, because there is no
> way, to say it all. Saying it all is literally impossible: words fail. Yet
> it is through this very impossibility that the truth holds onto the
> real.
>
> (Lacan, 1990: 3)

The relationship between speech and desire can be further clarified with
reference to Lacan's second seminar, *The Ego in Freud's Theory and in
the Technique of Psychoanalysis*. In the context of warning his audience
against the pitfalls and frustrations of assuming to interpret the analy-
sand's desire as always the same oversimplified conception of sexual
desire, Lacan claims that;

> what's important is to teach the subject to name, to articulate, to
> bring this desire into existence, this desire which, quite literally, is
> on the side of existence, which is why it insists. If desire doesn't
> dare to speak its name, it's because the subject hasn't yet caused this
> name to come forth.
> That the subject should come to recognise and to name his desire,
> that is the efficacious action of analysis. But it isn't a question of
> recognising something which would be entirely given, ready to be

coapted. In naming it, the subject creates, brings forth, a new presence in the world. He introduces presence as such, and by the same token, hollows out absence as such. It is only at this level that one can conceive of the action of interpretation.

(Lacan, 1988b: 228–9)

Desire, though it clearly always exists and imposes itself on the subject, cannot be reduced to any simple formula such as a reductive notion of 'sexual desire'. Desire as it imposes itself on the subject is necessarily such that it imposes itself idiotically. While desire is always the desire of the Other and is always constituted in relation to *das Ding*, to speak of such desire is always to speak of it in the abstract as a nebulous, pre-linguistic, Real force. Desire as it pertains to the subject has to be articulated in its singularity. Lacan's point here is that desire outwith the realm of the symbolic, as it is outside the realm of the symbolic, cannot be represented for or by the subject as it is. Desire, to the extent that it can be brought into line by the subject, and thus allowed to function for the subject, must be brought into the realm of speech. In so doing, the subject clearly does not access the primal force of pure desire and encounter *das Ding* or *objet petit a*. The desire named does not, as such, exist before it is named. Thus the desire which is brought into the world, which is created as 'a new presence' (Ibid.: 229), is the subject's own interpretation of desire. In such a process, the subject can be understood to be assuming the responsibility for his or her desire, placing themselves, through the process of articulation, in the position of the cause of their desire. That such a process does not result in the nullification of desire is due to the strict incompatibility between speech and desire. In bringing its desire into the realm of speech, the subject does not attain *das Ding*, the object of desire in the Real. Rather, the subject assumes the place of the cause of its own desire allowing desire to persist in relation to *das Ding*.

An important point to consider in this process of articulation is the distinction which Lacan draws between the subject of enunciation and the subject of the enunciated. Lacan's contention is that any utterance, any instance of speech, is symptomatic of the division inherent in the subject. Whatever is said, in the saying of it, pertains to two irreconcilable aspects of the subject, that of the enunciation and that of the enunciated or the statement. The subject of the enunciation would be that suggested in the instance of speech, the subject of the enunciated would be that suggested in that which is spoken of. The quintessential example here, as given by Lacan, is one which pertains to the content of the ninth commandment, that of lying. Were one to claim that one was lying, it is immediately apparent that the statement cannot, logically be true. If one is lying, then one's claim to be lying must necessarily be a lie, in which case one could not be lying. If one is not lying, then one's claim to be lying cannot be true, in which case one is lying. Either way, the statement reads back on itself to render it effectively meaningless. Effectively meaningless, that is, unless one assumes the presence of two subjects pertaining to the claim, the subject who is speaking and the subject who is spoken of. Clearly, if one were to make a similar claim about someone else, there would be no contradiction. One can accurately describe someone else as lying without the statement contradicting itself because the person described as lying is not the person making the claim and thus the claim itself is not brought into the question of the lying to which it attests. This is much what Lacan claims does occur in the claim to deceive. When one says that one is lying, there remains an element of truth in the statement, insofar as what is imbedded there is the desire to deceive.

To refer this back to the Graph of Desire, the subject of the enunciated or statement would be formulated on the lower arc between A and S(A), where the 'I' of the enunciated, the 'I' embedded in the statement 'I am lying', would be retroactively constituted as the signification of the signifying chunk 'am lying'. The 'I' attested to here is not, however, reducible to the subject invoked in the instance of speech, the unconscious subject of the enunciation. The 'I' at the level of the statement in a sense covers the 'I' behind the statement, the 'I' of the unconscious from whence the utterance emerges. What this would mean is that whatever is spoken at the level of enunciated cannot but indicate a 'deeper' truth emerging from the enunciation, from the unconscious, which, whatever the concern of the enunciated, attests to something of the truth of the subject's desire.

This same example is demonstrated with reference to the ninth commandment.

'Thou shalt not lie' as a negative precept has as its function to withdraw the subject of enunciation from that which is enunciated.

(Lacan, 1992: 82)

Importantly here, the commandment only functions as a commandment to the extent that it pertains to a subject who would recognise it as a part of their itinerary. That is, the commandment cannot somehow exist out there without a subject to whom it is addressed and who would receive it. It is in this sense that the subject is necessarily the author of the commandment for him or her self. The commandment must be 'spoken'. 'Thou shalt not lie', accepted as a commandment, is exemplary of the subject of the enunciated but also then necessarily indicative of the subject of enunciation, the subject as it speaks from the unconscious or, phrased otherwise, the subject of the unconscious constituting the subject in the field of signification. It is in this sense that the commandment 'Thou shalt not lie' includes 'the possibility of the lie as the most fundamental desire' (Ibid.).

What the prohibition against lying attests to then is the unconscious desire inherent to the subject. In such a prohibition, the law brings forth desire and points beyond itself to *das Ding* as that which both motivates desire and cannot be recuperated to the realm of law. The prohibition against lying entails a certain claim to refutation of the law itself, pointing to the very borders on which the law is founded. If, in lying, the subject would necessarily point to its own division – that of the subject of the lie which is spoken and that of the subject who betrays something of the truth of its unconscious desire through the speaking – then the prohibition against lying confirms the truth of its own status. The ninth commandment is a law, like all laws, which founds itself on the necessity of its being transgressed.

This point can be illustrated with the example of something like the function of a computer password. When asked to enter a password, there is no prohibition against lying. One simply cannot lie. It would mean nothing in this context. One can either type in the password or not. It is either correct or incorrect. Obviously one could guess the correct password or even break the code through the random generation of possible passwords, but one cannot lie, one cannot deceive the programme and make it believe that the password is something other than what it is. It is only with the subjective emergence in relation to the law that lying, transgression, would be possible and it is only with the possibility of transgression that subjective involvement becomes a possibility. In the context of this example, one could lie to someone else as to what one's password is. It is, put simply, only when one says something about it that the possibility of lying would arise. It would be in this sense that the law would require the subject. Without subjective involvement the law is not law as such. Without the subject's desire – in this case the desire to deceive – there is no law.

Law gives rise to the movement of the very desire it seeks to contain and, thus, inherent to the very foundation of the law is the necessary possibility of its own violation. The ninth commandment, concerned explicitly with speech as it is, points most clearly to this founding and necessary contradiction. If speech always contains a double articulation, if it always betrays the subject as divided, and thus emergent on two levels – that of enunciation and that of the enunciated – then the ninth commandment indicates that the law is not solely concerned with the maintenance of the subject on one side of the law but actually points to a reliance on transgression.

The law as that which gives rise to desire in prohibiting access to the impossible object cause of desire both functions in order to and relies for its own existence as law on the maintenance of a productive distance between the subject and desire. In this sense, the prohibition, while overtly condemning desire, creates the very possibility of desire emerging. The commandment not to lie, in creating a prohibition against that which cannot but be told, signals a pathway to desire as the (re-)emergence of that desire which would have been repressed.

Crucially, we should understand the prohibition against lying here as one of the conditions of all speech. Even if one lies – which one does – without the prohibition, without the general acceptance that one does not or should not lie, speech could not function. Without the distinction which the prohibition introduces between telling the truth and lying, all speech would descend into meaninglessness as it would no longer pertain to anything. Even the possibility of deception here would cease to exist as one can only meaningfully deceive when there is a possibility of not deceiving. What would effectively result would be babble. It is only with the constitution of the prohibition, that the possibility of both truth telling and lying emerge.

This point can be seen to pertain to the very possibility of society when one considers that the commandment Lacan presents as 'Thou shalt not lie' (Ibid.) is actually presented in the Hebrew as 'כרצר צר שקר לא תצנת' (Hebrew Bible, Exodus 20: 16), 'Thou shalt not bear false witness against thy neighbour' (King James Bible, Exodus 20: 16). With its more overtly legal sense, this representation of the commandment illustrates the necessity of a prohibition against lying not only for the possibility of speech and meaningful communication, but also the broader necessity for the principle of truthfulness or non-lying and, crucially, the existence of a distinction drawn between lying and non-lying for the possibility of founding and maintaining society. Clearly, without the possibility of language, the rules necessary for the foundation of society could neither be drawn up nor promulgated, but even logically prior to this, without a distinction between lying and non-lying, without a fundamental principle of truthfulness, there could be no possibility of the communion of people necessary to found a society as any such communion would require a base agreement of correspondence which simply could not exist when there is no possibility of distinguishing between the veracity and non-veracity of intentions and utterances. Clearly, the possibility of lying is also an outcome of the principle of truthfulness and it is thus that we can see that the 'true' function of the commandment is not so much the condemnation or prevention of lying but the creation of the possibility of the human condition, human society and language as a medium of speech.

We can then see that guilt in the juridical sense of being guilty of having transgressed this or that law is always subordinate to and differentiated from the notion of feeling guilty as a subjective response to the antagonism one faces in confrontation with one's own desire. Where the subject is always going to feel guilty because of the very relations of law and desire, because of the subjective response to desire and the interminable struggle between Eros and destructiveness, this does not necessarily mean that the subject has in actuality contravened this or that law, that the subject is guilty of transgression any more than the subject is necessarily and always guilty of desiring to transgress. The subject is, however, also guilty for (the possibility of) transgression, insofar as the subject is responsible for the law before which it stands. As we have seen, without the subject, the law is not as such. The law is always experienced as idiotic. What this would then suggest is that, in terms of ethics, the subject must be the one to ascertain its own guilt in the face of the law it author(ise)s. That is to say, beyond the essential and unavoidable guilt one would experience through the very fact of subjectivity, a guilt which is integral to desire, there is also the question of judging one's own guilt.

Returning to the conclusion Lacan proposes towards the end of his seminar on ethics, that 'the only thing of which one can be guilty is of having given ground relative to one's desire' (Lacan, 1992: 319), we can begin to unravel what might be at stake in such a proclamation. Clearly any interpretation must acknowledge the particularity of the terminology used here, that is, it must consider the sense in which the term guilt is being used, the complexities of the notion of desire and, crucially, what might be meant by or involved in the 'giving of ground' or 'ceding' with respect to desire which would render one guilty.

One could interpret this claim as suggesting that Lacan is advocating that it is unethical to renounce what one (truly) wants, that the only true ethical imperative is that one ought to discover and pursue one's wishes to the end and, if one does not, one has betrayed one's ethical duty. Here 'duty' would presumably have to mean 'duty to oneself'. This interpretation would hinge on a prioritisation of the relation between desire and *jouissance*, the idea that it is, ultimately, towards *jouissance* that desire is directed. This conception may be supported by a necessarily partial reading of the account of the meaning of castration which Lacan gives at the end of his essay 'Subversion of the Subject and Dialectics of Desire':

> Castration means that *jouissance* must be refused, so that it can be reached on the inverted ladder of the Law of desire.
>
> (Lacan, 1977a(viii): 324)

What renders such a reading partial is the fact that it relies upon a determined gliding over of the significance of the phrase 'the inverted ladder'. Such a reading, the suggestion that *jouissance* must be refused so that it can be attained elsewhere, occludes the fact that in being reached *elsewhere*, *jouissance* would no longer be what it was. That is to say, read carefully, the above quotation is pointing to the fact of two concepts of *jouissance* (Fink, 1995: 60). What should be recalled, in this context, is the fact that *jouissance* – as the pure pleasure of supposed unity retroactively understood to have preceded the division of the subject in language – is only ever accessible to the subject as an idea of *jouissance*. The subject, as constituted as divided from itself in the realm of the symbolic, could never actually attain what is, strictly speaking, a pre-symbolic notion or, more accurately, a symbolic projection of some*thing* which would have been prior to symbolisation, precisely because the subject can only come to be within the realm of the symbolic. As *jouissance* is that which cannot properly be brought within or experienced within the symbolic, the subject's access to it would necessarily entail its own subjective dissolution. It is in this sense that *jouissance* would signal the death of the subject. To (impossibly) attain *jouissance* the subject would have had to refuse the choice of 'meaning' in the *vel* of alienation, a refusal which, as we have seen, would constitute a refusal of the very grounds from which the choice or refusal might have been made. However, the subject also must maintain a certain relation with *jouissance* in order to continue to desire. Rather than rendering this an impossible contradiction, this is the very logic of the law which is constitutive of subjectivity. The law prohibits access to *jouissance* while maintaining the aim towards *jouissance* and so creates the productive distance which allows the subject to function;

> *jouissance* is forbidden to him who speaks as such, although it can only be said between the lines for whoever is subject of the Law, since the Law is grounded in this very prohibition.
>
> (Lacan, 1977a(viii): 319)

This maintenance of an aim towards *jouissance* while *jouissance* is in itself barred is possible through the very intervention of the law which, in prohibiting *jouissance* in itself, is also that which, we could say, gives rise to the idea of *jouissance*. Viewed from the retrospective angle from which it must necessarily be figured, there is something in the symbolic which speaks of *jouissance*, which suggests the promise of *jouissance*, and it is only through this signifier of *jouissance* that a(n impossible) relationship with *jouissance* can be maintained at all. This signifier of *jouissance* is what Lacan terms the phallus. Inherent in the foundation of the law, then, is a privation of *jouissance* which, in cleaving this *jouissance* from the subject, and thus allowing the subject to emerge, must also necessarily mark the place of this cleavage. This mark is the signifier of the phallus which will thus come to signify the sacrifice entailed in the refusal of *jouissance* and the persisting aim towards the impossible *jouissance* beyond.

> It is the only indication of that *jouissance* of its infinitude that brings with it the mark of its prohibition, and, in order to constitute that mark, involves a sacrifice: that which is made in one and the same act with the choice of its symbol, the phallus.
>
> (Ibid.)

Thus, the quotation, 'Castration means that *jouissance* must be refused, so that it can be reached on the inverted ladder of the Law of desire' (Ibid.: 324), does not refer to the possibility of refusing *jouissance* on one level, or in one place, and attaining it on or in another. Rather it refers to the impossibility of attaining it and its necessary supplement in the signifier which would maintain the perpetual movement of subjective desire.

In this sense, we can perceive the strict meaninglessness of the interpretation in which 'the only thing of which one can be guilty is of having given ground relative to one's desire' (Lacan, 1992: 319) could be rendered 'Do not give way on your *jouissance!*' (Johnston, 2001: 411). Not only is *jouissance* something the subject does not have and could not have, moreover, the very prohibition of and necessary non-attainment of it is constitutive of the very possibility of subjectivity. Put very simply, the transliteration of 'the only thing of which one can be guilty is of having given ground relative to one's desire' (Lacan, 1992: 319) into 'Do not give way on your *jouissance!*' (Johnston, 2001: 411) would effectively mean the advocating of putting an end to desire. This, quite obviously, runs in utter contradiction to Lacan's sense here.

Clearly, to rebound to the opposite and equally extreme position of interpreting Lacan's statement as meaning that the subject should simply maintain a relationship of desire is also impermissible as it results in what is effectively a tautology. Were it simply – and with an emphasis on simply here – a matter of maintaining the position of desiring subject, then the subject, as subject, could do little else as desire is, as we have seen, a necessary condition of subjectivity. To not desire would be to not be (a) subject. In a sense, these two extreme readings could be reduced to two sides of the same point. In attaining *jouissance*, one would have ceased to desire. In simply maintaining desire, one would simply be a subject as the subject is, by definition, the subject of desire. It is difficult to ascertain in what precise sense one might be guilty in either of these positions. In the former, because of the impossibility of subjective access to *jouissance*, there would be no subject to be guilty. In the latter, because of the condition of desire as constitutive of subjectivity, guiltlessness would be an inherent trait of subjectivity when, in fact, it would be closer to the mark to claim the opposite. Either way, the statement would seem to hold very little sense.

An alternative reading is that what Lacan is offering here in his conclusion, and, consequently, what he is offering throughout his seminar on ethics, should not be interpreted as a statement of ethics at all. Such an interpretation would suggest that the statement that 'the only thing of which one can be guilty is of having given ground relative to one's desire' (Lacan, 1992: 319) is nothing but a conclusion on the nature of 'guilt', that Lacan here is separating the notion of guilt from the field of ethics insofar as guilt would appear as an emanation from the 'greediness' (Lacan, 1990: 28) of the super-ego and, as such, actually stands in opposition to any successful furtherance of the field of human ethics (Johnston, 2001: 465). The question here, as suggested above, might be phrased as that of whether Lacan is concerned with feelings of guilt or of being guilty (Ibid.: 420).

Such an interpretation would centre on the formation and functioning of the super-ego in relation to the ego. As we have seen, the super-ego is constituted as an internalisation of an exterior prohibitive authority, subsuming as it does in this process not only the prohibitive force of the external authority, but also the aggressive force previously constituted against this external authority. It is this which renders the super-ego not only a formidable censor of the inclinations of the ego but also, and crucially, a censor which will not be appeased. Conjoined to this fact, the super-ego as internalised authority is privy to not only those desires which are acted upon but responds also, indeed more so, insofar as they are not vented, to the subject's inner, repressed desires. This structuration of the super-ego results in ever intensified feelings of guilt. It is not only that one might feel guilty because one has contravened the law, but one now feels guilty precisely because one has not contravened the law, because one has repressed the desire to contravene the law. As we have seen in the foregoing discussion, this situation is strictly unavoidable in terms of subjectivity. The very foundation of the law gives rise to the desire which it prohibits. Transgression, and thus the desire for transgression, is thus integral to the law. The result here is a somewhat depressing vision of humanity as stuck in an eternal bind of guilt. The very condition of subjectivity, constituted as it is in relation to a desire, is itself bound to the emergence of guilt.

Read in this way, the guilt referred to in the statement, 'the only thing of which one can be guilty is of having given ground relative to one's desire' (Lacan, 1992: 319), refers not to an ethico-juridical pronouncement but, rather, to the psychical effect of the super-ego's strictures upon the subject. What such a reading would seek to do would be to inscribe guilt as a necessary condition of subjectivity but not, as in the projected reading outlined above, where guilt would describe the ceasing of the movement of desire and the subsequent ceasing of subjectivity, but rather as a precondition of subjectivity, the conceptualisation and appreciation of which would allow us to separate guiltiness, as a necessary state, from any potential ethical construct. What this reading would effectively suggest is that fixating on guilt as an ethical 'category' is a stumbling block to ethics proper, as any ethical imperative, taken seriously, any attempted ethics, is inevitably going to engender feelings of guilt. This being the case, the statement could effectively be rewritten as 'the experience of guilt is the result of giving ground relative to one's desires'. This would then, supposedly, leave the way open for an examination, extrapolation or construction of a field of ethics which would be capable of situating itself beyond guilt, a 'beyond' here which would necessarily entail a recognition of the roots and mechanisms of guilt as a subjectively essential emanation of the existence and function of the super-ego without, however, encountering such a discovery as an impasse.

6
Judgement

At the beginning of *Seminar VII*, Lacan summarises the traditional question of ethics as, 'Given our condition as men, what must we do in order to act in the right way?' (Lacan, 1992: 19). To this he conjoins his own definitional emphasis and understanding that ethics 'essentially consists in a judgement of our action' (Ibid.: 311). He adds to this definition that judgement must be evident, albeit implicitly, not only from the exterior of the action, that is, that ethical judgement is not exclusively something one engages in or pronounces from the outside, but it, judgement, must also pertain to the action itself. The judgement necessary to ethics cannot be reduced to a juridical conferment which would be pronounced after the fact but must be inherent to the act itself in order for that act to be considered ethical as opposed to the act simply being judged right or wrong, beneficial or detrimental etc. on the basis of some pre-existing table of prescriptions. Without this last proviso, ethics would unavoidably be reduced to a posterior conclusion which would be identical, in structure at least, to the legal. The problem with such a reduction to the legal is that the content which would ensue is entirely arbitrary, being, as it would be, without any support. As we have seen before, the law must conceal in mythical obscurity its own impossible foundations. The judgement that *this* is right or wrong must necessarily rely upon a further level of reasoning or justification which explains or justifies why *this* is right or wrong, which in turn must rely upon a further level of reasoning or justification which explains or justifies why the previous reason is right or wrong, ad infinitum. The ultimate reason, if there were one, would have to have emerged *ex nihilo*, like the word of God to which many bodies of positive law do appeal. This, however, does not actually solve the problem. It simply shifts the ground, and the *reductio ad infinitum* moves to the question

106

of how we can justify our belief in this ground of law or how we can justify our interpretation of and from this ground of law.

While this might help us to understand why it is that an ethics cannot be reduced to a posterior judgement without becoming indistinguishable from the legal, it also raises a further problem in terms of the judgement which would have to pertain to an action. If any judgement in a legal sense must necessarily rely on an obscured ground, on an appeal to a mystical author(ity), then what, even if ethics is concerned with a judgement which would be integral to an act, stops it being reduced to the same problematic?

The answer lies in the very constitution of subjectivity, the necessary relationship between the subject and the law inherent in this constitution and the crucial fact that this constitution cannot reduce the subject and the law to the same instance. That is to say, although we are clearly not dealing here with a monadic subject who would somehow stand outside the law, who might assume a position of alterity to the law which would allow it to judge independently of the law as such, neither are we dealing with a subject who could be entirely subsumed within the law.

As we have seen, the law intervenes at the very moment of the constitution of the subject; the law, as commensurate with the realm of the Other, is the location into which the subject must become and such becoming is necessarily divisive of the subject, rendering it barred, $. What is essential here is the *idiotic* nature of the relationship between the subject and the law. The law, however universal it might be, must also impose here as the law for the subject.

The law in its prohibitory force creates the subject as divided. This division renders the subject as lacking. Arising from this lackingness is the conviction of a possible situation of non-lack, a conviction which is 'experienced' by the subject as the desire for the (impossible) return to unity which would be *jouissance*. It is, however, only through the intervention of the law that such a supposition might be made at all. Without the prohibitory effects of law, the cut it enforces, there would be no *jouissance* to be barred just as there would be no subject to be barred from and thus seek to attain *jouissance*. In this sense, *jouissance* is only ever retroactively posited as lost but is simultaneously, as retroactively posited, crucial to the very possibility of the subject.

The confrontation with this moment is the *vel* of alienation described earlier. The subject, in order to come to be as subject, must either choose the being as lacking (*manque-à-être*) of subjective existence in the realm of the Other, the lack of being (*manque-à-être*) which would be proper to the subject of the law, or it must refuse being altogether. The obvious paradox here is that in order to make such a choice, the moment must have already occurred. It is in this sense that the choice taken entails a retrospective positing of responsibility for that choice. The subject, in becoming subject, must assume responsibility for its own becoming subject. The alternative here is the foreclosure of this moment and the subsequent refusal of a subjective position as such. That is to say, the alternative is a perverse relation to the law which accredits the law or the Other with the responsibility for one's being.

The subject's assumption of responsibility is the emergence of the 'I' who would come to be in the place where the Other had dominated, who would come to be the cause of its own idiotic relation to the law. This is the logic inherent to the dictum *Wo Es war, soll Ich werden*; there where it was, 'I' must come to be.

Such an assumption of responsibility can be understood to be that which ceases the perpetual slide inherent in the search for or presumption of an ultimate foundation for and of the law. The law, as the realm of the Other, is, like the subject, lacking. This lack can be understood to be commensurate with the impossibility of its own founding moment. The law's necessary dependence on something outwith itself which would confer the authority of its own constitution means that it cannot be that which would guarantee one's position of or status as a subject. It is in this sense that the judgement entailed in the ethical would necessarily be a judgement made by the subject, a judgement, moreover, which could strictly not appeal to the law or the Other for its verification.

When Lacan says that 'the only thing of which one can be guilty is of having given ground relative to one's desire' (Ibid.: 319), this must be read with sufficient emphasis placed on the 'one's'. Lacan does not claim that *the only thing of which one can be guilty is of having given ground relative to desire*, he claims that 'the only thing of which one can be guilty is of having given ground relative to *one's* desire' (Ibid. my emphasis). This is what is not accounted for in the reading discussed in the previous chapter. The interpretation which concludes that what Lacan is engaged in here and, consequently, throughout the seminar on the ethics of psychoanalysis, can be reduced to the posing of the question of whether or not ethics can function beyond the super-ego, that is, whether or not there is a possibility of the subject moving beyond the confines of the relations of law, desire and guilt (Johnston, 2001: 420) misses the essential point that Lacan here addresses the very subjectification of desire and thus points to the assumption of responsibility which would render this potential position of having not ceded with regard to one's desire distinctively ethical. This emphasis on the subjective is borne out by Lacan's invocation of judgement as paramount to the field of ethics.

> let's say that an ethics essentially consists in a judgement of our action, with the proviso that it is only significant if the action implied by it also contains within it, or is supposed to contain, a judgement, even if it is only implicit. The presence of judgement on both sides is essential to the structure.
>
> (Lacan, 1992: 311)

We have here a complex definition of the conditions of an ethics. First, in order for an act to be considered ethical there must be someone or something which is capable of judging that act. This would further imply the existence of some criteria on which such a judgement might be based. So far, this is relatively uncontroversial. Most traditional forms of ethics would agree that ethics would be largely meaningless if there were not something to judge as ethical and 'someone' to do the judging. Where contention might arise would be the question of who or what might be in a position to judge and the related question of what might constitute a sufficient or worthy criteria for such judgement. The second part of Lacan's definition here also appears to fit fairly comfortably with more traditional forms of ethics. While some may argue that an act in itself might be judged to be right or wrong, they would still, most likely, agree that such an act would still require an actor and that some decision is involved in the enactment. That is to say, even in the most pressed of circumstances, someone does decide whether or not and in which way to act. This point is clearly attested to by Aristotle in his discussion of voluntary and involuntary actions where he contests that even actions committed under compulsion ought to be categorised as voluntary insofar as they are, despite the force of compulsion attendant to them, actually 'chosen or willed' at the point of acting.

> For at the actual time when they are done they are chosen or willed; and the end or motive of an act varies with the occasion, so that the terms 'voluntary' and 'involuntary' should be used with reference to the time of action; now the actual deed in the cases in question is done voluntarily, for the origin of the movement of the parts of the

body instrumental to the act lies in the agent; and when the origin of an action is in oneself, it is in one's power to do it or not.

(Aristotle, *Ethics*: 53)

This is not of course to rebound to a conception of subjectivity which would portray the subject as a clear and utterly free agent who has complete liberty over not only its actions but its very involvement in these actions and to the desire which would attend such actions. This would appear to be something that Aristotle would uphold and is something which would be upheld as a background of much of the tradition of ethical theory. That Lacan can commit to the definition of ethics above without committing to this notion of autonomous agency can be illustrated with reference to Aristotle's description here. If one accepts that, in Lacan's terms, one is not strictly free, insofar as one is conditioned by one's relation to the Other, that one is able to accede to subjectivity only in the place of the Other, that one is necessarily divided from oneself under the rule of law, then this still does not necessitate that one assumes a position of irresponsibility for one's actions. As in the example from Aristotle, one is still implicated in the most compromised of positions. This is the logic of the *vel* of alienation wherein, even when faced with the most forced of choices, one must still choose. The *vel* of alienation is not a mere example here which would serve to illustrate this point but is the very mechanism which underpins the logic at work here, a logic which insists on the situating of judgement in the action in order for that action to be perceived from a strictly ethical perspective.

In one of the cases Aristotle uses to illustrate his response to the question of voluntarism, for example, the choice one faces is whether or not, when asked to decide between committing a base act or allowing one's family to be executed, one is actually voluntarily choosing, that is, whether or not one is responsible for the choice made. For Aristotle, while most people would accept that the choice to commit the base act would not, as such, be a free choice, insofar as the alternative is so much worse, this decision is still one undertaken voluntarily. Similarly, for Lacan, the decision taken is very much a decision taken. The 'forced' nature of the decision does not excuse it.

This, as I have said, has quite a direct implication that passes all too often unperceived – when I tell you what it is, you will see that it is obvious, but for all that it is not usually noticed. One of the con-

sequences is that interpretation is not limited to providing us with
the significations of the way taken by the psyche that we have before
us. This implication is no more than a prelude. Interpretation is
directed not so much at the meaning as towards reducing the non-
meaning of the signifiers, so that we may discover the determinants
of the subject's entire behaviour.

(Lacan, 1977b: 212)

These 'determinants' of the subject's behaviour are ultimately that
posited and assumed by the subject itself. Insofar as there is no subject
before the *vel* of alienation, the subject, $, which comes about as a
result of the *vel* is necessarily that which retroactively posits itself in
the confrontation of the *vel*. Subjectivity is, as we have seen, only possible after the choice has been made and it is in this sense that the
entire choice, insofar as it is seen to have been made, is a subjective
assumption. The alternative here is to retroactively refuse the choice,
that is to foreclose one's very subjectivity. Interpretation here – the
judgement that *this* or *that* is the 'true' cause of the subject's desire, the
subject's very motivation as subject – can only be made by the subject.
And in being so made, it is not a description of something which
would have been already given, it is not an acknowledgement of a
cause which would have pre-existed as cause, it is not a refinding of
that which was there all along. The judgement made here is such that
it necessitates a creation. In coming to isolate the cause of its desire,
the subject is, in effect, assuming the weight of and as the cause of its
own desire, that desire which is in one. There is no other ground to
justify this desire, for any other ground would merely indicate a further
assumption.

This point can be seen in the famous example David Hume uses
of the billiard balls. Hume argues that in any occurrence which is
supposed to be an occurrence of cause and effect, it is not possible
to ascertain with any absolute certainty what, if anything at all, actually connects the two instances; 'One event follows another; but
we never can observe any tie between them' (Hume, 2002: 74). That we
do tend to accredit a relation of cause and effect between two events
is, according to Hume, due to the experience or the impression of
repetition.

when one particular species of event has always, in all instances,
been conjoined with another, we make no longer any scruple of
foretelling one upon the appearance of the other, and of employing

that reasoning, which can alone assure us of any matter of fact or existence. We then call the one object, Cause; the other, Effect.

(Ibid.: 74–5)

Such a conclusion is, however, for Hume no more than a supposition. That is to say, even in instances wherein we may feel convinced of the causal relation between two events, we have not actually uncovered any definite relation between the two other than the impression of like events tending to occur in a similar fashion. The flaw of reasoning here, as Hume is quick to point out, is that there is nothing in the repeated instances which would elucidate the connection any more than in one single instance.

The first time a man saw the communication of motion by impulse, as by the shock of two billiard balls, he could not pronounce that the one event was connected: but only that it was conjoined with the other. After he has observed several instances of this nature, he then pronounces them to be connected. What alteration has happened to give rise to this new idea of connexion? Nothing but that he now feels these events to be connected in his imagination, and can readily foretell the existence of one from the appearance of the other. When we say, therefore, that one object is connected with another, we mean only that they have acquired a connexion in our thought, and give rise to this inference, by which they become proofs of each other's existence: A conclusion which is somewhat extraordinary, but which seems founded on sufficient evidence.

(Ibid.: 75–6)

The point here is that there is an irreducible gap between what we would take to be the cause and what we would take to be the effect. The positing of this or that as a cause is never something which can be adduced as such; 'there remains essentially in the function of cause a certain *gap*' (Lacan, 1977b: 21).

Whenever we speak of cause ... there is always something anti-conceptual, something indefinite. The phases of the moon are the causes of the tides – we know this from experience, we know that the word cause is correctly used here. Or again, miasmas are the cause of fever – that doesn't mean anything either, there is a hole, and something that oscillates in the interval. In short, there is cause only in something that doesn't work.

(Ibid.: 22)

For Lacan, it is not the case that there is an error of reasoning which leaps too quickly in ascribing the position of cause to one event – for example, the phases of the moon – and the position of effect to another – for example, the movement of the tides. Rather, the gap which insists between cause and effect is the very condition of the concept of cause (and effect). Without the gap, there is no cause and effect as such. This would be what the concept signifies. In this sense, cause should be distinguished from that which is determined in a system. Cause, properly understood would be that which is exterior to the system itself, the 'wager' (Lacan, 1993: 192) on which the system could be founded. If, to return to the example of the *cogito*, we are to follow Descartes' logic in accepting that 'I think' confirms that 'I am' we are in fact accepting nothing which is not already inscribed in the system of natural language; that a predicate requires a subject. In itself, this linguistic analysis does not confirm anything else. 'I think, therefore I am' does not show any relation of cause between an agency and an action, it merely illustrates the structure of the system which would entail the postulation of a grammatical subject as the (supposed) agent for an action. The proper cause here, in Lacan's sense of that which would be indicative of a gap, of that which 'doesn't work' (Lacan, 1977b: 22), would be that which would pertain to the establishment of the system under discussion, the assumption that actions require agents or that every action is understood by necessity to have an agent.

The *vel* of alienation demonstrates this point insofar as it is indicative of the retroactively posited moment which would pertain to the limit of symbolisation, the impossible moment of emergence of that which was not into the realm of the symbolic where it will no longer be itself.

As soon as the subject comes to be, he owes it to a certain non-being on which he raises his being. And if he isn't, if he isn't something, he obviously bears witness to some kind of absence, but he will always remain purveyor of this absence, I mean that he will bear the burden of its proof for lack of being capable of proving the presence.

(Lacan, 1993: 192)

The retroactively posited emergence of the subject in the symbolic, posited as it necessarily is from within and in terms of the symbolic in which the subject would emerge, is thus impossibly posited, but, equally, necessarily posited, on the basis of a non-being. That the emergence of the subject is then indicative of a certain lack of being (*manque-à-être*), which is simultaneously a lack in being (*manque-à-être*), situates the assumption of being-as-lacking with the subject. What is, once again, crucial here is the retrospective logic of the assignation of cause. As there is nothing beyond the symbolic available within the symbolic from which the subject would posit a ground for its being subject and nothing positable at all outwith the symbolic, the subject cannot but assume the gap upon itself, whether such an assumption is acknowledged, repressed or even foreclosed.

It is this same sense of gap which necessarily pertains to the relation between the subject and desire and, thus, allows us to understand the necessity of the subjective assumption at work in the judgement which would characterise the ethical act. Desire is, as we have seen, always the desire of the Other but it is also necessarily desire of the Other subjectively mediated. Desire may be seen to emanate from the Other in the question *Che Vuoi?* but this question, or, more accurately, the impression of this question, does not in itself form the 'substance' of desire. The question of *Che Vuoi?*, and thus language itself, is indicative of the lack in the Other insofar as the Other would not be asking anything of 'me' were it not for its lacking some*thing* and thus desiring some*thing*. But, insofar as the subject is always necessarily the site of this question, the subject is that to which the question is addressed, that without which there could be no question, the desire of the Other is always a desire of the Other for the subject. It is thus that desire can be understood to be at one and the same time the desire of the subject and the desire of the Other. Desire, as desirousness, the very movement and possibility of desire emanates from the Other, from the realm of and the incompleteness of the symbolic order. Such desire, though, must be experienced by the subject in order for it to be recognised and thus instantiated as desire. It is in this sense that the desire in question, the desire which would be understood to be the cause of the subject, is particularly the desire of that subject, is 'one's desire'.

This is also to suggest, however, that the desire in question does not exist as such. If the desire were to exist prior to its being subjectivised, it would be exclusively the desire of the Other and would not thus be desire at all insofar as the Other would not be (experienced as) lacking and, thus, there would be no lack in relation to which the subject could emerge. It is thus that desire, as 'one's desire', must be brought forth in speech by the subject.

There is only one resistance, the resistance of the analyst. The analyst resists when he doesn't understand what he is dealing with. He doesn't understand what he is dealing with when he thinks that interpreting is showing the subject that what he desires is this particular sexual object. He's mistaken. What he here takes to be objective is just pure and simple abstraction. He's the one who's in a state of inertia and of resistance.

In contrast, what's important is to teach the subject to name, to articulate, to bring this desire into existence, this desire which, quite literally, is on the side of existence, which is why it insists. If desire doesn't dare to speak its name, it's because the subject hasn't yet caused this name to come forth.

(Ibid.: 228)

This process of naming could be understood to be conterminous with the subject's traversing of the fantasy. In response to the perceived question of and from the Other, *Che Vuoi?*, the subject is brought into confrontation with the limit of the symbolic order, a limit attested to in the lack in the Other which would be the condition of possibility of the advent and reception of the question. In order for the question to be received, the subject must (have) come to be in the realm of the Other and, thus, is constituted as recipient of the question only insofar as it, the subject, is lacking, is not all. This double lack, as it cannot be confronted as lack, is subjectively experienced as *objet petit a*, as that which would mark and cover the place of the lack, safeguarding the subject from experiencing the lack itself in its devastating lackingness. *Objet petit a*, insofar as it is no-thing, insofar as it has no content as such, insofar as it is that which marks the place of that which is by definition unsignifiable, must be determined with some 'content' by the subject. That is to say, the subject must, in order to maintain the functioning of the mark of the lack, put something in its place. This putting of something in the place of *objet petit a* is clearly not, however, to attain *objet petit a* or to attain any knowledge of what it might (impossibly) 'be'. In terms of *objet petit a*, whatever substantial content is conferred upon its place is never 'it'. If fantasy can be represented as the subject in relation to *objet petit a* ($\$\Diamond a$) it is always such that *objet petit a* is strictly not there, in the fantasy, as such. That is to say, that which would be the original cause of desire is not accessible for the subject. By naming its desire, the subject is not naming *objet petit a*. Rather, in naming its desire, the subject is naming that which, always unconsciously, has sedimented in the place of *objet petit a*. In a sense, in naming its desire, the subject could be understood to be naming its mistake. In this sense, naming one's desire or traversing one's fantasy is but a reconfiguration. It does not render fantasy obsolete but allows one to move beyond the illusion inherent in that fantasy. In so doing, it also entails a reconfiguration of the subject. In naming its desire the subject does not reveal itself as the hitherto eluded cause of its own desire. Rather, it assumes responsibility for the desire that is in it.

The point here is, thus, not that the subject could ever somehow be objectively shown to be the 'true' cause of his or her desire but rather that the very notion of cause requires an assumption. There cannot be a truth outwith a system which would determine it as true. Whatever is taken to be the cause of an effect is constituted in this relation by the subject who takes it as such. This is the case, *a fortiori* for the subject's desire. Even if one were to contend that the desire in one is caused by the Other and is thus the Other's responsibility, one has posited oneself as the cause of this thought or contention. If, in the analytic setting, one accepts the analyst's interpretation of the cause of one's desire as the accurate interpretation, then one has necessarily not uncovered the cause which would illuminate why one would (want to) accept the analyst's interpretation of the cause of one's desire. That is, one simply shifts the emphasis and postpones the properly subjective response. All cause, and thus, *a fortiori*, the cause of all desire, is ultimately something which has to be subjectively posited and thus subjectively assumed.

Judgement, then, pertains to both an act itself and stands against the act, in the sense that the subject must inscribe itself in the act and in the judgement of the act in order for the act to be considered a subjective act. That is to say, the conditions of an act being considered ethically would be the subject's positing of itself within the act and the only ethical judgement which could be made of the act would be one made by the subject in which the subject bore the whole weight of the judgement. There is, ultimately, no appeal to anything outwith the subject. It is in this sense that Lacan's ethics entails the adoption of 'the point of view of the Last Judgement' (Lacan, 1992: 313).

The question, 'Have you acted in conformity with the desire that is in you?' (Ibid.: 314) is the fundamental question of ethics insofar as it assumes 'the force of a Last Judgement' (Ibid.). Not giving ground relative to one's desire entails the assumption of the cause of one's desire.

This is not, however, a position one could ever assume once and for all. Assuming the locus of cause is to reconfigure one's position in relation to the Other and thus to reconfigure one's very subjectivity. The ethical point here would thus be a point of always re-beginning. That 'the only thing of which one can be guilty is of having given ground relative to one's desire' (Ibid.: 319) cannot be reduced to a description of the mechanism of guilt as it arises in response to the demands of the super-ego. Rather, it points beyond the ego/super-ego relation to the stance the subject would assume in the face of the law. Giving ground relative to one's desire would be tantamount to assuming a position of having no choice, a position which, in order to be assumed, would necessarily entail the denial of one's relation to the Other. Not giving ground relative to one's desire is to assume the responsibility for one's own position of subjectivity. It is the logic of *Wo Es war, soll Ich werden*, the moment in which the subject ($) assumes a position in that place which would otherwise be occupied by the law, by the Other.

Such a formulation of ethics is clearly one which cannot appeal to any pre-existent measure by which to adjudicate. In this sense, the ethical moment would entail a radical decision, *dêcaedêre*, a cutting away, insofar as it necessarily cannot rely upon the pre-existing order of things. If the moment of assumption is properly to be a moment of assumption, then this separates both the subject coming to be and the desire which would be attested to in the creative act of speech from what had gone before. If it does not, then there has been no assumption. That is to say, any recourse to the Other here would be tantamount to ceding on one's desire, rendering desire not 'one's' but (wholly and impossibly) the Other's. If the law, and thus the moral, can attest to no substantiation, then the weight of this responsibility, insofar as the law and the moral figure for the subject, must be taken up by the subject.

The logic at work here might be presented as the distinction between decision and calculation. A calculation would be that which would rely upon the pre-given, it would be internal to the logic of a system. A decision, on the other hand would be that which must necessarily be taken at the limit of the system. Calculation, as its mathematical use would suggest, is a process which would pertain to a system which would purport to be, as far as it goes, self-contained. Calculation is the enactment of or on the basis of formulae or prescription, it is that which would follow from a rule or law; if A, then B. Any such calculation would, however, necessarily point to its own limit in the same manner that the law necessarily points towards its own lack of ground or substantiation. As Derrida has pointed out, 'if calculation is calculation, the decision to calculate is not of the order of the calculable' (Derrida, 1992: 24). That is to say, the moment of subjective involvement would be indicative of the failure of the calculation to justify itself. There persists a gap wherein the subject emerges as the one who ascribes to the law or places itself before the law. Phrased otherwise, the subject necessarily assumes the responsibility for the decision to calculate in such and such a manner or assumes the responsibility to calculate at all. Such a moment, indicative of the insistence of the limit of the system or the law, would necessarily also be indicative of some*thing* of the outside of the law, some*thing* beyond the symbolic order, some*thing* of the Real.

This logic can be seen in the famous scene of Alan Pakula's film *Sophie's Choice* when Sophie is forced to choose which of her two children will be allowed to live and which will be taken to the gas chambers. What is crucial here is that there are effectively two choices which Sophie has to make, the emergence of the second contingent upon the first. Where what is usually emphasised is the horrendous choice Sophie has to make between her son and her daughter, who will be allowed to live and who will die, what this glides over is the fact that before this Sophie has to make the choice to choose. She is of course free not to choose at all, in which case both her children will die. The second choice, as to who will die, appears to be the impossible horrendous choice because it permits no appeal to a measure of calculation. There is no way of 'working out' which choice is the 'best' choice. It is a pure decision and, as such, the full weight of that decision falls on Sophie. The first choice can appear to be much more straight-forward. There is a clear appeal available here to a measure of calculation; the death of one child is preferable to the deaths of two. Understood in this way, one could argue that the first choice is not in fact Sophie's choice at all. There is nothing to decide here, only a 'simple' calculation to perform. What such a reading ignores is the fact that a choice is made despite the availability of a calculative measure. Sophie still chooses this calculation. She chooses to calculate and to calculate in this way. Why is it that the death of one child is preferable to the death of both? Sophie, in choosing, assumes the weight of this decision upon herself. One could even argue that a similar logic of calculation is evident in the second choice, that is, that it is conceivable that the preservation of the boy child is clearly the obvious choice to make. The politically correct 'unacceptability' of this second calculation serves to highlight the weight of subjective assumption in the acquiescence to the mode of calculation. That Sophie might have chosen the boy's life over the girl's would for many people be indicative of an unfounded choice, the appeal to 'reason' here, that boys are inherently more 'valuable', would be dismissed as barbaric chauvinism, that is, an untenable attempt at justification. What this would miss is that ultimately any justification, including the justification that one death is preferable to two, would be untenable. The decision made, the choice entered into, is, properly, the choice of this justification, thus assuming the ultimate weight of and for that justification. Conversely, the position many would take towards the film, that the second choice is utterly random, that there is no way to decide between the boy and girl, is equally to assume a position on the matter. Even the admission of incalculability, the submission to random chance, is a choice. The calculation, one death over two or boy over girl, may provide the answer to the choice but the subject of the choosing is still responsible for positing and accepting this mode of calculation. The assumption of the impossibility of calculation, the assumption that there is no relevant difference between the boy and the girl, also provides an answer, i.e. choose randomly. That this random choice must still be made allows us to observe what would have been less evident but ultimately just as existent in the case where a mode of calculation was available; that the choice made is made utterly by the subject.

This example illustrates again why it is that Lacan insists upon there being two moments of judging essential to the ethical. There is the judgement to act, which is necessarily the judgement to act in this or that way, and then there is the judgement of the act; was my choice to act and act in this way, the right choice? Importantly, the logic here is not chronological. The two instances of judgement on which Lacan insists cannot be simply reduced to a before and an after. Rather they are two instances of judgement which would insist at two different levels. The judgement to act would necessarily entail the judgement to act in this or that way, to act in what the subject believes to be the right way. A judgement conferred upon the act, similarly, would entail not only a judgement that this was or was not the right way to act, but also the judgement to judge at all. Judgement itself is an act.

The second moment in both instances of judgement here necessitates that the subject assumes the weight of the first, that this act (or this judgement) was in fact 'my' choice and in this sense the act is the act of assumption of responsibility. Clearly, there is no pre-given 'right way' against which to measure the judgement of the act. In this sense, the ethical can be seen to redouble to the position of assumption of responsibility. That there is no right answer, as such, at any level of acting, places the burden of ethics always with the subject.

That the subject does act is to indicate the existence and the insistence of desire. This is what would define the act as an act as opposed to mere behaviour or happening. An apple may fall from a tree, but it is not understood to have acted. It is only in the act, which is always and necessarily a subjective act, that desire manifests. This is then to suggest that the subject is always responsible for the act in which it is implicated. In assuming this responsibility upon itself, in assuming its own subjectivity in this act, the subject inscribes meaning to the act. The assumption of responsibility can thus be seen to be coterminous with the assumption of desire as 'one's desire'. As we have seen, such assumption of desire as one's 'own' cannot be reduced to the naming of something which is already there. Desire may well be the desire of the Other, but it is still desire of the Other in the subject.

What is crucial here is the non-totalisable nature of desire. Desire, in order to (continue to) be desire, must remain essentially unsatisfied. Desire, by its very nature, is incomplete. It is as such that desire can never be entirely subsumed on the part of either the subject or the Other. Both, as we have seen, are lacking and it is only as such that they (are understood to) desire. The naming of one's desire is thus necessary, insofar as that desire did not exist as a pre-given. It is not a case of recognising the desire of the Other in the sense of what would be absolutely the Other's desire. Neither, however, is it a case of simply creating desire in the nominative process. Desire as desirousness, what we might call pure desire, will, because of this displaced nature, always persist. Naming one's desire, like the attainment of that which would have sedimented in the place of *objet petit a*, is always and necessarily going to be a case of *not-all*. In this sense, there is always something ineffable in desire. This ineffable core would persist in the insatiable *Che Vuoi?*

What this would point to is that the assumption of responsibility cannot be reduced to a subjective self-sufficiency. That any judgement, while it cannot be reduced to the Other, to law, also necessarily entails a re-inscription in the field of the Other. This re-inscription can be understood in the dialectic of speech. While language, which can be understood as coterminous with the Other, would be a necessary condition of speech, the two are also radically incommensurate. Language does not in and of itself have meaning. Language does not speak. Speech, as the subjective intervention in the field of language, which necessarily relies on language, is the forging of meaning. But speech, as we have seen, must also be speech for someone. Thus, the ethical moment, while it is radically subjective, while it entails a subjective assumption of responsibility, is also and still deeply bound to not only the field of the Other but to the other in the sense of another being supposed to understand.

In terms of the ethical and its relation to the legal or moral, this would mean that the judgement taken must re-inscribe itself as a law in the sense of an inscription of right and wrong. In this way we can further clarify the distinction between the ethical and the legal. The legal is inscribed as permitting and prohibiting. What can never be accounted for in this inscription is the moment of acceptance, the ground of the law, the final reason which would uphold the law. This grounding can only be assumed by the subject. This moment of assumption would define the ethical in contradistinction to the law, in that it cannot in itself be reduced to the law but at the same time it cannot subsist outwith the law and would require the inscription of the law in order to be made at all and the re-inscription as law in order to be seen to have been made at all. The ethical would be (indicative of) the breach in the symbolic, in the law, and, as such, cannot exist in utter separation from the symbolic, utterly independent of the law. At the same time, the ethical, the moment of subjective judgement, must be brought into the realm of the symbolic in order for it to be understood to have been enacted or made. In this sense, it can be seen that the ethical is not something which could be dwelt within or taken up once and for all. The ethical is necessarily pulsatory and, as such, must be taken up again and again.

What the foregoing discussion also points to is the fact that the ethical is also inextricably bound to the other, in the sense of the other person, what Lacan, following Freud, refers to as the *nebenmensch*, the neighbour. This ethical relation to the neighbour, this relationship to the neighbour as ethical, this relationship of ethics as entwined with the neighbour, can be adumbrated on three levels. It is in encounter with the neighbour that the subject would encounter language, bringing with it the whole barrage of division which would be constitutive of the subject. It is, thus, also in encounter with the neighbour that the subject would encounter desire. Coupled with this last point, it is in encounter with the neighbour that the subject would experience the persistence of *das Ding*.

It is at this point that that reality intervenes, which has the most intimate relation to the subject, the *Nebenmensch*. ... The *Ding* is the element that is initially isolated by the subject in his experience of the *Nebenmensch* as being by its very nature alien, *Fremde*.

(Lacan, 1992: 51–2)

Lastly, it is to the other as interlocutor that the subject addresses the meaning of its desire. It is in response to the neighbour that the subject assumes, by expression, the responsibility for its desire and thus for its position as subject. Ethics, so understood, then, would be an ethics necessarily in relation to the other. What this would not explain, however, is the extent to which ethics would be a responsibility to or for the other. Traditionally ethics has insisted upon certain prescriptions in terms of one's behaviour towards other people, most succinctly and extremely in the sixth commandment, 'Thou shalt not kill' (King James Bible, Exodus 20: 13). Remaining within the terms of Judeo-Christian morality, we might phrase this question as that of why one ought to love one's neighbour. Even given that ethics as we have defined it is necessarily related to the other, what is there in this relation, if indeed anything at all, which would suggest that it ought to be a relation of preservation, respect or love? That is to say, given that ethics entails a relationship with the other as 'neighbour', as well as the Other as the symbolic realm, what does it say about this relationship?

Part III
The other

7

Misrecognising the other

In the fifth chapter of *Civilization and Its Discontents* Freud broaches the directive that 'Thou shalt love thy neighbour as thyself' (King James Bible: Leviticus 19: 18 and Matthew 19: 19) and responds to this with what we might, following Lacan, characterise as 'horror' (Lacan, 1992: 186). For Freud, love of one's neighbour is something which would impose as an excess, an affront to the love that one would give to those closest, one's partner, one's friend, one's community. Where the sexual relationship can be understood as being the paramount case of relating to another, for Freud, the love given therein cannot be extended beyond the pair involved to encompass a wider world of people;

> sexual love is a relationship between two people, in which a third party can only be superfluous or troublesome, whereas civilization rests on relations between quite large numbers of people. When a love relationship is at its height, the lovers no longer have any interest in the world around them; they are self-sufficient as a pair, and in order to be happy they do not even need the child they have in common. In no other case does Eros so clearly reveal what is at the core of his being, the aim of making one out of more than one; however, having achieved this proverbial goal by making two people fall in love, he refuses to go further.
>
> (Freud, 2002: 45)

Consequently, for Freud, the pre-eminent question which arises in the face of this injunction to love one's neighbour as one's self is 'how shall we manage to act like this? How will it be possible?' (Ibid.: 46). Freud considers one's love to be something one would value or treasure. Love is not something which should be squandered. Love can be given to the other on the basis of desert and such desert is categorised on the basis of identification.

> If I love another person, he must in some way deserve it. ... He deserves it if, in some important respects, he so much resembles me that in him I can love myself.
>
> (Ibid.)

One may love another insofar as one identifies with this other to the extent that one's loving them is effectively one's loving oneself. One loves oneself in the other. Beyond this, one may love another who excels one's own self-image but only insofar as, in so doing, one loves an idealised projection of oneself, the self one might (desire to) become. One would, in addition, love, by extension, those who are beloved by the one one loves. The example Freud offers here is of loving a friend's son. Such a love is comprehensible as one identifies with the friend and thus will share in the pain the friend experiences if harm were to befall their loved one(s). Beyond this proximity, for Freud, it becomes very difficult to see how love might be given. Moreover, it becomes questionable whether love should be shown towards such strangers as, in the economy of love, this would cheapen the love rightly shown to those closest. Love here, in Freud's understanding, can be seen to be characterised with an essential preference. To love all equally, as the biblical directive appears to imply, is necessarily to extinguish preference and, thus, cannot but be detrimental to the love one would have given to one's friends and family. When love extends to all, regardless of their qualities, then, effectively, those qualities are disregarded (Ibid.: 46–7).

What we can see in Freud's exposition here is that love is, initially, founded on the basis of identification with the self. As we have seen, however, such identification is by no means straightforward. Not only is the subject not self-identical, but, moreover, the subject, in order to identify with another, must first constitute the image of its own identification. Such an image, the ideal ego (*i(a)*) is never adequate to the subject. It is always, in Lacan's terms, a *meconnaissance*, a misrecognition of the self. Consequently, the other who would come to be identified as *like* the subject is, in fact, only ever reminiscent of the ideal ego. This logic would pervade any notion of intersubjectivity based upon identification. Recognition of the other as that with which one can identify is necessarily misconstrued as what one is inevitably seizing upon as identifiable is a misrecognition of the other based on its similarity with one's own misrecognition of oneself. We can see this logic at work in Lacan's rereading of the Hegelian master-slave dialectic.

If the love one would give to another or experience towards another is based on misrecognition, then this would suggest that the other is experienced in an objectified form, an objectification which necessarily obfuscates and protects one from the unfathomable in the other. Insofar as this unfathomable aspect of the other 'demonstrates that something is there after all' (Lacan, 1992: 52), that there is something available which 'will be there when in the end all conditions have been met' (Ibid.), the other can be understood to be experienced as indicative of that towards which desire would be directed. However, insofar as this object is unattainable, the likelihood is that the other, particularly in terms of a sexual relationship, is going to function as an object of fantasy, *a*. If the other is conceived on the basis of an identification with the ideal ego, then this would be to say that the other is conceived in such a way that it functions to cover over the unfathomable it would bear in its approach, *das Ding*. This is not, however, to suggest that the incomprehensible in the other is somehow neutralised and rendered domesticated. The other in the mode of fantasy can, as we have seen in our discussion of *objet petit a*, only ever shield the subject from the encounter with the Real. *Das Ding*, as the persistence of the Real, would continue to persist.

For Lacan, the union of two people under the aegis of Eros, which Freud invokes as the paramount and most proximate instance of loving the other, is never more than a matter of misrecognition. We can see this in two examples Lacan provides; the poetry of courtly love and his reading of Freud's case of Dora.

Even if we do follow Freud in taking the example of the sexual relationship as being exemplary of the relationship or encounter the subject has with the other, it is still an encounter grounded in misrecognition. What is crucial to acknowledge here is the imaginary status of such a relation and the fact that this imaginary status is incapable of entirely diminishing the persistence of that which would exceed imaginary representation. In terms of proximity at least, such a relationship or encounter might be understood to be that of the closest kind but, even in the most proximate of relations, there is something in the other which resists comprehension. The other cannot be totalised. The image one would construct of the other on the basis of identification is never the other as such. What persists is the unfathomable in the other which necessarily imposes a questioning of the subject.

The very unfathomability of *das Ding* as it is encountered in the other persists in the double articulation of the question of *Che vuoi?* As indicative of the lost object which 'one is supposed to find again' (Ibid.) *das Ding* would give rise to, or in its insistence would be experienced as, the question of what the subject wants. But conjoined with this, again, insofar as *das Ding* is unfathomable, insofar as it resists representation, it will be experienced as the question of what the other wants from the subject. The problem here, for the subject, is that there is no way of knowing the answer to either facet of the question. Not only does the subject not know what its own good would be, but neither can it know what the other's good would be. It does not know what the other wants. As the subject will then adopt various objects as its good, none of which will be *it*, it also will tend to suppose that the *it* it has adopted, which is never *it*, might be *it* for the other. This is exemplified in the story of Saint Martin when he gives his cloak to the beggar. How, Lacan asks, in this most benevolent of gestures, does he know that it is the cloak that the beggar wants? Although the answer here, clearly, is that he does not know, the question persists as to how we might love the neighbour when we do not know what he wants. How, in Freud's terms, will it be possible?

In *Freud's Paper on Technique: The Seminar of Jacques Lacan, Book 1: 1953–1954* (1988a), Lacan presents a version of Hegel's master-slave dialectic which furnishes us with an initial answer to the question of why we might relate to the other in a manner which would entail a certain responsibility to and for that other. For Hegel, the very possibility of self-consciousness depends upon recognition; self-consciousness '*is* only by being acknowledged or recognised' (Hegel, 1967: 229). Clearly, however, such a moment of recognition, if it is to provide a grounding for consciousness of the self, cannot be a simple recognition of each by the other as already existing as conscious selves. In order to be recognised by the other, one would have to have recognised the other as a consciousness, something capable of bestowing the kind of recognition sought. But, in order to recognise the other, one would have to have already recognised oneself as something capable of bestowing such recognition, something other than a mere object of existence. It is this impasse which, for Hegel, would lead to the struggle between the two selves. The problem here is that the outcome of a struggle for domination is not and cannot be the recognition sought. The 'victor' may show himself to be an independent entity but would have negated the status of the other who might recognise him. That is to say, in the resultant situation of master (dominator) and slave (dominated), there would no longer be the possibility of mutual recognition necessary to attain any recognition. The master, having reduced the slave to something 'less' than an independent consciousness would have negated the possibility of his own being recognised. Clearly, too, the slave loses, as, reduced to the status of slave, he is not recognised as an independent entity. He will have become, rather, an object for the master. It is, however, beyond this impasse, the slave who eventually does attain something of his aim insofar as he is set to work and, through his engagement with the world, his working on the things in the world, he affects a change in himself, attaining the self-consciousness he was initially unable to attain through recognition from the master.

> in fashioning the thing, self-existence comes to be felt explicitly as his own proper being, and he attains the consciousness that he himself exists in its own right and on its own account.
>
> (Ibid.: 239)

For Hegel, this possibility of attaining self-consciousness through labour is not an independent possibility which could have been attained without the prior stages of the struggle. That is, the fear experienced in conflict with the other and the fact of being put to work, the order, discipline and obedience inherent in being put to work, are necessary stages in the slave's attainment of self-consciousness. Without what Hegel terms 'absolute fear' (Ibid.: 240), the slave would have remained in a 'determinate mode of being'. That is, it would not have attained the independence of self-consciousness but rather a 'stubbornness' (Ibid.), a reactive and dependent mode of being. Coupled with the necessary disturbance of absolute fear, the fact of the slave's engagement in formative activity allows the possibility of his shaping not only this or that particular thing but a 'universal power over the entire objective reality' (Ibid.).

In Lacanian terms, the scenario Hegel presents can be understood as instructive of the subject's relations to and within the realms of imaginary and the symbolic. In Lacan's reading, the scenario of the struggle of master and slave is necessarily posited as mythical and it is as myth that it can be understood to conjoin the imaginary and symbolic realms.

> Its point of departure, being imaginary, is hence mythical. But its extensions lead us on to the symbolic plane.
>
> (Lacan, 1988a: 223).

The myth can be understood as a double inscription of the functioning of the imaginary order insofar as, not only is the myth itself posited as an imaginary scenario, but the recognition which would be attained within the myth would be of an imaginary order. However, for Lacan, this double inscription at the level of the imaginary also points towards a double inscription at the level of the symbolic, indicating the fact that from the subjective perspective the imaginary would have to already be structured by the symbolic. This would then indicate that imaginary recognition, including imaginary self-recognition, is always maintained or posited within the terms of the Other. The very positing of 'oneself' and the other, as another person like 'oneself', relies upon inscription in the symbolic.

Working within the terms of the master-slave myth itself, we can see that the recognition sought therein is imaginary. Each party implicated in the scenario seeks recognition in order to attain a sense of self-consciousness. In order for this to be possible, each party would have to recognise the other party as worthy of bestowing the desired recognition. This would then suppose that each party had already recognised the other party as at least potentially worthy of bestowing the desired recognition. However, in order for this to happen, each party would already have to have recognised themselves as capable of recognising the other as worthy of bestowing the desired recognition. The logic is impossibly circular. Neither party could recognise the other without already having recognised themselves as recognising the other. It is only insofar as we understand the myth as an imaginary scenario that sense can be made of this impossible circle.

This becomes clearer if we turn to Lacan's formulation of the Mirror Stage. In the mirror stage, as we have seen, the infant is confronted with an image which, through a process of identification, is mis-taken as the model for the infant's own self, thus conferring a sense of unity and mastery which would pertain to that self. What is crucial here is that there is strictly speaking no unity and mastery at work. The infant sees what it takes to be a unitary form and assumes to model itself, that is its self-image, on that form. That is to say, the infant has modelled its unified self-image on the mis-taken unity of the image it sees before it. In a later reference to the mirror stage, Lacan indicates what we might understand as the necessary intersubjective (or symbolic) moment of the infant then seeking confirmation of this unity in another, for example, by turning to the parent 'as if to call on him to ratify this image' (Evans, 1996: 116).

What is accounted for in both stages here, the child's initial mis-recognition of itself and its dependence on another for ratification, is the purely imaginary identification of the self or ego. In each stage, the identification in question can be understood to attest to a division insofar as the infant who recognises itself in fact recognises something outwith itself, the mirror image, and this recognition needs to be supplemented by another who is clearly also outside. Moreover, as in the master-slave myth, the other would have to have already been recognised as worthy of conferring ratification. The recognition in question is necessarily misrecognition. It is this function of *méconnaissance*, misrecognition, which, for Lacan, 'characterizes the ego in all its structures' (Lacan, 1977a(ii): 6).

The identification which would both proceed from and be necessary to the mutual recognition sought in the myth would be of a purely imaginary order. The subject, in assuming to be a unified entity in itself, would seek to recognise this in a similarly unified entity which would be both modelled after and be the blue-print for the subject's own misrecognised self, its ego. Such identification, however, must also partake of the symbolic order. The very differentiation between self and other would only be possible on the basis of a differentiating structuration.

Such differentiation is what would give rise to the aggressivity attested to in the Hegelian version of the myth. The subject, in attaining its idea of itself as unified in an image which appears outside itself and, additionally, in confronting the other as unified, becomes aware of its own fragmented status. The other here – whether as other person or as the image confronting the infant – because of its mis-perceived wholeness, is taken as accentuating the fragmentation of the subject and thus threatening its desired or assumed wholeness.

Arguably the key to the forms of recognition here lies in the retroactive positing of the whole scenario. That 'the myth itself can only be conceived of as already bounded by the register of the symbolic' (Lacan, 1988a: 223) points to the fact that the subject, in order to be seen to be divided in its own misrecognition, would always already have to appear as divided in the field of the symbolic, that is, in the locus of the Other. This suggests that it is not only the wholeness which would be desired which is assumed, in all its fragility, in the posited encounter with the other, but also the fragmented self, the lack of wholeness which the image of wholeness would seek to repair. The myth can thus be understood as an instance of fantasy, wherein the subject, $\$$, as already divided in relation to the symbolic, posits itself in relation to an idea of wholeness, a; ($\$ \Diamond a$).

This would suggest that the mode of intersubjectivity attested to in the dialectic of the master and slave is only ever of an imaginary order but, as myth, points, in a double inscription, towards the subject's (dis)location in the symbolic order. Not only does the Hegelian myth itself result in confirming the symbolic, in the guise of order and labour, as the ultimate locus of identity but the very myth itself can only be posited on the grounds of, in terms of, the symbolic order.

The symbolic, as we have seen, is itself a finite realm, the order of the Real imposing itself as its limit. This is the logic we encountered previously in the impossibility of a closed symbolic order. It would be this impossibility which would open up the space of desire which is necessary for subjective constitution. It is also, for Lacan, this impossibility, this insistence of the Real, as *das Ding*, which constitutes the possibility of the ethical. This opening, as we have seen, is encountered in the other, the *Nebenmensch*.

If the other as other person appears to the subject as an imaginary entity, this is not to say that the other as other person is something which would be entirely constructed or projected by the subject. The subject is liable to encounter the other insofar as the other is recognisable as being the same but this cannot in itself account for the other; there is necessarily something in the other which escapes comprehension. This is the logic Lacan reads into Freud's description of the subject's encounter with the *Nebenmensch* in *A Project for a Scientific Psychology*. Freud asks us to suppose that,

> the object which furnishes the perception resembles the subject – a *fellow human-being*. If so, the theoretical interest [taken in it] is also explained by the fact that an object *like this* was simultaneously the [subject's] first satisfying object and further his first hostile object, as well as his sole helping power. For this reason it is in relation to a fellow human-being that a human-being learns to cognize. Then the perceptual complexes proceeding from this fellow human-being will in part be new and non-comparable – his *features,* for instance, in the visual sphere; but other visual perceptions – e.g. those of the movements of his hands – will coincide in the subject with memories of quite similar visual impressions of his own, of his own body, [memories] which are associated with memories of movements experienced by himself. Other perceptions of the object too – if for instance, he screams – will awaken the memory of his own experience of pain. Thus the complex of the fellow human-being falls into two components, of which one makes an impression by its constant structure and stays together as a *thing*, while the other can be *understood* by the activity of memory – that is, can be traced back

to information from [the subject's] own body. This dissection of a perceptual complex is described as *cognizing* it; it involves a *judgement* and when this last aim has been attained it comes to an end.

(Freud, 1966: 331).

We can detect in Freud's passage the relations of the symbolic and imaginary which would govern the subject's relation with its counterpart. Clearly, there is here recognition on a visual plane, an identification with the other as appearing similar or comparable. The other person appears as like or reminiscent of objects already constitutive of the subject's psychic economy, the subject's recalled object of satisfaction, the subject's recalled object of hostility, the subject's recalled object of support. What this recalling already points to is the fact of structuration, the engagement with the world in terms of the symbolic order. Without the possibility of structuring and, in Freud's terms, cognizing that which is encountered and that which has already been encountered, the very process of imaginary recognition could not take place. This is why, as we have seen, the mirror stage cannot be reduced to a purely imaginary moment but is always already structured by the symbolic.

We can thus understand Freud as pointing to the fact that in the encounter with another person there are two processes at work. There is the process of identification wherein one recognises as the same that which would correspond to elements of one's prior psychic economy. Then there is the process of cognition wherein one would make the same that which does not immediately correspond to elements of one's prior psychic economy. What this initial reading would not account for is a third possibility, that which refuses reduction to the same. It is this third point which Lacan reads into Freud's passage in terms of the reference to that which 'stays together as a *thing*' (Ibid.).

Lacan presents what he terms the 'climactic sentence' of this passage as:

Thus the complex of the *Nebenmensch* is separated into two parts, one of which affirms itself through an unchanging apparatus, which remains together as a thing, *als Ding*.

(Lacan, 1992: 51)

By emphasising the phrase 'unchanging apparatus' (Ibid.), Lacan draws our attention to the fact that the *thing* under discussion here cannot be reduced to something which would attain coherence in the symbolic, in our cognition of our 'experience' of it.

In the previous section of *A Project for a Scientific Psychology* Freud has described the process whereby one would distinguish, in the complex experience of same and other, what he terms 'similarity', on the basis of that which is experienced as that which 'on the whole remains the same' and that 'which for the most part varies' (Freud, 1966: 328). Freud links this process explicitly to the function of grammar, claiming that language would call the former 'the *thing*' and the latter 'its activity or attribute – in short, its predicate' (Ibid.).

Lacan's point, in his reading, would appear to be that, despite the references to activity, gestures etc., in the passage of Freud's to which he refers, the *thing* attested to in the encounter with the fellow human-being, the *Nebenmensch*, cannot be reduced to this previously disclosed explanation in terms of grammatical subject and predicate, noun and verb. The *thing* in this second instance, the thing which would be encountered as an 'unchanging apparatus' (Lacan, 1992: 51) is not the same *thing* as the *thing* which would be recuperated as a grammatical certainty.

> It has nothing to do with an allusion to a coherent whole that would occur in the passage from a verb to a noun, quite the contrary.
>
> (Ibid.: 51–2)

Lacan's point here would be that in addition to the imaginary and symbolic relations we would entertain with others, both of which would be forms of recuperation – the imaginary being a recuperation to that image of ourselves we had fixed in the constitution of the ego, the symbolic being a recuperation to the system of knowledge we have at our disposal – there is an aspect of the encounter which cannot be recuperated. This third aspect would be the Real, attested to by *das Ding*.

Failure to account for this last aspect would render the other as no more than a projection of one's ego, a mirror of that which is, in itself, but an imaginary construct. For Lacan, it is clearly not that actual people do not do this. The point is rather that in doing this one is necessarily not recognising the other as other. Coupled with this, as the image of the other one would have recuperated would have been recuperated on the basis of its similarity to one's 'self', one's own ego, which is but an image of completion, the image one would have recuperated cannot, itself, be other than incomplete.

The ego is an object. Any recognition attributed to the other on the basis of its resemblance to the ego would then also be recognition as an object. To so recognise the other as an object is to miss something of the other.

The complex of the object is in two parts; there is a division, a difference in the approach to judgement. Everything in the object that is quantity can be formulated as an attribute; it belongs to the investment of the Ψ system and constitutes the earliest *Vorstellungen* around which the destiny of all that is controlled according to the laws of *Lust* and *Unlust*, of pleasure and unpleasure, will be played out in what might be called the primary emergences of the subject. *Das Ding* is something entirely different.

(Ibid.: 52)

We can understand this distinction between object and non-objectifiable in terms of the distinction we drew in Chapter 2 between drives and desire. Where drives maintain their course in terms of an impermeable aim, fixating on an object and trajecting that object, achieving their satisfaction in the repetition of the circuit of that object, desire, properly, has no object. It 'aims' towards *das Ding*. Drives, then, can be understood as concerned with a refinding, with re-cognition;

the first and most immediate goal of the test of reality is not to find in a real perception an object which corresponds to the one which the subject represents to himself at that moment, but to find it again, to confirm that it is still present in reality.

(Ibid.)

This endeavour of refinding is exemplified by Freud in the case of a child encountering the breast from an angle which does not present it as immediately corresponding to the wished for image. The child encounters the breast from the side where the nipple is not apparent but recalls a previous experience of suckling wherein a movement of its head presented the side image it now experiences. By linking the head-movement to the previously experienced side image the child is now able to reverse the movement and achieve the wished for image of the front view with nipple apparent. In such a way, by conjoining images already, accidentally, experienced, the child is able to achieve a return to and of that object experienced as the object of satisfaction (Freud, 1966: 328–9).

Das Ding, however, is that which escapes cognition and cannot be recuperated as an image. It is beyond the realm of the imaginary. As such, it is experienced as 'strange and even hostile on occasion, or in any case the first outside' (Lacan, 1992: 52). In its insistence as absent, as that which cannot be grasped or brought to rein within the symbolic nor fixed in the imaginary, *das Ding* suggests the presence elsewhere of something which could solve the lack in the subject.

> It demonstrates that something is there after all, and that to a certain extent it may be useful.
>
> (Ibid.)

It is in relation to this impression which cannot be grasped, which can be recuperated to neither an imaginary nor a symbolic relation, that the subject's desire manifests and around which the subject's representations are governed.

Das Ding is experienced as the desire of the Other attenuated to the other but, as that which will also motivate desire in the subject, it is also the desire of the subject as the desire of the Other. What we can understand from this persistence of *das Ding* is that the unity of the object which is accomplished in the imaginary is only a unity insofar as it excludes from consideration *das Ding* as that ununifiable, irrecuperable kernel of the Real which would persist both in the subject and in that which the subject would attempt to comprehend or cognize.

In this way we can understand that the image which would constitute or provide the possibility of the complex of identity and identification, recognition of the other and self-recognition, is never actually 'it'. That is to say, in its failure to account for, to comprehend, to take in *das Ding* – the impossible kernel of the Real as it imposes on the subject, particularly in its encounter with the *Nebenmensch* – the image at one and the same time becomes that which would (impossibly) conceal the failure of comprehension and that which would point to the failure to conceal the lack of comprehension. The false unity inherent in the imaginary relation is indicative of the non-unity of the object of comprehension.

What this then suggests, in terms of the subject's relation to another person, is that what is grasped as identifiable, what is mis-recognised, is necessarily not all. The other apprehended as another ego, an alter-ego, necessarily brings with it some*thing* which cannot be reduced to recognition, some*thing* unrecognisable. This would be the other, not as another ego, but as absolutely Other.

> The world of our experience, the Freudian world, assumes that it is this object, *das Ding*, as the absolute Other of the subject, that one is supposed to find again.
>
> (Ibid.: 52)

This persistence of *das Ding* as the absolute Other in the other is further elucidated by Lacan in reference to the example of the poetry of courtly love which, for Lacan, serves as an example of the object-ification of the other at its most extreme. What must necessarily be dis-entangled in Lacan's example here is the literary figure and the actual existing person for whom, or in place of whom, the literary figure would stand. The poetry of courtly love, ostensibly the troubadour poetry of the eleventh to thirteenth centuries, is concerned with the presentation of a female character who is exalted and inaccessible. Typically, the Lady of courtly love poems is described in a formulaic manner, thus serving to empty her 'of all real substance' (Lacan, 1992: 149). As Lacan points out, 'courtly love was, in brief, a poetic exercise, a way of playing with a number of conventional, idealizing themes, which couldn't have any real concrete equivalent' (Ibid.: 148). This is not, however, to suggest that the poetry of courtly love was solely con-cerned with fictional characters. That the women cited in the poems actually existed – the names at least were those of actual existing people – clearly indicates that the poetry in question is not limited exclusively to the imagination. There is here a divergence in the func-tioning of the poetry insofar as it both addresses actual people and renders those actual people fictionalised, deprived of the complexity of their actuality.

> This love that led some people to acts close to madness was addressed at living beings, people with names, but who were not present in their fleshy and historical reality.
>
> (Ibid.: 214–15)

The crucial point here is that, insofar as the discussion of the poetry of courtly love might allow us to understand something of the relation of the subject to the other, it is a relation here without relation. The other attested to in the poetry is reduced to an object. But she is reduced to an object in such a way that she is exalted to a position of extreme unattainability. The poetry addresses an actual existing woman but in such a way that her 'reality' is covered over by the irreality of the poetic creation. This is not, however, a case of replacing the available woman of social reality with an exalted and exaggerated fictionalised version. For Lacan, what is evident here is the fact that both the actual woman and the poeticised Lady are unattainable, only in different ways. The construction of the poetry and, with it, the Lady of the poetry as unattainable, serves to obfuscate the fact that the actual woman was always already unattainable;

> courtly love ... is a highly refined way of making up for (*suppléer à*) the absence of the sexual relationship, by feigning that we are the ones who erect an obstacle thereto.
>
> (Lacan, 1998: 69)

The replacement of the actual woman by the fictional version not only serves to obfuscate the actual woman, but, crucially, serves to obfuscate the fact that the actual woman was already unattainable. It is not, thus, that the poetry of courtly love seeks to 'improve' upon the 'naturally given' woman by rendering her more beautiful, more perfect. It is rather that the poeticisation seeks to posit a certain mastery over the woman's unattainability, her ungraspability. This point becomes more evident when we consider that the poetry of courtly love was not exclusively concerned with aggrandisement, but would also on occasion serve to reduce the woman in question to a hideous caricature (Lacan, 1992: 162).

As we have seen, the other brings with it the encounter with *das Ding* as that in the other which is neither reducible to the other nor recuperable to the subject as self or ego. In the example of the Lady of courtly love, Lacan shows one manner in which the subject can be seen to deal with *das Ding* as it impresses itself in the encounter with the other. As we have seen in the examples of the Hegelian master-slave dialectic and in the mirror stage, the subject is inclined to absorb the other as a projection of and ratification of its own self image as it is experienced in the constitution of the ego. This absorption necessarily fails insofar as the subject cannot absorb that of the other which escapes symbolic and imaginary recuperation i.e. *das Ding*. In the example of courtly love poetry this failure is circumvented by elevating the object to the place or status of *das Ding*. This is clearly not to say that the Lady in question is encountered as *das Ding*. Quite the contrary. It is by elevating her in the poetic imagination to the place of *das*

Ding that the very encounter with *das Ding* in all its impossible horror is avoided.

> The object that specifies directions or poles of attraction to man in his openness, in his world, and that interest him because it is more or less his image, his reflection – precisely that object is not the Thing to the extent that the latter is at the heart of the libidinal economy. Thus, the most general formula that I can give you of sublimation is the following: it raises an object – and I don't mind the suggestion of a play of words in term I use – to the dignity of the Thing.
>
> (Ibid.: 112)

But raising the other as object to the dignity of *das Ding* in no way obliterates *das Ding*. It does not solve the enigma of the other, the inescapable otherness of the other. It merely, albeit in a rarefied manner, covers over this enigma with a less threatening enigma, an enigma which is or can be domesticated. The Lady raised to the dignity of *das Ding* is the veil of *das Ding*.

> If the Thing were not fundamentally veiled, we wouldn't be in the kind of relationship to it that obliges us, as the whole of psychic life is obliged, to encircle it or bypass it in order to conceive it. Whenever it affirms itself, it does so in domesticated spheres. That is why the spheres are defined thus; it always presents itself as a veiled entity.
>
> (Ibid.: 118)

It is thus as veiled and only as veiled that *das Ding* can be encountered not as *das Ding* in itself but as what Lacan terms 'the Other thing' (Ibid.); *das Ding* as it is 'represented by something else' (Ibid.). The representation of *das Ding* is thus not only the elevation of some*thing* else to the dignity of *das Ding* but, through this very process, the representation of the place of *das Ding* by something in the signifying field. It is *das Ding* veiled, but then necessarily also marked, by a signifier. This then returns us to the operation of the pleasure principle as that which regulates the mechanisms of the subject's desire. If *das Ding* is veiled by and thus represented by a signifier, this would serve to displace the subject's desire onto some*thing* other than *das Ding*, thus at one and the same time avoiding the destructive encounter with the Real and allowing desire to proceed in a domesticated environment.

Clearly, the logic of sublimation at work in the example of courtly love is akin to that of fantasy. It is the 'replacement' of that in the other which would motivate desire – *das Ding* – with a posited object of desire – *objet petit a* – and thus the subject's positioning of itself in relation to something other than the absolute (otherness of the) other; ($\lozenge a$).

> Hence, what emerges with the term by which Aristotle designates it is quite precisely what analytic experience allows us to situate as being the object – from at least one pole of sexual identification, the male pole – the object that puts itself in the place of what cannot be glimpsed of the Other. It is inasmuch as object *a* plays the role somewhere – from a point of departure, a single one, the male one – of that which takes the place of the missing partner, that what we are also used to seeing emerge in the place of the real, namely, fantasy, is constituted.
>
> (Lacan, 1998: 63)

We should recall here that fantasy functions to cover over a lack in the symbolic artifice, that lack in the big Other which would be experienced as the motivation of desire. As we saw earlier, the formulation and persistence of fantasy offers the subject an illusory sense of its own identity, the formation of the ego and, concomitant with this, an illusory perception of the social reality within which the subject would posit its (illusory) existence. Here we can see more precisely the conjunction of these two aspects of this operation, a conjunction which, properly, renders them as one, not two. The *meconnaissance* of self-identity achieved in the realm of fantasy is achieved, and only achieved, in relation to the *meconnaissance* of the social reality which would be read as being beyond the subject. Bound within this *meconnaissance* is the subject's *meconnaissance* of the other as other person, one of those who would be experienced as populating the social reality in relation to which and within which the subject's own *meconnaissance* of its 'self' is bound. As we saw earlier, the subject's fantasy arises and functions as a response to the question of *Che vuoi?* as it is experienced as being addressed to the subject from the Other. That the subject might posit its misconstrual of the other in the place of the answer to this question is no accident. To the extent that the other is perceived as being that which, or the one who, has an answer to the question, the other can function as the hope of the subject's own attainment of the/an answer.

This logic can perhaps be seen more clearly in another example from the psychoanalytical canon, Freud's case of Dora, or, more precisely, in Lacan's reading of this case. As is perhaps evident, and as Lacan remarks himself in the above quotation from *Seminar XX* (Lacan, 1998: 63), the mechanism of sublimation in the example of courtly love is particularly male. It should be noted here that in Lacan's usage the terms 'male' and 'female' refer less to any biological determination of the sexes and more to the 'determined choice' of structural position the subject assumes. The mechanism which Lacan detects in the case of Dora allows us an understanding of the relation ascribed more typically to the hysteric, structurally female, subject.

It is important to consider in our reading of the Dora case that what we are presented with in Freud's original 'Fragment of an Analysis of a Case of Hysteria' (1977), and consequently as can be traced in any subsequent commentary or critique based on this fragment, is never more than a particular representation of a young woman and the circumstances, events and symptoms pertaining to her as understood, described and interpreted by Freud. That is to say, as with the example of the lady of the poetry of courtly love, what we have at our disposal here is once again a woman 'not present in [her] fleshy and historical reality' (Lacan, 1992: 214–15) but rather a woman represented, a woman 'as signifier' (Ibid.: 215). In this sense, it might be argued that the 'facts' of the case of Dora say more about Freud's desire than they do about Dora's (or Ida Bauer's – the proper name of the patient whose treatment the case describes).[4]

What we can appreciate in Lacan's reading of the case is that he is not so much claiming to have somehow uncovered the 'truth' of Dora's (or Ida's) desire but that he is, rather, concerned with demonstrating an understanding of the functioning and structure of hysteria. Whether such functioning would have pertained to Ida Brauer is another question entirely. Neither is the point here to generate a 'rule' of hysteria from the singular example of the Dora case, but rather it is to consider the structural relations evident in the case study and the potential insights that uncovering such structures would allow. Such uncovering can allow us an insight into the mechanism – and the complexity of the mechanism – of desire as it can be adduced in and through the example. Where for Freud the case study can be

---

[4]For further discussion of the complexity of interpretation pertaining to the Dora case, see Bernheimer and Kahane (eds), 1985.

understood to constitute an example of the hysteric's desire – who or what it is that Dora herself desires – on Lacan's reading we can begin to see that the case study, rather than unproblematically representing Dora's desire, can be understood to present the question of desire, the question, that is, of 'who desires in Dora' (Lacan, 1993: 174). The text, and the context, of the case study can thus be understood to alert us not only to Dora's desire – in that she is the subject of the analysis – but also to the desire of the other 'characters', specifically Herr K. and Dora's father – in that their desire can be understood to be operative on and conjectured by Dora – and Freud – in that he is the author of the text – and, by extension, the desire of subsequent interpreters of the text, such as Lacan and ourselves. With this complexity of desire in mind, we can perhaps appreciate that the case of Dora, 'A Fragment of an Analysis of a Case of Hysteria', functions as significantly more than a mere example of hysteric desire as evident in one patient. That is to say, (the text of) the case study can be understood to function as an example of the very impossibility of locating desire with any certainty, the impossibility of any unquestionable objectivity in the field of desire. Just as in the example of the Lady of the poetry of courtly love, we can understand Freud, in his presentation of the case of Dora, to have rendered her an object. In response to this reading, Lacan allows us to ascertain the strict impossibility or failure of any such reduction of the other, the strict impossibility of ever knowing the other's desire as such.

In Freud's presentation of the case, the eighteen-year-old Dora is brought to him suffering from hysterical symptoms which, in Freud's interpretation, can, at least in part, be explained by her entanglement in a complex 'family romance'. Dora's father is engaged in an affair with a family friend, Frau K. and, meanwhile, Dora is the object of amorous advances by Frau K.'s husband, Herr K., advances with which, it appears, her father is quite complicit insofar as Dora could be understood to have been 'handed over to Herr K. as the price of his tolerating the relations between her father and his wife [Frau K.]' (Freud, 1977: 66). While, initially, Dora complains of this situation, opposing both her father's relationship with Frau K. and his embroiling of her in this relationship through Herr K., Freud concludes from her analysis that she is actually quite complicit with the whole scenario, that 'She had made herself an accomplice in the affair' (Ibid.: 67) and 'had given every possible assistance to her father's relations with Frau K.' (Ibid.). The apparent contradiction between her complicity and her protestations is, according to Freud, due to the conflict between, on the one hand, her love of her father and, on the other, her love of Herr K. For

Freud, Herr K.'s amorous advances are met with opposition from Dora precisely because they 'brought forward and reinforced her old affection for her father' (Ibid.: 92), feelings of affection which 'had now become distressing to her' (Ibid.). That is to say, for Freud, there exists in Dora a conflict between her object choices, an obstacle to the progression from her first object choice – her father – to 'a more normal object, namely, another man' (Lacan, 1993: 90). In addition to this conflict of feelings, Freud detects a certain 'current of homosexuality' (Freud, 1977: 95) evident in Dora's affection for Frau K. and the manner in which Dora would praise her 'in accents more appropriate to a lover than to a defeated rival' (Ibid.: 96–7). In a later footnote to the case, Freud remarks that Dora's 'homosexual (gynaecophilic) love for Frau K. was the strongest unconscious current in her mental life' (Ibid.: 162).

Picking up on this latterly posited centrality of Frau K. to the case, Lacan, in his reading, concurs that it is in fact Frau K. who should be understood as the object of Dora's attention. Lacan's point, contra Freud, is not to indicate the resurgence in Dora of a commonplace 'homosexual predisposition' (Ibid.: 95) but rather to demonstrate the 'unusual object relations' (Lacan, 1993: 90) typical of the hysteric subject. In unravelling the complex of relations evident in the Dora story, Lacan suggest that, rather than seeing Herr K. as the object of Dora's 'suppressed' love (Freud, 1977: 92), as the successor in her affections for her father, we might understand Herr K. as being little but a tool or a pawn;

> Dora in fact uses Herr K. as her ego, in that it is by means of him that she is effectively able to support her relationship with Frau K. ... It's only Herr K.'s mediation which enables Dora to sustain a bearable relationship.
>
> (Lacan, 1993: 91)

In Lacan's reading, Dora can be understood to identify with both Herr K. and her father in order to gain access to Frau K. Herr K., in such a reading, stands in relation to Dora's father not so much as a rival but rather as a surrogate. That is to say, where Freud would contend that Herr K. was the 'normal' object of Dora's affections and that her assenting to his advances was blocked due to, for example, her jealousy over his attention towards a servant and the correspondent wound to her pride in his repetition of the very same words to both her and the servant (Freud, 1977: 147), for Lacan, Herr K. is not essential to Dora for any attribute of his own, but rather he is significant in the access he provides to developing an understanding of Frau K., her father's object choice, and, more generally, what it is *in* a woman that a man would desire. It is in this sense, rather than in the sense of object choice, that Herr K. can be understood to function as a replacement for Dora's father. It is Herr K.'s desire, understood as resembling her father's desire, which interests Dora, an interpretation which is supported by the diminishing of Dora's interest in Herr K. after he tells her that he is not in fact interested in his wife (Lacan, 1982: 70), when he tells her, 'I get nothing out of my wife' (Freud, 1977: 147).

For Lacan, Dora's relationship with her father is imbued with both 'identification and rivalry' (Lacan, 1993: 91) and it is this complex which both situates Frau K. as an object of attention and Herr K. as a necessary foil. Her identification with her father leads to the assumption of the 'same' object of desire, Frau K. Her rivalry necessitates that a fourth figure, contra her father, is introduced to the scenario. What is crucial here is that, for Lacan, Dora assumes her father's desire for Frau K. in both senses of 'assumes'. It is not important here whether or not her father had actually elevated Frau K. to a position akin to that of the Lady of courtly love, an idealised or perfected object of desire. We do not, in any case, have sufficient information to discern this. What is crucial is that Dora can be understood to have assumed that he does. Having made such an assumption, Dora can then be understood to have taken this same imaginary object to be the object of her 'own' desire.

It is thus that Lacan can assert that the crucial question one must ask here is not that of the object of Dora's desire so much as that of who it is 'who desires in Dora' (Ibid.: 174). It is a matter of locating Dora's ego. As we have seen in the mirror stage, the ego is constituted in relation to a complex misrecognition based on an exterior model. Here the function of the 'exterior model' is assigned to Herr K. It is thus that we might understand that it is the structurally male point of view which comes to operate in Dora.

> Herr K. is Dora's ego. The function filled by the specular image in the schema of the mirror stage, where the subject situates his sense so as to recognize himself, where for the first time he situates his ego, this external point of imaginary identification, is, for Dora, placed in Herr K. It is insofar as she is Herr K. that all her symptoms adopt their definitive sense.
>
> (Ibid.: 175)

That we can thus understand the desire operative in Dora as being structurally male is not to say that we should understand Dora herself as being structurally male. Crucial here is the logic of assumption at work in the narrative. As symptomatic of the functioning of hysteric desire, the mechanism we have in operation here is that of the assignation of the object of desire assumed to be the object of the structurally male obsessional to the hysteric subject. Clearly this not to equate the two structures insofar as they might be understood to have taken the same object, rather, it is to indicate a dissymmetry between the two insofar as the movement of desire detected is radically different. The hysteric, in adopting the desire of the other, can be understood to experience desire in a manner irreducible to the obsessional both in spite of and because of the assumption of the 'same' object. Neither is this by any means to suggest that the structurally male or obsessional subject somehow has a more direct access to or experience of desire, that his desire would be truly his while the hysteric's desire is a mere semblance or copy of this 'authentic' male desire. In both cases – that of the hysteric and that of the obsessional – the desire experienced is the desire of the other (Lacan, 1988b: 269). It would be the function of analysis to allow the subject to traverse such a position and come to assume the place of the cause of their desire.

Significant here, in terms of locating and nominating the cause of desire in Dora, is the point made earlier concerning the textual status of the case study and thus Freud's status as author. In so emphasising Dora's authored status, we can understand that the answer to the question of 'who desires in Dora' (Lacan, 1993: 174) is necessarily doubled. While on the level of Freud's narrative we can see that it might be Herr K. and her father who 'desire in her', who function as models for her desire, we can also discern, on the level of Freud as narrating, as authoring the text before us, that it is also Freud who desires in Dora (Lacan, 1982: 68). In each case, what we are presented with is a man's desire assumed as the model for the young girl's.

In this way, Lacan's reading of the Dora case allows us to detect the mechanism of assumption evident in any attempt to ascertain the other's desire. Dora, as here presented, desires what she assumes the other, Herr K., her father, desires. But in addition, we cannot ignore the fact that Dora, as presented, is necessarily mediated by the desire of the other and thus 'her' desire, as (re-)presented, is always, to an extent, coloured by the desire of the other; most notably, Freud. This then indicates less a clear access to or apprehension of the (hysteric) other's desire than it does an impasse, the impossibility of discerning the other's desire with any veracity or certainty, the impossibility of accessing the other's desire beyond or entirely outwith the mediating effects of one's own.

In understanding both these examples, the example of the poetry of courtly love and the example of the case of Dora, in terms of the logic of fantasy, we can see how both offer answers to the question of *Che vuoi?*, the fundamental and traumatic encounter with the Other as experienced as a question of the subject's very subjectivity. In the example of courtly love poetry, an answer to the question *Che vuoi?* is offered in the form of the Lady encapsulated and created in the poetry, a logic we can see as carried over into the presentation of Dora in 'A Fragment of an Analysis of a Case of Hysteria'. This answer, however, must be understood to be an answer which comes from the Other. As Lacan stresses, the poetry in question is rarefied, highly ornate and constructed in accordance with rigorous poetic convention;

> courtly love was, in brief, a poetic exercise, a way of playing with a number of conventional, idealizing themes, which couldn't have any real concrete equivalent.
>
> (Lacan, 1992: 148)

It is a linguistic answer. An answer in the terms of the Other. The very fact that the woman in question is radically divorced from any actual, historical, flesh and blood person and, rather, follows predetermined prescriptions and descriptions, points to this. 'She' is literally 'pre-scripted', a poetic cliché, an answer taken from, already inscribed in, the Other, rather than one offered singularly by the subject. The 'person' involved in the poetry is 'transformed into a symbolic func-tion' (Ibid.: 149); *a*. A similar logic of transformation should be under-stood as occurring in Freud's presentation of the Dora case. Dora is transformed into symbolic function. She is written.

In Lacan's reading of the case of Dora, operating at a level which we might describe as interior to the narrative itself, we can understand the answer to *Che vuoi?* as being, 'what the other wants', insofar as the hysteric's desire is directed towards the desire of the other, that which the other is perceived as desiring. This is not to suggest that the hysteric, through the other, has access to pure desire or access to *das Ding* as that towards which desire would aim. The other's desire is not directed towards *das Ding* in itself but rather towards a surrogate thereof. The other no more has the 'answer' than the hysteric. The question of the hysteric might then be, what is it in this *thing* that would be the answer to what the other wants? This incessant question-ing is further conjoined to the attempt to identify, which, as we have seen, is inherent to the logic of fantasy. The hysteric, here, chooses another woman as the object of her fantasy in order not to possess but rather to discover what it is *in* the other woman which would make her desirable. The question is then, ultimately, *'What is it to be a woman?'* (Lacan, 1993: 171). The prevalence of this question can, in addition, be detected in the very writing of the Dora case insofar as we can understand that it is not only Dora who asks this, but also Freud and, by extension, the reader.

The hysteric, so understood, chooses to identify with the other in the belief that he can provide the answer which otherwise eludes her. The gap in the symbolic, the fact of the symbolic's necessary incompleteness, that it is Ⱥ, is in a sense denied by assuming that the other has the answer. Where, for the male-obsessional, the gap in the Other impresses as that which cannot be signified, as the answer to his own failed identification, for the hysteric-female, that which is taken to be that which would fix the gap is taken to be with the other. In either case the answer to the question is out of reach.

In this sense we can understand that in its encounter with the other the subject is interminably faced with a question of its own existence. Where for the obsessional this question would be characterised as its asking of itself, 'Why is he here? Where has he come from? What is he doing here? Why is he going to disappear?' (Ibid.: 179), for the hysteric, as we have seen, it would be characterised as the question *'What is it to be a woman?'* (Ibid.: 171). The imposition of this questioning and the form of questioning the subject would adopt is inseparable from its emergence in the field of the Other, the choice retrospectively taken in the face of the *vel* of alienation. The subject is, as we have seen, impossibly divided from itself, incomplete, barred, $. This very incompleteness of the subject instigates a search for the answer in the Other. As the Other can be understood to be commensurate with the field of signification as it is encountered by the subject, the answer sought is going to be sought as a signifier. What we see in Lacan's reading of the Dora case and his discussion of the poetry of courtly love is the demonstration of these different possibilities of approaching the insistence of this questioning, different possible means of responding to the asymmetric lacks in the subject and the Other. Where in the poetry of courtly love the answer constructed would be that of a signifier which would function as the mask of the lack in the Other, in the case of Dora we might understand that it is the fact that the Other might have or at least have access to the answer which functions as the mask to the subject's own lack of answer. If we recall that the subject, whether hysteric or obsessional, is such that it is constituted as barred, as $, that is, that it is not possible for the subject to attain any complete, objective identity, then we can understand the two different modes of questioning here to indicate two possible responses to the condition of lack (both in terms of the lack in the subject and in terms of the lack in the Other). Crucially, these two possible responses are both marked by necessary failure (Glynos, 2000: 214). It is in this sense that we can understand the woman as being the phallus and the man as having the phallus.

As we saw previously, the (symbolic) phallus is another name for that master signifier which would solve the lack inherent in the subject. In suggesting that the woman, as other, is the phallus, we should understand this in the terms of the poetry of courtly love, where the other in question is not another person so much as a signifier, the other person reduced to a signifier. In suggesting that the man, as other, has the phallus, again, we should not understand this as meaning that the other *actually* has the phallus so much as the other is perceived to have the phallus. Thus the hysteric can be understood to identify with the other as he who would have the phallus, the answer, as 'a means of approaching this definition that escapes her' (Lacan, 1993: 178), utilising the phallus she believes he possesses 'as an imaginary instrument for apprehending what she hasn't succeeded in symbolising' (Ibid.). The other, however, is as incapable of attaining, of having, the answer as she is.

If we can understand the different approaches here to be essentially failed, this is clearly not to suggest that there is another, successful approach. Fantasy, as we have seen, is that which supports desire, which is to say it is essential to the possibility of subjectivity. The fantasy as exemplified in the poetry of courtly love supports desire by positing a surrogate answer to the question of desire, *objet petit a*. The fantasy exemplified in Lacan's reading of the case of Dora is shown to support desire by assuming that the answer lies elsewhere. In both cases, *the* answer is necessarily avoided. This is not, however, to suggest that the answer can ever be accepted, or even posited, as not existing. Even a refutation of the possibility of an answer would function as an answer. The answer given is always *not it* and yet the answer that there is no answer is also *not it*.

In terms of the encounter with the other and the experience of *das Ding* that this would bring, we can understand both these modes of fantasy as responses towards and defences against the trauma that such an encounter would entail. By elevating the other to the status of an object, as in the example of courtly love, the subject both marks the place of *das Ding* and renders the other, as the harbinger of *das Ding*, as 'neutralized' or 'non-threatening'. On the other hand, as in Lacan's reading of the Dora case, by rendering the other as availed of the answer, the hysteric subject also covers over the insistence of the Real the other would bring by rendering the other as having attained the signifier necessary to fill their lack. In both cases, crucially, *das Ding* continues to persist. That fantasy covers the lack, as we have seen, is not to suggest that fantasy solves the lack. *Das Ding*, as the insistence of desire in the other necessarily persists insofar as the subject's answer, the subject's fantasy, is never adequate to the gap it would seek to cover.

In addition to the mechanism of desire illustrated in Lacan's reading of the Dora case – what we have called a level interior to the narrative – his commentary on the case and the shortcomings of Freud's conclusions can also be understood to underscore the central impossibility here of ever knowing or encapsulating the other and its desire. While the image of the lady of the poetry of courtly love and the understanding of Dora with which we are presented are only ever re-presentations – and, within this latter representation, the mechanism of desire illustrated as hysteric is itself indicative of a logic of assumption as to what it would be that the other desires – the 'truth' of the other's desire, the other *qua* other, in each case, necessarily eludes the subject. The other's desire, the other *in-itself*, is essentially inaccessible.

8
Loving Thy Neighbour

When the other is reduced to an imaginary effect, the semblance of the subject's own misrecognised ego, such a reduction necessarily entails a remainder, that of the other which refuses, which escapes, the reductive process. This 'remainder' would be the insistence of *das Ding*. This insistence of the lack, the lack of *the* answer, the impossibility of knowing and thus adequately responding to or accommodating the other's desire, is evident in the story of Saint Martin and the beggar. Saint Martin, presumably with all the best of intentions, gives the beggar his cloak but, how, Lacan asks, does Saint Martin know that the cloak is what the beggar truly wants? He may want Saint Martin to 'kill him or fuck him' (Lacan, 1992: 186).

Lacan presents the example of Saint Martin in the context of discussing Freud's 'horror' (Ibid.) in the face of the commandment to love one's neighbour. As we have seen in Chapter 7, Freud rejects the directive to love one's neighbour, protesting that such a directive runs counter to reason. It is reasonable, in Freud's perspective, to love those closest, those with whom one can identify oneself. The directive to love one's neighbour would constitute an affront to those who would be deserving of love and, in so doing, an affront to the subject and the love he would hold precious. What, according to Lacan, Freud misses in this protestation is the 'opening on to *jouissance*' (Ibid.) that the encounter with the other would offer.

What is crucial here is the indeterminacy of *das Ding*, that in its strangeness it is impossible to characterise *what* it might be. *Das Ding* is the suggestion, the promise with no guarantee, of something beyond the realm of the symbolic. It is that which would solve the lack in the subject and thus it, in all its unknowability, functions as that towards which desire would be directed. *Jouissance*, as we have seen, is only ever retroactively posited as that which would be attained and experienced in this beyond, in this impossible grasping of *das Ding*.

It is as unknown that *das Ding* can become the site, for the subject, of the emergence or possibility of both good and evil. As the insistence of the realm of the unknown, *das Ding* avails itself to encapsulate that which cannot be explained in the terms of the symbolic order. It marks the limit or, better, indicates the beyond-the-limit of the symbolic.

It is in this sense that Lacan discusses *das Ding* in conjunction with the question of creationism. As we have seen in both the logic of the origin of law and in the notion of the signifying realm as essentially marked by its own limit, there is a fundamental problem in the conception of origins or limits. Any limit always necessarily and impossibly points to its own *beyond*. The necessity here lies in the fact that without a beyond, there can be no limit. The impossibility lies in the fact that to conceive of the *beyond* is recuperate it to within the limits of the system. *Das Ding* functions as an attempt to conceive this limit/beyond in all its radicality. *Das Ding* is the pure insistence of the limit without imputation of content. It cannot, thus, be said, that that of which *das Ding* is indicative is 'good' or 'bad' and yet it is still indicative of the insistence of the possibility of good or bad. The very fact of the insistence of *das Ding* on the subject who is rendered incomplete in its emergence in the symbolic avails the positing of good and evil in the beyond of which it, *das Ding*, is indicative.

The gap or opening of the Real which would be indicated in the insistence of *das Ding* is the gap in the Other. The Other as the site of the subject's emergence is also constitutive of the incompleteness of the subject, $\math$. In this sense *das Ding* can be conceived as commensurate with what Lacan terms 'the human factor' (Ibid.: 124).

> The Thing is, in effect, involved insofar as it is defined by the fact that it defines the human factor – although, as we know, the human factor escapes us.
>
> (Ibid.)

The human factor escapes us insofar as it is conditioned in relation to a beyond, the beyond of the signifying order, the beyond of the domesticated satisfactions of the pleasure principle. That such a beyond refuses categorisation, that it is beyond signification, is indicative of the error inherent to any question of humanity's fundamental moral nature; whether humanity 'is fundamentally good or bad' (Ibid.: 125). The posing of such a question already assumes the limitations of what the answer might be. As Lacan, insists, the question cannot be reduced to such a binary but must rather be 'a question of the whole' (Ibid.).

Das Ding, as we have seen, is experienced as the suggestion of that which would exist which would render us complete. It is the insistence of that lost *Thing* which, at one and the same time, gives rise to the sense of incompleteness in the subject and 'promises' the solution to this incompleteness. The paradox here is that in introducing the concept of completeness, the subject effectively models it on something which is not there. Lack is only experienced as lack in the light of the impression of something which would shore this lack but this something is strictly inconceivable.

> The fact is man fashions this signifier ['whole' or 'wholeness'] and introduces it into the world – in other words, we need to know what he does when he fashions it in the image of the Thing, whereas the Thing is characterized by the fact that it is impossible for us to imagine it.
>
> (Ibid.)

This impossibility of imagining *das Ding* indicates once again the fantastic nature of the subject's relation to the other. If the other brings with it something irrecuperable to the subject, something which radically refuses incorporation, the attempt to displace the intrigue of this alien aspect onto a fantasised image of the other is essentially to attempt to avoid the unknowability, the incomprehensibility, of this alien aspect. Whether one conceives or imagines the other as hostile or benevolent, one necessarily misses, in this conception which cannot but be a retreat to the imaginary, that of the other, that which insists in and with the other, which cannot be imagined. This is one sense in which Freud can be seen to be over hasty in his dismissal of the injunction to love one's neighbour. In his contention that the neighbour is hostile or evil, Freud himself can be understood to have *imagined* the other as hostile, to have refused that of the other which cannot be known.

As Lacan illustrates with the example of the story of Saint Martin, the good one gives towards the other, insofar as the other is imagined as the counterpart of one's own ego, is liable to be the good as one conceives of it for oneself. Saint Martin encounters a beggar one winter night as he is entering a city. The beggar stops him and asks him for alms but, as Saint Martin has no money, he can only give what he has, his cloak. So, he takes his sword and cleaves his cloak and gives one half to the beggar. For Lacan, this example, which might be held in the Christian tradition as the epitome of loving one's neighbour, actually says very little. The good that Saint Martin takes to be the good of the beggar is nothing but his own good transposed onto the beggar, a point attested to in the story by the fact Saint Martin keeps one half of the cloak for himself. The other as conceived on the basis of its identification with the subject's own image of itself, its ego, leads to the good of the other being similarly conceived on the basis of the subject's misconception of its own good.

> It is a fact of experience that what I want is the good of others in the image of my own.
>
> (Ibid.: 187)

What Saint Martin does not account for here is that in the other which escapes identification. He does not know what the other wants.

> Perhaps over and above that need to be clothed, he was begging for something else, namely, that Saint Martin either kill him or fuck him.
>
> (Ibid.: 186)

What Lacan is pointing to here is the fact that it is not a question of an either/or. That Saint Martin sees the beggar as wanting or needing clothing to stay warm is not necessarily a mistake. The beggar, in all probability, was quite grateful for the cloak. The point is that this does not exhaust the beggar's desire, there is, beyond that in the beggar which can be recuperated by Saint Martin, something excessive, a desire which cannot be reduced to the services of goods, i.e. *jouissance*.

This conjunction of goods serves to illustrate the error Freud commits in assuming that the other is evil and harmful. The good one assumes for oneself, the object which would satisfy, serves to safeguard against the encounter with unbearable *jouissance*. In imputing this good to the other in an exclusive fashion – that is, as the Good – the subject would necessarily fail to account for the fact that this good was never *the* good for them, but only ever a surrogate and, thus, necessarily not *it*.

As the subject is constituted as the subject of desire in relation to a lack in its own being, a lack which is necessarily extimate, that which can be understood to be most central to the subject is also necessarily beyond the subject;

> [It is] that which is most myself in myself, that which is at the heart of myself, and beyond me, insofar as the self stops at the level of

those walls to which one can apply a label. What in French at least serves to designate the notion of self or same (*même*), then, is this interior or emptiness, and I don't know if it belongs to me or to nobody.

This is what my sophism signifies; it reminds me that my neighbor possesses all the evil Freud speaks about, but it is no different from the evil I retreat from in myself. To love him, to love him as myself, is necessarily to move towards some cruelty. His or mine?, you will object. But haven't I just explained to you that nothing indicates that they are distinct? It seems rather that they are the same, on condition that those limits which oblige me to posit myself opposite the other as my fellow man are crossed.

(Ibid.)

Das Ding is that in the subject and that in the other which would be encountered as desired and as abhorrent. It is hostile, but it is the same hostility the subject would encounter in itself. The abhorrence of the *jouissance* of which *das Ding* would be indicative is that beyond the meagre enjoyment afford by the pleasure principle. It is that which would bring a pleasure unbearable for the subject insofar as it would be the destruction of subjectivity as such. But it is an abhorrence inseparable from the very symbolic order constitutive of the subject insofar as it is that which would be indicated at the very constitutive limit of the symbolic order, that lack in the symbolic which would be inherent, as limit, to the symbolic. *Das Ding* would then be that which would mark the limit encountered in the attempt to integrate the other. That of the other which refuses identification is, paradoxically, inseparable from that in the subject which refuses identification. Or, phrased otherwise, that in the other which refuses identification is indicative of that in the subject which refused identification. It is, then, precisely this *Thing* which binds me to the other. This would suggest that the occlusion of the other through its reduction to an image modelled on the ego is, effectively, an occlusion of *jouissance*.

It is at this point that we can return to Freud's discussion of the directive to love one's neighbour as one's self introduced in Chapter 7. Freud's initial refusal of the directive is centred around the fact that it appears to advocate a non-preferentiality which would, for him, deny the very possibility of the love that it sets out to promote. Love for one's neighbour which would be love without preference is wrong, 'for my love is prized by my family and friends as a sign of my preference for them; to put a stranger on a par with them would be to do them an injustice' (Freud, 2002: 47). It is, for Freud, the very distinguishing qualities of the object of love, most notably those qualities in which the lover can find a point of identification, which confers on love the value which would be proper to it.

> If I love another person, he must in some way deserve it. ... He deserves it if, in certain important respects, he so resembles me that in him I can love myself. He deserves it if he is so much more perfect than myself that I can love in him an ideal image of myself. I must love him if he is my friend's son, for the pain my friend would feel if any harm befell him would be my pain too; I should have to share it. But if he is a stranger to me and cannot attract me by any merit of his own or by any importance he has acquired in my emotional life, it becomes hard for me to love him.
>
> (Ibid.: 46)

In his *Afterword* to *Revolution at the Gates* (2002), Žižek critiques Kierkegaard in a manner which would allow us to see him as joining with Freud in opposition to the directive to love one's neighbour in favour of preferential love. In *Works of Love*, Kierkegaard argues that the love attested to in the directive to love one's neighbour is the highest form of love precisely because it does not distinguish on the basis of preference. For Kierkegaard, the love one might have towards one's partner, the beloved, or one's friend is but a form of self-love.

> self-love and passionate preferential love are essentially the same, but love for the neighbour – that is love. ... For this reason the beloved and the friend are called, remarkably and profoundly, to be sure, the *other self* and the *other I*.
>
> (Kierkegaard, 1995: 53)

In opposition to exclusively preferential love, Kierkegaard advocates love of one's neighbour as non-preferential, as a love which renounces distinctions. Such love is the perfection of love precisely insofar as it is not dependent on any extraneous perfection in the object. Love predicated on a perceived perfect object cannot, for Kierkegaard, be perfect love because it is by definition limited to and by the object which would condition it. He compares such limited love to the health of a person which only subsists in one particular and favourable location. Clearly, Kierkegaard argues, we would not consider this person's health to be particularly excellent. We may consider the conditions or arrangements excellent, insofar as these conditions and arrangements are what allow the person's health to subsist. But the person's health itself we would no doubt find frail in that it is dependent upon these limited conditions. So it would be for love reserved only for persons who would display the kinds of particularities that Freud advocates as the proper aim for love. Such love is limited and, thus, while perfection may well reside in its object, the love itself is by definition poor, imperfect.

> Thus, the perfection of the object is not the perfection of the love. Because the neighbour has none of the perfections that the beloved, the friend, the admired one, the cultured person, the rare, the extraordinary person have to such a high degree, for that very reason love for the neighbour has all the perfections that the love for the beloved, the friend, the cultured person, the admired one, the rare, the extraordinary person does not have.
>
> (Ibid.: 66)

Love for one's neighbour, in Kierkegaard's understanding, is perfect love precisely because it does not distinguish. It is perfect as love in that it is not dependent on the qualities of the object on which it befalls. Indeed, as perfect, it falls on every object equally.

Concerning himself with the object here, Žižek contends that, following Kierkegaard's argument, the only good neighbour is a dead neighbour. Death might be understood as that which would remove all distinctions and, thus, in death, the neighbour can be fully loved, can attain to that perfected love which renounces distinctions.

Žižek, accurately, perceives in Kierkegaard a desire to delimit a non-pathological love, in the Kantian sense of non-pathological, where there would be no subjective incentive or attachment in the act of love, where love is 'motivated not by its determinate object, but by the mere *form* of love – love for the sake of love itself, not for the sake of what distinguishes its object' (Žižek, 2002: 213). In order to do so, Kierkegaard is not advocating that the only good neighbour is a dead neighbour. To do so would be to treat death as the distinction *par excellence* and thus miss the very point at which he aims; a love which is not predicated on any distinction at all. This would properly be, as Žižek claims, the love of the poet who can valorise the object of his love in death not because this erases distinctions but precisely because death here distinguishes the beloved above all else. What Kierkegaard, in Žižek's reading, appears to be advocating is rather that we treat the neighbour – that is, each individual – equally, as 'already dead, erasing his or her distinctive qualities' (Ibid.: 214). This, Žižek maintains, indicates the failure of Kierkegaard's argument. This, he says, is 'where Kierkegaard cheats' (Ibid.). This non-pathological love, for Žižek, would precisely miss what is difficult in love, the work of love which would describe it as authentic. Kierkegaard's love for the neighbour, devoid of any particularity, is, for Žižek, an 'easy feast' (Ibid.). Against this, and we can perhaps understand this as a support for Freud's rejection of the directive to love one's neighbour, Žižek suggests that we 'love the other *because of his or her very imperfection*' (Ibid.). What Žižek clearly has in mind here is that some*thing* in the other which would render them different.

Contra both Freud and Kierkegaard, Žižek isolates the imperfection as that which would render the other as worthy of love, the difficult work of love. Kierkegaard and Freud appear to be very much in agreement on the fact that that which commonly renders someone worthy of love is their identification with the lover. For Freud someone deserves love when they 'so resembles me that in him I can love myself' (Freud, 2002: 46). Similarly, for Kierkegaard, 'passionate preferential love is another form of self-love' (Kierkegaard, 1995: 53). We can clearly understand this identification in self-love which Freud defends and Kierkegaard criticises as the imaginary objectification of the other. One loves the other here, as Kierkegaard and Freud both point out, inasmuch as the other resembles oneself. Or, to be more precise, one loves the other inasmuch as the other is misrecognised as resembling one's misrecognition of one's self. A misrecognition of the self which originates in the other.

> it is from this fellow as such that the misrecognitions which define me as a self are born.
>
> (Lacan, 1992: 198)

Against such identification on the basis of misrecognition, Žižek would appear to advocate a love which, difficult as this may be, is predicated on difference, a love which would celebrate that in the other which could not be reduced to or recuperated to an identification. This resistant some*thing*, he argues, is *objet petit a*.

> Lacan's name for this 'imperfection', for the obstacle which makes me love someone, is *objet petit a*, the 'pathological' tic which makes him or her unique.
>
> (Žižek, 2002: 214–15)

Where Žižek's argument falters is in that which he identifies as constituting the other as the proper object of love is precisely the fantasy object which would shield the 'annoying excess' (Ibid.: 214) which would render the other imperfect and deserving of authentic love. Žižek confuses the object of fantasy with that which it would serve to conceal. As we have seen in Lacan's reading of Freud's *A Project for a Scientific Psychology*, the encounter with the other can be separated into two aspects, 'one of which affirms itself through an unchanging apparatus, which remains together as a thing, *als Ding*' (Lacan, 1992: 51) 'while the other can be *understood* by the activity of memory – that is, can be traced back to information from [the subject's] own body' (Freud, 1966: 331). That is to say, in the encounter with the other there is necessarily a process of identification and there is necessarily some*Thing* which cannot be reduced to this process of identification. Without the process of identification, the other would not be recognised as another person. Without the remainder, that which would resist identification, the other would not constitute an*other*. In the terms of Lacan's reading here, we can understand that what, in Freud, we might term 'deserving love' and what, in Kierkegaard, we might term 'love of the self in the other' are commensurate with that in the other which can be 'understood by the activity of the memory – that is, [that which] can be traced back to information from [the subject's] own body' (Ibid.). That is, it is love based on (mis)identification with the other, identification of the other as the counterpart of one's ego. Against this, however, *objet petit a* is not the 'unchanging apparatus' (Lacan, 1992: 51) but rather that which would simultaneously be indicative of and protective against the 'unchanging apparatus' (Ibid.). To fixate on the object of fantasy and, moreover, to impute this object to the other, to make of this object a distinctive *part* of the other, is precisely to refuse to acknowledge one's own part in the constitution of this object in the relation of fantasy.

It is that in the other which refuses identification which, paradoxically, for Lacan, is necessarily already the *same*, that which would lie beyond the positive distinctions the subject would draw between itself and the other. It is not the same, however, in the sense of a recuperation to the self, but rather because it is that which is in the subject more than the subject itself, that which is extimate to the subject. It is that which both insists upon the subject and cannot be reined within the subject. It is precisely that which would lie beyond all distinctions.

In this sense, we can see, contra Žižek, that, despite the apparent morbidity, Kierkegaard's claim is perfectly valid. Where Kierkegaard might be understood to falter himself is in the idea that such removal of all distinctions might be possible. Though, to be fair, it is not clear that Kierkegaard is actually making this claim at all. The love for the neighbour which would be a love oblivious to all earthly distinctions is in his own words not something which should 'abolish dissimilarity, neither dissimilarity of distinction nor of lowliness' (Kierkegaard, 1995: 88). Rather, he advocates that dissimilarity should be seen, in loving the neighbour, as hanging 'loosely on the individual, as loosely as the cape the king casts off in order to show who he is' (Ibid.).

> In other words, when the dissimilarity hangs loosely in this way, then in each individual there continually glimmers that essential other, which is common to all, the eternal resemblance, the likeness.
>
> (Ibid.)

Kierkegaard seems not to be so much advocating a renunciation of the recognition of positive differences, those aspects of the other which would set that other apart in their unicity, their particularity, as he is indicating that such differences are necessarily an imputation of the subject who would perceive them. Kierkegaard's point is to admonish those who would seek to validate self-love on the illusory ground that it is love of the other in all their individuality. In indicating that dissimilarity may be made to 'hang loosely' on the individual, Kierkegaard is indicating precisely that this is no easy feat. Relations with the other are such that they are bound in a logic of identification. The danger lies in allowing such identification, such love (or hate) of the *'other I,* the *other self'* (Ibid.: 53) to be *mis*taken as *true* recognition of the other's 'particular characteristic' (Žižek, 2002: 214). To refer to one of Žižek's preferred examples, the mole on Cindy Crawford's lip is not *her objet petit a,* it is precisely Žižek's *objet petit a,* that which Žižek perceives in her which renders her unique and desirable for him, that which allows her to be escalated to the status of an object of fantasy *for him.* For Kierkegaard, we should struggle to allow, to remain with this example, Cindy Crawford's mole, to 'hang loosely', that is precisely to acknowledge the objectifying perspective in which we might place 'her', to accept that the other necessarily exceeds the image, and thus the relation with the image, we would have constructed of them.

This is to suggest that the relation with the other entails a certain impossibility, an aporia wherein the other can neither be reduced to a point of identification nor experienced exclusively in their otherness. Any relation with the other is such that it would necessarily entail a process of identification, but an identification which is necessarily a recuperation to the *meconnaissance* of the subject in the form of the ego, an identification, that is, which is necessarily a misidentification which cannot but point to its own limitations. In so pointing to the limitations of identification, both in the sense that such identification is limited to recuperation and in the sense that such identification is necessarily *not all*, any relation with the other necessarily entails a beyond of identification but a *beyond* which must be understood as entailing a *with*. It is beyond identification and recuperation that we would experience the otherness of the other but such a beyond cannot be experienced in itself, that is, it can only insist at the limits of the symbolic and imaginary frameworks and, thus, only figure in subjective experience as the limitations of the symbolic and imaginary frameworks.

The logic of such a conjunction of the same and other, the impossibility of either a reduction to the same or the reduction to exclusive separation of otherness, can be adduced in Husserl's phenomenological investigation of the experience of the other in his *Cartesian Meditations*.

> *How* can my ego, within his peculiar ownness, constitute under the name, 'experience of something other'. precisely something *other* – something, that is, with a sense that excludes the constituted from the concrete make-up of the sense-constituting I-myself, as somehow the latter's analogue?
>
> (Husserl, 1991: 94)

If the experience of the other is precisely something differentiated from the subject's own experience of his or her self, then what is there that would substantiate such an experience while still marking it as distinct from the experience of an object? On the one hand, if it were possible to experience subjectively the very subjectivity of the other, then there would be nothing to differentiate such an experience from one's own experience of one's self. On the other hand, if the other is merely experienced as *being there*, as another object in the world, then on what basis would one be justified in assuming its attributes to extend beyond this physical appearance?

> if what belongs to the other's own essence were directly accessible, it would be merely a moment of my own essence, and ultimately he himself and I myself would be the same.
>
> (Ibid.: 109)

In response to these dilemmas, Husserl argues for a deduction of the other on the basis of an analogy with the subject. The subject, for Husserl, experiences itself 'as *uniquely* singled out' (Ibid.: 97).

> there is included in my ownness, as purified from every sense pertaining to other subjectivity, *a sense*, '*mere nature*', that has lost pre-

cisely that 'by everyone' and therefore must not by any means be taken for an abstract stratum of the world or of the world's sense. Among these bodies belonging to this 'Nature' and included in my peculiar ownness, I then find my *animate organism* as *uniquely* singled out – namely as the only one of them that is not just a body but precisely an animate organism: the sole Object within my abstract world-stratum to which, in accordance with experience, I ascribe *fields of sensation* ..., the only Object 'in' which I '*rule and govern*' *immediately*, governing particularly in each of its 'organs'.

(Ibid.: 96–7)

That is, the subject perceives its own 'psychophysical self' as the only *noema* which is not merely the perception of a physical body but is conceived as that which is 'reflexively related to itself' (Ibid.: 97). In order to conceive of the other as similarly capable or productive of such self-experience, such governing, the subject must conceive of the other analogically as the same but different. The essence of the other cannot be directly experienced without this effectively amounting to a recuperation to the self of the subject. It can, however, according to Husserl's argument, be deduced as existent through the logic of recognition and analogy.

The analogy here would be one drawn by the subject on the basis of its recognition in the imaginary of a similarity between the appearance of the other and the image it, the subject, has of itself. This would be what in Lacan's terms we might call 'ego identification'. It is, however, not, in Lacan's understanding, so easily reducible to an identification by analogy of the other with the self. As we have seen in the mirror stage, the subject can be understood to have constituted its own image of it*self*, its ideal ego, on the basis of a misrecognition of the other. Any identification with the other on the basis of an analogy with the self is thus necessarily an identification of the other with the ideal ego, rendering the other analogous, not with the subject as such, but with the subject's misrecognition of itself which was necessarily already constituted in misrecognition of the other as something other than the subject.

That is to say, the (mis)recognition of other on the basis of imaginary identification, precisely because it is misrecognised on the basis of imaginary identification, cannot account for the other in all its alterity. As imaginary identification would be, by definition, partial, that is, as it is only identification with the ideal ego, the other so comprehended or so constituted on the basis of such identification is necessarily not all. Something of the otherness in the other still persists as unknown. The very possibility of encountering the unknown in the other arises from this possibility of a point of perceived resemblance. Without such, there would be no suggestion of encountering the other as anything other than an object. It is insofar as the other is encountered as analogous to the subject that it is encountered as other than or more than an object. Insofar as the other is encountered as a speaking being or potentially speaking being, the otherness perceived in it insists on the subject.

Significant in Husserl's discussion of the possibility of intersubjectivity is his emphasis on the point of perception. True to the phenomenological method, Husserl's assertion of a distinction between *himself* and the other *noemata* is based on *his* own role of perceiver. As *he* perceives or intends the objects of his consciousness, *he*, as perceiver, is already there, already engaged in the conscious act. Such apperception of course speaks only of consciousness. The noema of the physicality of the self is concluded through the consciousness of *his* own body being governed by *himself*. Through the perception of *his* touching an object and the contrastive perception of *his* touching a part of himself, Husserl concludes that *his* relation to the body doing the touching and the thing touched is not the same. The analogous deduction of the other as another self, must then also follow from the logical priority of the perceiver. The other as other is necessarily logically subordinated to the self insofar as the self is construed as the perceiver.

Where, clearly, the Lacanian formulations we have been following complicate such a picture is in their theorising of the subjective basis upon which any such analogous deduction might be said to take place. Any identification configured as an identification on analogy is dependent on the starting point with which the analogy is made. *Other* is necessarily thought as *other than*. *Same* is necessarily thought as *same as*. Either render themselves logically dependent upon that which would be located at the point of comparison. Whether A is other than B or A is the same as B, in both cases the identity is determined by B. The question in such a formulation would be that of initially identifying B in order to, subsequently, determine the otherness or sameness of A. What Lacan allows us to do is to understand that such a starting point is only ever a pure assumption.

Insofar as the encounter with the *Nebenmensch* brings with it that which can be recuperated to the understanding, the familiar, and that which remains alien, *das Ding*, we can understand that in such a formulation, to remain with our simplified terms, A^1 is the same as B and A^2 is other than B insofar as A^1 is that which is taken to be recuperable to an identification with that of *B* which was constructed on the basis of a misrecognition of or misidentification with a prior term and A^2 is taken to be irrecuperable to such an identification. By recognising this bifurcation or separation in *B*, that there is a B^1 and a B^2, where B^1 would represent that which had been constructed on the basis of misrecognition and B^2 would represent that which refused any reduction to such an identification on the basis of misrecognition, that which would be excluded from any such identification, we can understand that A^1 is (taken to be) the same as B^1 and A^2 (is taken to be) the same as B^2 with the proviso that it is only as A^2 and B^2 are only identified by their non-identity, by the impossibility of construing them as such, that A^2 and B^2 can be understood to be the same. So far, within such an abstraction, the terms of each pair, $A^1 = B^1$ and $A^2 = B^2$ would appear to be quite reversible. What renders the pairings irreversible is the fact of perception, or the starting point. A^2 and B^2 cannot strictly speaking be construed as reversible insofar as they are, effectively the same thing. There are not two points here to reverse. From the point of view located in the symbolic order there is that which cannot be known, that which would resist all representation. The insistence of this unrepresentable excess, *das Ding*, is what would be indicated in A^2 and B^2, the insistence of a beyond of the symbolic and the imaginary both in or with the subject and in or with the other. As such, the two terms are not so much reversible as never reducible to two terms as such in the first instance. It is only from the question of perspective that the separation of the points into two might arise, a separation which would be properly understood as a misconstrual. The very question 'His or mine?' (Lacan, 1992: 198) asked of the indeterminate 'interior or emptiness' (Ibid.) is, properly, inappropriate insofar as there is nothing which 'indicates they are distinct' (Ibid.). The otherness, the alien in the other as *Nebenmensch* is irreducible to a reversible relation not because of a fixed priority of one term over the other but rather because of a radical impossibility of distinguishing two points at all.

It is thus only in the case of A^1 and B^1 that a reversibility might be considered possible. Here reversibility is only conceivable on the basis of the hypothesis of a third external vantage point, one which would consider both elements from an equal distance. It is in the very impossibility of such an external vantage point that the irreversibility of the elements in question imposes itself. The only vantage point is one of the elements itself. Consequently, regardless of the formal identity of the two components, a formal identity which is at best illusory, constituted as it is on the basis of a double misrecognition, there imposes a contextual dissymmetry insofar as one point is necessarily the point of perspective, a requisite condition which necessarily repudiates the hypothesis of reversibility. Where A^1 stands for the other, the *Nebenmensch*, and B^1 stands for the ideal ego, the subject's misrecognised self-image, we can understand that, beyond the insistence of *das Ding*, both A^2 and B^2, where these terms are understood to be not so much formulated on the basis of an identity as to be misconstrued as two separable terms, there is another factor which renders the pair irreversible; that of the point of perception.

This is not, however, to suggest that the point of perception is in any way a pure given, that there is something which would independently insist apart from misrecognition or *das Ding* which would radically differentiate a from $i(a)$. The point of perception is rather that point which must be assumed, the $I \rightarrow it$ (*Ich* $\rightarrow$ *Es*) of *Wo Es war, soll Ich werden*. What differentiates a from $i(a)$ is the fact that $i(a)$ is constituted as the image of what *I* would be, the ideal image one would have of oneself, and a, as the other, is constituted as what would be other than *me* for *me*. Both points are constituted as *for* but inadequate to the subject, but, in being so constituted, both points are located or imagined separately for the subject.

What this allows us to understand is that in any attempted or projected identification between the subject and the other, there is (1) imaginary identification on the basis of misrecognition, $i(a) \rightarrow a$; (2) *das Ding*, as that which insists but refuses a recuperation to identification and thus refuses any allocation to either the subject, $\cancel{S}$, or the other; and (3) a necessary point from which the other is perceived as identifiable. What ought to be clear here is that the point of perception cannot be reduced to $i(a)$, that on the basis of which (mis)identification with the other is construed. It is rather because of the inherent proximity of $i(a)$ to that which would perceive it, that $i(a)$ is constituted as an (illusory) image of the self, that the process is deemed irreversible.

It is important here to acknowledge that this imaginary identification must also partake of symbolic mediation. That is to say, beyond or in addition to identification in the imaginary order, the subject, in order to be constituted as a subject must enter the realm of the symbolic. This 'secondary identification' (Lacan, 1977a(i): 22) can be understood to emerge in the process of the Oedipus complex with the intervention of the father, or as we have seen previously, in the process of castration which would be synonymous with the subject's emergence in the field of the symbolic. The initial stage of the Oedipus complex (though, this, for Lacan, should be understood as a logical rather than a chrono-logical sequence) can be understood to be commensurate with the ima-ginary identification we have been discussing. In encountering the mother as lacking, the child, as we have seen previously, seeks to situate itself as the object of her desire. Since the child is incapable of accom-plishing this, is incapable, that is, of completely satisfying the mother, it encounters itself as also lacking. The 'second' stage of the Oedipus complex would be characterised by the intervention of the imaginary father, that is, the perception of desire as prohibited. It is in the third stage that the Real father is understood to intervene and display that he has the 'phallus', that which would satisfy desire. Crucial here is the point that the Real father is a function and is not essentially bound to the biological father. Rather, the Real father would be defined precisely in terms of that which is understood to possess the phallus, 'the signifier of the desire of the Other' (Lacan, 1977a(vi): 290), that which would satisfy the mother's desire. The intervention of the Real father can be under-stood as allowing the child access to the symbolic through the process of renunciation of the always failed attempt to situate itself as the cause of the mother's desire. This can be understood as the inauguration of law and, thus, the Real father can be understood in terms commensurate with the mythical father of the primal horde; he who would satisfy the women of the group, he who would be without lack. Through identification with the Real father, the subject can be understood to have adopted and inter-nalised the prohibitionary strictures understood to have been imposed by the father. This is the moment of incorporation we have seen in terms of Lacan's reading of the myth of the primal horde.

> Freud shows us, in fact, that the need to participate, which neutral-izes the conflict inscribed after the murder in the situation of rivalry between the brothers, is the basis of the identification with the pater-nal Totem. Thus the Oedipal identification is that by which the subject transcends the aggressivity that is constitutive of the primary sub-jective individuation. ... it constitutes a step in the establishment of that distance by which, with feelings like respect, is realized a whole affective assumption of one's neighbour.
>
> (Lacan, 1977a(i): 23)

This 'secondary', symbolic, identification can be understood to be con-stitutive of the ego ideal, *I(A)*, that on the basis of which one would internalise the law and the symbolic order. In identifying with the father, in incorporating the father as prohibitory force, the subject locates itself in terms of the phallus, the signifier of desire which would be understood to be inaugural of the signifying chain. The position so assumed is one of symbolic identification. The phallus, as the signifier of desire, would be that in relation to which the subject would symbolically constitute itself.

> It is in so far as the function of man and woman is symbolized, it is insofar as it's literally uprooted from the domain of the imaginary and situated in the domain of the symbolic, that any normal, completed sexual position is realized.
>
> (Lacan, 1993: 177)

It is the different positions adopted in relation to the phallus which would determine the symbolic and sexual identity of the subject. This can be seen most clearly in the formulae Lacan adopts in his schema of sexuation in *Encore*. Where the subject who would be structured as male would be understood to be wholly determined by the signifier, the subject who would be structured as female is not. Where the phallus is understood as the signifier of desire and thus, inseparable from this, the signifier which would be understood to introduce lack, it can be understood to be constitutive of the subject. It is thus only through symbolic identification that the subject can come to 'be' in the symbolic order and the precise manner in which this identification is undertaken or experienced is determinative of the particular (sexed) position the subject will take up. It is only from such a position that the misrecognition on the basis of the *same* and *other* can be understood. That is to say, without symbolic structuration, there is, properly, no position from which to perceive the (mis)identification in question. The subject as symbolically constituted, as barred, $, is the position of perception which would be assumed, not an already constituted or existent position in front of which such processes of identification would unfold. As we have seen, though, *das Ding*, as that which is beyond both imaginary and symbolic recuperation, would be that which would persist beyond both imaginary and symbolic identification.

Where the Husserlian conception of adduction of the other through the process of empathy is such that there is the suggestion of the other as a mere reduplication of the ego, in a Lacanian conception what stops a reduplication is the persistence of that which cannot be recuperated to such an identification, that which was never reducible to the ego and – where the *and* here does not necessitate any suggestion of consequence – is not reducible to any alter-ego. That the irreducibility of *das Ding* in either instance is not predicated on a logic of consequence is attested to by the fact of the impossibility of any firm exterior starting point. If, as is suggested in Husserl's formulation, the alter-ego were construed or perceived on the basis of an originary ego, then it might be possible to claim that that which insists as an excess in impossible relation to the ego is subsequently or consequently read into the perception of the alter-ego construed on analogy with the original model. The problematic to such an understanding that Lacan allows us to grasp is the fact of there being no clear cut original from which to work. As the mirror stage indicates, not only is the ego itself construed upon a misrecognition of some exterior model – the child's own image, the parent or even a toy – but also the whole scenario of (mis)recognition is only ever received in a retroactive movement. That is to say, there is not available any comfortable, linear progression from ego to analogous ego formulated on a basis of identification of similarity but rather a disrupted circle or *reductio ad infinitum* of misrecognition from *i(a)* to *a* to *i(a)* .... What would disrupt such a knit of misrecognition is not only the fact of misrecognition – that is, that each moment would entail an encounter with that which could not be accounted, *das Ding* – but also the fact of the point of perception. In order for the process of (mis)identification to be seen to have taken place, there must be, no matter how obfuscated, a point from which the process is seen to have taken place. Both *i(a)* and *a*, the ideal ego and the other, are such that they are only ever taken to be. They are imaginary effects. They are construed by the subject, $, and, as construed by the subject, form part of the psychical make-up of the subject. As we have seen previously, such a subject is by no means a pre-given unity but rather a position which must be assumed. The subject in coming to be can be understood, as we have seen previously, as the very split between the imaginary 'self-present ego' and the indeterminable, unfathomable otherness within itself. It is this location of the subject as barred, $, not so much *in* as *as* the very disjunction of these two positions, which should be seen as the point of perspective. What this indicates is that the point of perspective is not in any predetermined sense the truth of the subject, its original or proper position. Rather, the point of perception is the position the subject would come to assume and thus from which the subject would retroactively posit the very disjunction it could not inhabit.

Clearly here such a point is going to be unstable. As we have already seen, the assumption of the *I* in *Wo Es war, soll Ich werden* is only ever pulsational, it is not a matter of an assumption once and for all, but rather an assumption to be made again and again.

9
Beyond Difference

We misrecognise ourselves in the image of the other and through this misrecognition come to constitute an idea of ourselves, an identity which is fragile and predicated on that which is external to us. Such an understanding necessarily problematises any straightforward distinction between same and other insofar as I misrecognise the other as *like* me on the basis of my own misrecognition of myself and I fail to grasp that which is truly other in the other just as I fail to grasp what is truly other in myself. Where then does this leave ethics in relation to the other? In *Ethics: An Essay on the Understanding of Evil* (2001), Alain Badiou presents what might be understood to be an intervention on this very point. Against what he characterises as the 'ethical predication based upon recognition of the other' (Badiou, 2001: 25), Badiou posits what we might understand as an ethics of the same, that is, for Badiou, 'the real question [of ethics] ... is much more that of *recognising the Same*' (Ibid.). For Badiou, any theory of ethics which would purport to found itself on a notion of difference from the other is destined to, at least philosophical, failure insofar as the positing of any foundational difference between self and other is necessarily ignorant of the constitutive difference which would entail to everything including the self itself.

> Infinite alterity is quite simply *what there is*. Any experience at all is the infinite deployment of infinite differences. Even the apparently self-reflexive experience of myself is by no means the intuition of a unity but a labyrinth of differentiations, and Rimbaud was certainly not wrong when he said: 'I am another.'
>
> (Ibid.: 25–6)

Isolating Emmanuel Levinas as the originator of contemporary ethics of difference, Badiou argues that such ethics are, in their Levinasian form at least, essentially religious and as such cannot be 'gathered under the name of philosophy' (Ibid.: 23).

In Badiou's reading, Levinas refuses traditional metaphysics on the basis of its prioritising of the Same. Such prioritising would be exemplified in the Husserlian notion of analogy considered in Chapter 8. Any conception of the other on the basis of analogy with the self is tantamount to a reduction to the Same wherein the other would not be experienced as other as such.

> The dialectic of the Same and the Other, conceived 'ontologically' under the dominance of self-identity [*identité-à-soi*], ensures the absence of the Other in effective thought, suppresses all genuine experience of the Other, and bars the way to an ethical opening to alterity.
>
> (Ibid.: 19)

This impossibility of adequately thinking the other from the basis of a system of thought predicated upon a notion of self-identity necessitates the adoption of another mode of thinking, one which does not rely upon the prioritising of the same but, rather, conceives of any posited identity as necessarily posterior to the encounter with the other. Levinas, according to Badiou, finds such an alternative in the Talmudic tradition wherein the law describes, not the presence of identity but the demand of and, thus, responsibility towards the other which would thus necessarily be prior to any conception of identity, whether the identity of the self or of the other. The quintessential or ultimate mode of so experiencing the other is, on Badiou's reading, what Levinas has termed 'the face to face' (Levinas, 1969: 202), the encounter with the other as 'the epiphany that occurs as a face' (Ibid.: 196). Levinas's point in his invocation of the face of the other is that such an encounter, the appearance of the other as absolutely other, the epiphany of the face, is that which cannot be reduced to the logic of the same.

> The face resists possession, resists my power. In its epiphany, in expression, the sensible, still graspable, turns into total resistance to the grasp.
>
> (Ibid.: 197)

From this encounter with the face of the other, with that which would be indicative of the ungraspable, Levinas argues that we find ourselves in a position of irreversible responsibility for the other.

In his use of the term 'face' and his insistence on its resistance to recuperation or comprehension, Levinas is clearly not intent on evoking the mere corporeality of the human face as we understand it in its everyday or biological sense. At the same time, however, the term 'face' cannot easily be reduced to a mere metaphor. Rather, Levinas's use of this term should be understood as inclusive, signifying the empirical presence of the other as other person and transcending any attempted reduction to such a presence. The face marks the appearance of the other and announces the epiphany of that in the other which cannot be reduced to a mere object of experience.

> The face is present in its refusal to be contained. In this sense it cannot be comprehended, that is encompassed. It is neither seen nor touched – for in visual or tactile sensation the identity of the I envelops the alterity of the object, which becomes precisely a content.
>
> (Ibid.: 194)

In this emphasis on the impossibility of comprehension, the fact that the face is such that it cannot be subsumed within the 'I', we should understand that the face is not the disclosure of the other, an unveiling of that which had hitherto been inaccessible. The face marks the advent of that which will remain beyond comprehension and yet insists.

> The presentation of the face, expression, does not disclose an inward world previously closed, adding thus a new region to comprehend or to take over. On the contrary, it calls to me above and beyond the given that speech already puts in common among us. What one gives, what one takes reduces itself to the phenomenon, discovered and open to the grasp, carrying on an existence which is suspended in possession – whereas the presentation of the face puts me into relation with being.
>
> (Ibid.: 212)

It is insofar as the face can neither be refused nor grasped that, for Levinas, it demands a response. Such a response cannot be reduced to the kind of reaction one would give towards an object of comprehension precisely insofar as the response is a response towards that which cannot be grasped. Where one reacts to an encounter with that which is familiar by identifying it, by compartmentalising it with its type, such luxury is not afforded by the epiphany of the face which announces that which would have no compartment, which is beyond typification. As such, for

Levinas, the response invoked in the encounter with the face of the other cannot be maintained in a straight-forward one-to-one relation. That which cannot be grasped cannot be assigned to the other exclusively. To do so would be to assume to know, precisely to grasp or comprehend it and thus to assign it a place in one's world. As ungraspable, the beyond evoked in the face of the other remains beyond and thus irreducible to *that* other as an object of my interest or perception.

> *The existing of this being*, irreducible to phenomenality understood as a reality without reality, is effectuated in the non-postponable urgency with which he requires a response. This response differs from the 'reaction' that the given gives rise to in that it cannot remain 'between us', as is the case with the steps I take with regard to a thing. Everything that takes place here 'between us' concerns everyone, the face that looks at it places itself in the full light of the public order, even if I draw back from it to seek with the interlocutor the complicity of a private relation and a clandestinity.
>
> (Ibid.)

The indeterminate and over-determined status of the face points to the fact that it is the name for one of those border concepts, a marker for a limit point 'between' the familiar and the unfamiliar. The face marks that which refuses comprehension and yet manifests as an appearance. As comprehension would entail comprehension in language, that which could be conceptualised within, in Lacanian terms, the symbolic order, the face, as that which refuses comprehension, marks the limit of language. In so doing, for Levinas, it marks the origin, the very possibility of language. In Levinas's formulation, the face-to-face is the 'primordial event' of signification which 'makes the sign function possible' (Ibid.: 206). That is to say, the face marks not only the limit of the comprehensible and thus the limit of the signifiable – where the possibility of comprehension entails the possibility of signification – but also, in so doing, and because it does so, it indicates the very possibility of language or signification in the first place. For Levinas, the subject cannot be reduced to a 'transcendental consciousness' such as Husserl propounds, a consciousness which would be constitutive of the phenomena of its experience and, in terms of intersubjectivity, as we have seen, constitute the other on the basis of an analogy with its own apperception of itself. Rather, for Levinas, the subject can only be conceived after and on the basis of the encounter with the other not because the other would somehow provide a model in which the subject might recognise itself or from which it could constitute its own identity but because it is in encounter with the other that the very possibility of language and signification, that which would allow the possibility of comprehension, arises. For Levinas, the 'primordial essence of language is to be sought ... in the presentation of meaning' (Ibid.), the advent of the possibility of such meaning would be contemporaneous with the advent of the other and the face to face encounter. The other both precedes language and announces the possibility of language.

Clearly, Levinas's argument here does not attest to a conventional chronology. To insist on such a conventional chronology would be to assume that language comes once and for all. That is to say, the commonsensical view which would uphold that when one encounters another person one already has language at one's disposal and thus that Levinas's insistence on the constitutive status of the face to face clearly misses the 'fact' that in any encounter with another person one is already furnished with linguistic armoury or saddled with linguistic baggage, is ignorant of the pulsative status of the subjectivity described here. The encounter with the other is, as the primordial point, not something which could then be relegated to the past but must insist again and again through every encounter with the other, through every appearance of the face of the other. Every instance of language, as discourse, as thought, is, for Levinas, invocative of and dependent upon the instantiatory face to face encounter.

> Meaning is the face of the Other[5], and all recourse to words takes place already within the primordial face to face of language. Every recourse to words presupposes the comprehension of the primary signification, but this comprehension, before being interpreted as a 'consciousness of', is society and obligation.
>
> (Ibid.: 206–7)

It is for this reason that Levinas can claim the primacy of responsibility. If 'the essence of language is the relation with the Other' (Ibid.: 207), then this relation with the other cannot be reduced in any way to an already constituted consciousness as such consciousness would necess-

---

[5]'Other' with a capital 'O' is Lingis's translation of Levinas's 'autrui' (the personal other), distinguished from 'autre' (the impersonal other) and should, thus, in no way be understood as commensurate with Lacan's big 'Other', the field of language. See translator's footnote, Levinas, E. (1969), pp. 24–5.

arily depend upon language for its conception. In this way the encounter with the other calls into question the fragile identity of the subject and necessitates its being constituted again. As Levinas states earlier in *Totality and Infinity*,

> To be I is, over and beyond any individuation that can be derived from a system of references, to have identity as one's content. The I is not a being that always remains the same, but is the being whose existing consists in identifying itself, in recovering its identity throughout all that happens to it. It is the primal identity, the primordial work of identification.
>
> (Ibid.: 36)

Identity is not something that can be fixed but is better understood as a process. What defines the subject, for Levinas, is not its identity in the sense of knowing what it *is*, but rather its identification in the sense of its perpetually constituting itself. Such constitution is necessarily subsequent to the encounter with the face of the other.

If the very possibility of language, of thought, of comprehension relies upon the encounter with the other, then all thought, including any thought of oneself, is only possible on the basis of a relation with the other. Language, for Levinas, is not the tool of consciousness but, rather, that which arises as a possibility only from the other and thus consciousness or self-identification can only be posterior to the encounter with the other. Not only would this suggest that the traditional view of recognition of the other on the basis of their identity with the self is misguided insofar as there is no identity of the self before encounter with the other on the basis of which the other might be recognised but also that, in locating the encounter with the other prior to any self-identity, we would locate an openness to sociality before and as a condition of any self-conception, a self-conception which in turn would necessarily be reliant on this sociality. As the other, in the encounter one would have with them, puts into question one's identity, this encounter can be understood not only as a beginning but also as a demand.

The encounter with the face of the other, for Levinas, is characterised by 'expression'. Such expression cannot be reduced to any conventional notion of language in use insofar as what is expressed in expression is not the articulation of terms which would somehow already refer to a meaning within the totality of a system. The expression evident in the face of the other precedes any such 'circle of understanding' (Ibid.: 201). The expression in the face of the other is rather the limit point where the system of language can no longer offer a guarantee, where the assemblage of inter-referential signs of language can no longer hold. It is because of this 'lack', this failure of language, that responsibility manifests in the face to face encounter. For Levinas, the demand entailed in the encounter with the other, constitutive of language and, thus, outwith any recourse to the guarantee of language, necessitates bearing witness to oneself and, crucially, providing or becoming, assuming oneself as, the guarantor of this attestation. Where the confines of language can no longer provide the security of identity, one must assume one's identification upon oneself. Such an assumption cannot, for Levinas, be a solitary assumption insofar as the questioning and command which would give rise to the necessity of assumption, which would render the assumption possible in the first place, only comes from the appearance of the other. One is thus responsible for oneself but only insofar as one is already responding to the other. Response and responsibility are thus conjoined and one is, insofar as one is called upon to respond, responsible in this responding not only for oneself but, before this, for the other.

Crucially, for Levinas, the encounter with the other in the face to face cannot be reduced to or maintained as a simple relationship of one for the other. Insofar as the face of the other, understood as the epiphany of that which would be beyond comprehension, cannot be reduced to a monadic entity, the face of the other is indicative of humanity.

> It is not that there would first be the face, and then the being it manifests or expresses would concern himself with justice; the epiphany of the face qua face opens humanity.
>
> (Ibid.: 213)

The encounter with the face of the other can be understood as evocative of justice, a responsibility which exceeds the duality of the one for the other, precisely because the face of the other cannot be reduced to a comprehensible singularity. Always, for Levinas, in the face of the other there is a reference to a third party, a third party which would be understood as 'the whole of humanity which looks at us' (Ibid.).

For Levinas, this 'whole of humanity' cannot be understood in the logic of a genus wherein individuals would be united in resemblance or already constituted points of definition or identity. Biologically defined, *homo sapiens* may constitute a genus but this is, by definition, only a biological genus. Humanity understood as community is, for Levinas, a fraternity of unique parties. If identity, as we have seen, can only be understood as a process of identification wherein there can be no self-contained and stable identity which would precede the encounter with the other, then there can be no identity which could be understood as already common on the basis of which community might be founded. The very possibility of identification and thus of community arises from the encounter with the face of the other but, at the same time, it would appear the very possibility of encountering the other qua other, in order to be recognisable in any way, arises from the possibility of a human community.

This possibility of a human community would be such that it would necessitate individualities whose very identity is constituted in their singular response to the other. However, if the possibility of such a constitution of identity, albeit identity as process, is reliant upon the encounter with the other qua other, then something else, beyond the response commanded by the face of the other encountered must be understood to initiate the possibility of the fraternity to which this would attest. That is to say, if the possibility of a human community relies upon the unicity of individuals whose identity would be constituted in the response to the face of the other and the epiphany of the face of the other evokes the whole of humanity, then, without the instantiation of an exterior point of reference, we can be understood to have resumed the very 'circle of understanding' Levinas sought to escape. This exterior point, for Levinas, is suggested in the very term he chooses to describe the community which would be a community beyond mere biological identification; fraternity. Fraternity clearly implies a paternity (not to mention a maternity), a single source from which 'we', the community-to-come attested to in the encounter with the face of the other, would emerge. Levinas is, however, quick to insist that paternity – and this is perhaps what would set it apart from a maternity – is not reducible to a causality. Paternity is, rather, for Levinas, the 'establishment of a unicity with which the unicity of the father does and does not coincide' (Ibid.: 214). The father-child relationship is not one which could be reduced to a pure resemblance, an emission wherein the father simply causes the son to be. Rather for Levinas, the father-son relationship 'designates a relation of rupture and a recourse at the same time' (Ibid.: 278). The fraternity which would emerge from the paternal, which would have the paternal as its source, entails a double relation with this paternal, a relation both of attachment and disjunction. The son has recourse to the father insofar as the father is that without which the son would not be but the son is also necessarily separate from the father, a separation without which the son would not be.

> The son resumes the unicity of the father and yet remains exterior to the father: the son is a unique son. ... The unique child, as elected one, is accordingly at the same time unique and non-unique. Paternity is produced as an innumerable future; the I engendered exists at the same time as unique in the world and as brother among brothers. I am I and chosen one, but where can I be chosen, if not from among other chosen ones, among equals.
>
> (Ibid.: 279)

It is, for Levinas, the existence of the father and, more specifically, the love of the father, the father's love, which allows for the possibility of a human community. The love of the father for the son, insofar as it is understood to entail the love between unique (separate) but dependent (inseparable) individualities, is, for Levinas, the 'sole relation possible with the very unicity of another' (Ibid.).

> The very status of the human implies fraternity and the idea of the human race. Fraternity is radically opposed to the conception of a humanity united by resemblance, a multiplicity of diverse families arisen from the stones cast behind by Deucalion, and which, across the struggle of egoisms, results in a human city. Human fraternity has then two aspects: it involves individualities whose logical status is not reducible to the status of ultimate differences in a genus, for their singularity consists in each referring to itself. (An individual having a common genus with another individual would not be removed enough from it.) On the other hand, it involves the commonness of a father, as though the commonness of race would not bring together enough. Society must be a fraternal community to be commensurate with the straightforwardness, the primal proximity, in which the face presents itself to my welcome. Monotheism signifies this human kinship, this idea of a human race that refers back to the approach of the Other in the face, in a dimension of height, in responsibility for oneself and for the Other.
>
> (Ibid.: 214)

We might here recall the discussion of the significance of the father in Freud's 'scientific myth' (Freud, 2001a: 135) of the primal horde. There too the father emerges as the figure essential for the possibility of the constitution of a fraternity. For Freud, as we have seen, inherent in the relation of the sons to the father is an ambiguity of feelings, an entwining of love and aggression, a simultaneous bonding and separation. Again, for Freud, it is from this relation to this figure of the father, and the love and aggression which would characterise this relation, that the very possibility of community, of society emerges through the murder and consumption of the father, that is, through destruction and identification as the catalysts for the inauguration of the social pact and the institution of law. What, as emphasised by Lacan, is crucial in Freud's myth is its very status as myth. The scene of the primal horde works as an explanation of the origins of society and law not insofar as it is a historical event which would have happened but insofar as it is a myth which illuminates something of the psychic relations of the subject who subscribes to the myth. The events of the myth, the pre-eminence of and the surpassing of the father, function as a retroactively posited situation, the 'truth' of which resides only in its postulation, not its occurrence. In order for the relationship with the father, in all its ambiguity, to function as the ground of the possibility of a fraternal community for and from within which the myth can be retroactively posited, the fraternal community must already have emerged. Just as the events of the myth, as we saw in Lacan's reading of Freud, would be inconceivable without the law of which the myth is supposed to have been constitutive, so in Levinas's postulation of a father as constitutive of the community of fraternity which would ground the possibility of the encounter with the other, the community must already exist in order for the paternal origin to be posited as its origin. That Levinas here invokes the example of monotheism might be understood as his appealing to God as the 'missing' ground which would guarantee the fraternity which would be the necessary context for the face to face encounter with the other. If, however, we read Levinas with Lacan, we might understand this less as the unjustifiable postulation of a 'higher entity' than as the assumption of a necessary but necessarily retroactively posited *aitia*. If, as we have seen, the law which would substantiate the possibility of any community necessitates a ground it cannot itself provide, then this ground can only be postulated as prior to that which it would be understood to have founded from within that which is founded. It is only in an appeal to something external that the *reductio ad infinitum* of authorisation can (be seen to) be halted.

If the face to face encounter is that which would initiate the possibility of subjective identity, if it can be understood to be instantiative of language as that which would refuse the complicity of a self-sufficient one to one relation, if it can, that is, be understood as testimony to the insistence of the wider human community, a community, moreover, which would be understood as a community of equality, a fraternity, then this community and the possibility of language which would bind the community must be inaugurated from outwith the terms constituted in the face-to-face encounter. It would thus be for this reason that some*thing* other than the other person insists in the encounter with the other as other person. It is this other than the other which Levinas terms the absolute other.

What this indicates is that the otherness encountered in the other is not reducible to any 'concrete', cultural, psychical or even inherent difference between the subject and the other. The otherness of the other is rather invocative of an otherness which would exceed the other in both their corporeality and in any impression the subject might have of them. That is to say, the otherness of the other, what Levinas terms 'an other absolutely other' (Levinas, 1969: 218), is such that it would resist any recuperation to identification by the subject. This is, consequently, a strictly asymmetric relation in that the absolute otherness attested to can only be attested to in the first person relating of a relationship.

> These differences between the Other and me do not depend on different 'properties' that would be inherent in the 'I', on the one hand, and, on the other hand, in the Other, nor on different psychological dispositions which their minds would take on from the encounter. They are due to the I-other conjuncture, to the inevitable *orientation* of being 'starting from oneself' towards 'the Other'.
>
> (Ibid.: 215)

As we have seen previously, the approach of the other must necessarily pertain to a particular perspective. There is not available a third position from which the relation of 'I' to the other could be perceived objectively. Any claim to such a third position would necessarily become, once again, a particular perspectival position. The absolute otherness to which the face of the other attests must then at one and the same time appear only to the 'I' and be differentiated in this particularity. There is, in Levinas's terms, no available 'correlation from which the I would derive its identity and the Other his alterity' (Ibid.). The relationship of the *I* to the other necessitates the assumption of the position of the *I* from which the relation is perceived. To assume to see the relationship in or as a totality is to assume to adopt an impossible position outwith the relationship. That is to say, there is no position from which the other can be seen to be other in the simple sense of being different from the *I*. Such a judgement would assume to 'see' two comparables which could be distinguished on the ground of their similarity or difference. On the contrary, for Levinas, the relationship can only be experienced, and thus be 'seen' to occur, from within the terms of the relationship itself. The assumption of the occupation of a third point is merely a reduplication of the problem. The encounter with the face of the other thus refuses any totalisation and thus necessarily opens towards the absolute otherness which would be indicative of the inherent limitation of finitude.

> The identity of the I comes to it from its egoism whose insular sufficiency is accomplished by enjoyment, and to which the face teaches the infinity from which this insular sufficiency is separated. This egoism is indeed founded on the infinitude of the other, which can be accomplished only by being produced as the idea of Infinity in a separated being. The other does indeed invoke this separated being, but this invocation is not reducible to calling for a correlative.
>
> (Ibid.: 216)

The encounter with the other as other person, as the relationship cannot be recuperated to any totality, is necessarily indicative of an infinity beyond the finitude of the *I* and of any attempt to recuperate the other to the *I* on the basis of identification or recognition. This would be the absolute otherness with which the *I* would find itself in an asymmetric relation.

For Badiou, this absolute otherness is 'obviously the ethical name for God' (Badiou, 2001: 22). It is perhaps, however, not quite so obvious that this is, or has to be, the case. Levinas's description of the altogether other as that which would insist in the encounter with the other, that which would refuse totalisation in any recuperation to the Same or the ego of the self, is, at best, ambiguous. At the same time, it ought to be acknowledged that Levinas does, as we have seen above, appeal to some*thing* beyond finite relations which would ground or guarantee the relations of alterity which would emanate in the approach of the other. The question is whether the persistence of such a guarantor, the paternal to the fraternity of humanity, operates as an assumption within Levinas's thought or whether it rather, as with Lacan and Freud, assumes the place of a theoretical conjecture. That is to say, the question might be phrased as whether or not Levinas is claiming that this primordial father actually exists or whether he is claiming that the postulation of such a figure functions in the psyche as a necessary limit to and thus assumed guarantee or guarantor of the order of relations which would be commensurate with and necessary to the functioning of society. To characterise that which is by definition beyond comprehension would be to impossibly reduce it to a moment of subjective comprehension. To declare that the 'Altogether-Other ... is quite obviously the ethical name for God' (Ibid.) is to read Levinas as positing that which is by definition beyond the knowable as something which could be known.

The invocation of the term God, both by Levinas and Badiou, perhaps obfuscates the issue here. Badiou's claim appears to be that God, as a name for unity, for Oneness, is not tenable. To make a claim for the unity of what lies beyond comprehension is to have claimed that what lies beyond comprehension can at least be characterised. While it may not be possible to comprehend such Oneness in its totality, it remains characterised and thus comprehended, albeit theoretically, as a Oneness, as a totality. As we have seen with Lacan, such a claim for totality is only ever a postulation arising from the experience of incompleteness. The very concept of a totalising oneness is self-refuting insofar as oneness must, in order to be thought, be posited against some*thing* else and thus engender difference.

That which would persist beyond comprehension is described by Levinas as the Infinite, not in the sense that it would be infinity positively experienced and impossibly embraced in itself as infinity but, rather, as that which would necessarily mark the limit of conscious experience itself; that which cannot be thought. The limit of the finitude of understanding is indicative of the infinitude of what cannot be understood. It is in the encounter with the other, before the face of the other, that, for Levinas, one would experience infinity as that of the other which would exceed '*the idea of the other in me*' (Levinas, 1969: 50).

Insofar as Levinas can be understood to be characterising that which would be beyond comprehension as a definite One, he would be guilty of claiming to know, to have brought within the circle of understanding, that which would by definition refuse any comprehension, any understanding. Insofar as this is not the case, insofar, that is, as that we read Levinas in a manner significantly more commensurate with Lacan, and thus understand this beyond of comprehension as insistent but ungraspable, as structurally untotalisable but, equally, irrefusable, then we need not read Levinas's absolute other as 'the ethical name for God' (Badiou, 2001: 22) but might rather read it along the lines of Lacan's 'absolute Other' (Lacan, 1992:52), that is, as *das Ding*.

Consenting to such a reading is not, however, to dismiss utterly Badiou's characterisation of Levinas's ethics as religious or as a pious discourse. The encounter with the absolutely other in the face of the other, precisely insofar as it is incommensurate with comprehension throws into question the totality of comprehension which would have otherwise contained subjective self-identity. Such questioning necessarily demands a response, a reconfiguration of identity. Such a reconfiguration cannot, however, be something given but must always be subjectively assumed. Moreover, insofar as the very possibility of identity is reliant on the language of and encounter with the other, that is, insofar as the throwing into question which would allow the possibility of the process of identification is necessarily preceded by the face of the other, the identity assumed by the subject is always an assumption in response to the other. Such response becomes responsibility precisely because in assuming the weight of the guarantee of one's own identity and thus one's relation to the other, one is also, necessarily, assuming the weight of the guarantee for the other with whom one takes oneself to be in relation. Such an assumption of responsibility is, as we have seen before, to assume the location of and as one's own cause. As such an assumption, following the logic of the cause we have outlined earlier, is such that it can appeal to no ground upon which to guarantee itself, it is what we might rightly characterise as a leap of faith, insofar as we understand such a leap of faith to be coterminous with a pure assumption.

Levinas's idea of ethics would then entail a certain religiosity, not only because it invokes, or can be read as invoking, God as the name for that which would exceed comprehension, that which would mark the limit of thought and, thus, that which in the other, as in the subject itself, refuses any recuperation to understanding. Beyond this, what we might characterise as a certain religiosity would be the pure assumption without ground which necessarily insists at the limit of any system of thought, including any philosophy, including Badiou's philosophy. This is a point that Badiou himself would appear to concede when, for example, he notes that the mathematical ontology upon which he founds much of his philosophy is, itself, established 'in the constraint of options of thought whose choice no purely mathematical prescription can norm' (Badiou, A. (1998), *Petit manuel d'inésthétique*, Paris: Seuil, 37. quoted in Hallward, 2003: 312).

It is precisely such a leap of faith, such a decision which 'no purely mathematical prescription can norm' (Ibid.), which places the subject in relation with not only the other, as other person, but also with itself. It is the pulsational emergence of the subject in the instance of assumption, in the *Wo Es war, soll Ich werden*, which renders any relation with the other, the Other and with the subject possible. Such a leap of faith or assumption can be understood as coterminous with what we have termed the subjective perspective. This is not, then, to deny Badiou's point that infinite alterity is 'quite simply *what there is'* (Badiou, 2001: 25). It is merely to add the clarificatory note that while infinite alterity is 'quite simply *what there is'*, such infinite alterity must still allow for the assumption of an, albeit fragile and pulsative, position from which such infinite alterity might be experienced.

Badiou claims that,

> Even the apparently reflexive experience of myself is by no means the intuition of a unity but a labyrinth of differentiations, and Rimbaud was certainly not wrong when he said: 'I am another.' There are as many differences, say, between a Chinese peasant and a young Norwegian professional as between myself and anybody at all, including myself.
> As many, but also, then, *neither more nor less.*
>
> (Ibid.: 25–6)

Badiou's assertion here, that there are *'neither more nor less'* differences 'between myself and anybody at all, including myself' (Ibid.) should not be understood as an attempt to equalise difference such that difference becomes once again a unity. The One is not. To read Badiou's *'neither more nor less'* (Ibid.) as a recuperation of unity would be to miss the point. It is rather the case that in the pure multiplicity there is no warrant to distinguish the difference between differences. To isolate, separate and prioritise the difference one experiences in the other is to refuse the difference one necessarily experiences in oneself.

This is precisely the point made by Lacan in his discussion of the assignation of evil to *das Ding.*

> that which is most myself in myself, that which is at the heart of myself, and beyond me, insofar as the self stops at the level of those walls to which one can apply a label. What in French at least serves to designate the notion of self or same (*même*), then, is this interior or emptiness, and I don't know if it belongs to me or to nobody.
> This is what my sophism signifies; it reminds me that my neighbor possesses all the evil Freud speaks about, but it is no different from the evil I retreat from in myself. To love him, to love him as myself, is necessarily to move towards some cruelty. His or mine?, you will

object. But haven't I just explained to you that nothing indicates that they are distinct? It seems rather that they are the same, on condition that those limits which oblige me to posit myself opposite the other as my fellow man are crossed.

(Lacan, 1992: 198)

As Lacan makes very clear, the evil 'my neighbour possesses ... is no different from the evil I retreat from in myself', 'nothing indicates that they are distinct', 'they are the same' (Ibid.). Again, however, the orientation attested to in such experience is crucial here. The otherness one experiences in oneself may be no different from the otherness one experiences in the other, which is precisely not to say that the otherness the other experiences in themselves and the otherness the other experiences in its neighbour is no different from the otherness I experience in my neighbour and in myself. To seek such a generalisation would be to assume to take an impossible position outwith oneself. The other always remains other and while, as Rimbaud claimed, in quite different circumstances, 'je est un autre' (Rimbaud, 1963: 268), it is the perception *from*, the otherness *from*, which renders the experience radically asymmetrical. Just as, for Lacan, there is no Other of the Other (Lacan, 1998: 81), also there can be no experience of what would be other for the other. In assuming itself as its own cause, the subject necessarily assumes the cause of 'all' insofar as this 'all', like the law, like the system, like the other, appears only for the subject. Crucial here, however, is that the position of subjectivity remains within the infinite of multiplicity. If the otherness encountered in the other cannot be separated from the otherness encountered in the self, then this is neither to recourse to a position of atomistic individuality nor to recourse to a conception of subjectivity as but a part of an unceasing flux of difference. Where the former would suppose a certain self-sufficiency of the subject which would set it apart from the other, a totality of the self, the latter would suppose the very oneness Badiou shows to be impossible, a totality of the cosmos. In opposition to these two positions, the position of subjectivity assumed is necessarily both other to the other and other to itself without these othernesses being reducible to a one, insofar as a one would be comprehendible. It is in this sense that we should understand Lacan's characterisation of '*das Ding*, as the absolute other of the subject' (Lacan, 1992: 52). *Das Ding*, as otherness, is extimate to the subject, it is 'strange to me, although it is at the heart of me' (Ibid.: 71).

The other is not, then, some*thing* which could be adduced in any certainty as a separate and coherent entity. The other is, insofar as the other attests to a subjective experience, necessarily divided between a misrecognition and absolute otherness. That is to say, there is that of the other which the subject can recuperate to an understanding, which is necessarily the other reduced to the terms of the same, and there is that of the other which refuses any recuperation. In neither instance, however, can the other be separated absolutely from the subject insofar as the other is only the other insofar as it is experienced by the subject. This is, however, not to place the subject in some position of absolute priority. The subject's experience of itself is only possible on the basis of an experience of the other both in terms of the language of the other and in terms of the constitution of its own image of itself in response to the experience of the other. One is dependent upon the other in order to be 'called into' subjectivity and, as such, subjectivity can never be reduced to a monadology. Such an encounter with the other, as it is dependent itself on the possibility of the Other, the symbolic network which would facilitate and describe the contours of community, can neither arise nor be maintained in an isolation of one for the other. The subject, as it is not a monad, cannot be understood to *be* the ground of its own position but must assume this ground.

This is clearly, though, to propound a theory of ethics which does not explain what one must do, how one must act. That is to say, it is not to offer an ethics with any positive contents. In assuming the ground of its own subjectivity, the subject clearly is given no access to the truth of a good which would guide its actions. It is rather to posit a freedom from any such truths as there is no ground available other than the fragile ground of the subject's own assumption. Any other posited ground would necessitate beyond it the assumption that *I* accept or endorse it, which would return us to the same point. Insofar as no system of explanation or system of morality can account for its own constitution, its own justification, the limit point of any such system must lie with the subject.

This is not, however, to posit the notion that somehow anything goes. The subject, as we have seen, even in assuming the weight of its own cause, even in assuming the position of ultimate justification for that which it would endorse, is bound to the Other (the symbolic order) and the other (in the sense of other person) without which it would have no position of subjectivity to assume. That is to say, the subject in assuming the location of its own cause is necessarily doing so, to paraphrase Levinas, in the face of the other, that is, in response to the other but also, with Lacan, the subject is assuming such a place in the place of, within the confines of, the Other, the symbolic order, without which subjectivity would not be possible.

Clearly then, this is not to advocate a certain conception of the good that one might bestow upon the other. But neither is it to endorse the free reign of any evil we would enact upon the other. The good is not some given which could be received and made available for all. Rather the good is that which is posited as what would ultimately motivate one's desire, as the impossible beyond. What the subject chooses to locate in the place of this good, what the subject nominates in assuming responsibility for the desire that is in them, in naming and thus specifying their desire, is the good configured for and by that subject. Any such attempt to generalise the good is unwarranted insofar as to do so would be to reduce the other to a pure point of imaginary identification, an object. To do so would be to refuse the very otherness of the other, that in the other which would refuse any such recuperation. In this sense, we do not and cannot know what the other's good is.

Similarly, to impute evil to the other and, thus, to seek to justify the aggression one might enact upon the other is also to assume to have somehow impossibly gained access to the very otherness of the other which is by definition beyond comprehension. As we have seen, the evil I detect in the neighbour 'is no different from the evil I retreat from in myself' (Lacan, 1992: 198). To justify the aggression one would take out on the other on the basis of the evil one detects in him or her is to, again, reduce the other to an imaginary object, the object of a fantasy in which the other would be taken to be the cause of, and thus proper object of, one's aggression. That is to say, the aggression the subject would 'take out' on the other is always misdirected insofar as the other, as other, is never *it*, never the proper cause and thus proper recipient of such aggressivity. This point is illustrated in the Hegelian master-slave scenario and in Lacan's formulation of the mirror stage discussed above. The threat of the other which might be taken to give rise to aggressivity is only ever taken as such on the basis of an imaginary relation. This is not also to suggest that aggression arises only as an imaginary effect and should or even could somehow be relinquished. What it is to suggest is that the cause of aggression, like that of desire, can only properly be assumed by the subject. To assume that the other is in some way responsible for the evil one would impute to him or her is to deny oneself as the cause of one's own position of subjectivity. To justify one's aggression towards the other is to blame the other for what is properly one's own responsibility.

Returning to the question of the love of one's neighbour and, particularly, Freud's questioning, 'how shall we manage to act like this? How will it be possible?' (Freud, 2002: 46), we can see that the question is misplaced insofar as it assumes that the narcissistic love predicated on identification is somehow the norm from which love for the less proximate other would be a deviation. Love for those closest, those with whom one might forge a bond on the basis of recognition is precisely that which would reduce the other to the status of an object of identification, an alter-ego, a reduplication or conjecture based on one's own misrecognition of oneself. Such love is not predicated so much on positive differences but, rather, on positive similarities. Moreover, as the so-called 'self', as the measure against which such similarities or differences would be judged, is none other than the ideal ego, the ego's idealised image of the self – not the subject – and such an ideal image is only ever founded on the basis of a mis-identification with the other in the first place, then any such identification is necessarily illusory and alienating. Put simply, such an identification on the basis of similarity or, on the flip side of this, such difference adduced on the basis of a lack of similarity, necessarily fails to account for both the otherness which would be proper to the other, that of the other which cannot be recuperated to an already constituted image, and the otherness which would be central to the constitution of the subject itself.

It is only in moving beyond such imaginary ego identification that the subject can assume a position of subjectivity and, in so doing, assume a position in relation to the other which is not one of recuperation and dismissal. That is, a position wherein the subject assumes both the weight of responsibility for its own position and opens itself to both the absolute otherness of the other and the absolute otherness in itself; there is nothing to suggest that they are distinct (Lacan, 1992: 198).

This logic is one of impossibility and it is only as such that we can understand the movement necessary here. If the other, insofar as the subject encounters them, is inevitably split between that which could be recuperated on the basis of identity and that which refuses any such recuperation, this is not to refuse the unicity of the other. That such unicity cannot be accounted for or understood, or precisely insofar as this unicity cannot be accounted for or understood, is to suggest that the only position the subject could entertain towards the other is one of perpetual openness. Such openness should not be understood as a positive moral imperative, *thou shalt be open to the other*, but rather arises from the very impossibility of totalising the other, of capturing what the other *is*. Beyond the imaginary other configured on the basis of one's misrecognition, one encounters the otherness of the other which refuses any identification. What is imputed to this otherness, what is imagined to lie beyond, can clearly neither be verified nor assumed to be exhaustive. Moreover, in transcending the imaginary relations with the other one necessarily acknowledges at least the potential unicity of the other. To refuse such a potential is to immediately recuperate the other to a limited understanding.

It is in this sense that Badiou is quite right to dismiss the culture of 'right to difference' (Badiou, 2001: 24) on the grounds of its underlying and deep rooted hypocrisy.

> the self-declared apostles of ethics and of the 'right to difference' are clearly *horrified by any vigorously sustained difference*. For them, African customs are barbaric, Muslims are dreadful, the Chinese are totalitarian, and so on. As a matter of fact, the celebrated 'other' is acceptable only if he is a *good* other – which is to say what, exactly, if not *the same as us?*
>
> (Ibid.)

The problem with such 'respect for difference' (Ibid.) is that it precisely assumes to objectify the other, to distinguish the other on the basis of positive differences, characteristics which can only be differentiated from the same on the basis of identification or lack thereof. As such, any difference adduced is only the difference between one's image of the other and one's image of one's self. That of the other which refuses comprehension is precisely not respected but is rather reduced to an object of thought, an object which is, properly, the responsibility of the one to whom it occurs.

This is not, however, to conclude that no relation with the other should be sought. The otherness of the other necessarily does insist and, moreover, forms the basis of the possibility of subjectivity. The point would be that beyond any narcissistic and aggressive reduction of the other to a point of identification the otherness of the other still demands a response. Insofar as any recuperation is, by definition, necessarily inadequate to that which would insist, any recuperation necessarily entails a remainder which must then persist.

In assuming responsibility for one's position as subject one is necessarily assuming responsibility for the manner in which one construes the other but one is also then necessarily maintaining an openness towards that of the other which one cannot construe. To assume to contain the other as one's image of the other, to assume to be able to totalise the other is to reduce the other to an object of fantasy. The imaginary identification in fantasy is, as we have seen, precisely that which would support desire. To relinquish the fantasy would be to encounter the abyss of *jouissance*, the unbearable impossibility which would be destructive of the subject. To fixate on the fantasy and refuse one's own place as the cause of desire would be to relinquish one's subjectivity, the responsibility one has for one's choice to be subject.

What is therefore essential here is the fact that we are not faced with a strictly either/or situation. It is not a choice between either the object of fantasy or the renunciation of identificatory distinction in fantasy, but, rather, the assumption of the cause of one's own fantasy and, through this, recognition of the fantasy as, albeit necessary, fantasy and, concomitant with this, the recognition of the persistence of some*Thing* both in the other and in the self which cannot be reduced to or resolved as a fantasy object.

Das Ding is extimate to and constitutive of the subject insofar as it is indicative of the site of lack in relation to which the subject's desire would aim. *Das Ding*, then, is, properly, neither of the subject nor of the other. It is, however, also inseparable from the subject in the sense that without it the subject would no longer be subject. It is this necessary and necessarily extimate (non-)relation which allows Lacan to formulate *das Ding* as the *same*, as 'that which is most myself in myself, that which is at the heart of myself, and beyond me, insofar as the self stops at the level of those walls to which one can apply a label' (Lacan, 1992: 198). *Das Ding* is outwith the realms of both the symbolic and the imaginary and as such can neither be properly ascribed to the other or to the subject. To do so would be to, impossibly, render it in the order of the symbolic or to postulate it as an image of identification. Rather, *das Ding* is that which insists but of which one cannot know 'if it belongs to me or to nobody' (Ibid.).

Thus the hostility one perceives in *das Ding* as it persists in the encounter with the neighbour, the hostility beyond the rational(ised) hostility one might conjecture to the neighbour (this former being but another mode of identification) cannot be distinguished from the hostility inherent to the subject. Beyond the symbolic order, the social structures, the law and language which would organise the subject's relations with the other, beyond the imaginary order which would allow the subject to identify (with) the other, *das Ding* would remain and insist as that which is the absolute other of the subject, an absolute other in the subject more than itself.

The paradox here is that this absolute other we encounter in the other, this absolute other which cannot be distinguished, is always our own. The very irreversibility of the subject in relation to the other and the Other necessitates that *das Ding* is always experienced in relation to the subject. As we have seen previously, the very lack constitutive of the subject's position as subject which it experiences in the insistence of *das Ding* is only ever retrospectively posited. As such, *das Ding* is necessarily encountered from a particular perspective. It is always *das Ding* in relation to the subject in all its singularity. This is the irreversibility of the subject's relation towards the other which would necessitate that, in its very indistinguishable otherness, in its persistence as unknowable, neither belonging 'to me or to nobody' (Ibid.), *das Ding* is still uniquely experienced in relation to the subject.

It is this very indeterminacy which would bind the subject to the other in a fashion that cannot be reduced to a symbiosis. *Das Ding* encountered in the other as hostile and evil and as the promise or suggestion of the good is the beyond towards which the subject's desire would be directed. The fantasy, the other constituted in fantasy, would be that which would support such desire without allowing it to extinguish itself in impossible satisfaction. Traversing the fantasy, and thus reconstituting itself as the cause of its own desire, would be for the subject to constitute itself in a relation with the other which maintains the necessary support of fantasy without imputing the lack inherent in itself to the other. Moreover, in this very irreversibility of the assumption of responsibility, the subject necessarily assumes the burden of the other's lack.

This would be the maintenance of an openness which would then necessarily extend beyond the closest, the familial, the beloved, precisely insofar as any such limitation would entail a restriction on the basis of identification and difference. This would also, however, suggest that one cannot respond to the multitude of the other(s) *en masse*, assuming otherness to be but a category of sameness which would be somehow equally dispersed over all others. The otherness experienced in the other, just as the otherness experienced in the subject itself, cannot be reduced to a unity as doing so would be once again to reduce it to a comprehension. Totalising the other as a (social) category as that which would be beyond the subject is also to reduce the other, each other, to an aspect of fantasy. While the unicity of the other cannot be experienced as a positive entity, neither can it be dismissed as an impossible fiction. The unicity of the other, though it cannot be certified as an actuality, must rather, as it can no less be rejected as an actuality, be maintained as a possibility and responded to *as if* it were there.

This then both necessitates and illustrates the passage beyond a precarious logic of a generalisation which cannot be generalised. To maintain an openness to the other, all others, is to maintain a certain universal stance in the face of the other but only insofar as in so doing one is maintaining an openness to the otherness of each other idiotically, in their potential for unicity. It is thus a generalisation which functions as the basis of a stance which would refuse generalisation, that would open to the other one by one and again and again, an advocation of a universality which recognises the impossibility of universality.

Part IV
The Social

10
Ethics and the Other

As we have seen, for Lacan, the subject's desire arises not only in the face of the lack it would experience in and as itself but, irreducibly conjoined with this, the subject's desire is also always the desire of the Other. That is to say, the subject can only be and can only experience itself as subject in the encounter with the lack inherent to the Other. This double movement of lack and desire allows us to conceive of the subject as interminably constituted in the field of the social. That is to say, with the Lacanian subject there is no possibility of assuming a delimited private realm which would somehow subsist independently from the social or public realm. To assume to occupy a position outwith the social would be to assume the impossible position of independence from the Other without which the possibility of subjectivity would be foreclosed.

The Other, as the subject's experience of structuring organisation, as the possibility of law, is that which, at one and the same time, prohibits and engenders that which would be experienced as the impossible good of the subject. As we have seen, it is the very impossibility of totality in the law, the failure of the system to found itself and the failure of the system to encapsulate that which it would exclude, that renders the ethical and the subject possible. The ethical in this sense should be understood to arise *against* the law. This is not to reduce ethics to an 'anarchy', a condition simply without law or rule. Defined as *against* the law, the ethical remains dependent on the law without which it could not arise. This is also, clearly, not to make of the ethical the straightforward inversion of the law. If there is no given or attainable good, then neither the moral nor the legal can be defined in terms of a content (which would necessarily be this impossible good). To invert the letter of the law would then, on a formal level, be to maintain precisely the structure of the law. As the content is never *it*, the maintenance of the structure of the law is precisely the maintenance of the law; the maintenance of the law of the law. An ethics which is *against* the law is thus neither an inversion of the law nor something which could be maintained outwith the structures of the law. Law and ethics are thus co-substantial without either being reducible to the other. The ethical, as the moment of subjective assumption, necessarily occurs in response to the law without any determination as to content. As the law itself is anarchical, in the sense that it is without ground, without *arche*, the ethical necessarily entails an assumption without precursor. The ethical is, then, the necessary subjective supplement to the law without it being reflective of the law.

Such an understanding of the relation between ethics and the law indicates that the law in and of itself cannot be ethical. This is not to say, as indicated above, that what is ethical must somehow be contrary to the letter of the law. The problem is rather a structural one. As the law cannot provide its own moment of foundation, its own ground or justification, any such ground or justification must lie outwith the law and can only be assumed idiotically or uniquely by the subject. Such an assumption must, however, in order to be conceived at all, be (re)inscribed in the law. That is to say, it is only within the terms of the law, of the Other, of the symbolic order, that anything could (be seen to) be justified at all. This emphasises once again that the ethical, like the subject, can only be figured as a pulsational moment. The ethical cannot be figured as an alternative to the law in any absolute and permanent sense, but must, rather, be seen as the necessary other of the law, in the sense that it is both irreducible to and inseparable from the law. The ethical is the subjective response before the Other.

Might this then suggest that any law, from the perspective of ethics, is as good as any other? If the good is necessarily unattainable, and the ethical cannot be governed or predetermined by the law, then might not the ethical arise in the context of any law whatsoever? Clearly, this is to an extent the case. Were it not, it would be tantamount to proclaiming that in certain regimes, under certain laws, the ethical was impossible. Which would be to assert the impossible totalising reach of those laws or conditions in question. This is not, however, to recourse to an extreme of suggesting that each actual law or system of law is as good as every other. It is rather to separate conceptually the structural necessity of law from any particular content which might be enacted as law. Clearly, as there is no ultimate external authority to which one might appeal to adjudicate the rightness of any particular law or body of law, the appropriateness or acceptability of any law can only be attested to by those who encounter it. This is then to acknowledge subjective responsibility in the face of the law. At the same time, however, it is also to acknowledge that any such subjective responsibility always already entails the assumption of a subjective position which must be, to some extent, conditioned by and bound in relation with the Other.

The subject only arises as a possibility in the context of a social order. Without the Other, as the network of symbolic and social ordering in the place of which the subject can assume a position, the subject has no possibility of becoming at all. Such subjective constitution is, however, as we have seen, necessarily precarious. The subject constituted in, and in the terms of, the social field is also such that it will necessarily experience itself as excluded from the social field. For the subject to be subsumed utterly by the Other would be the negation of the very possibility of the subject. Coupled with this, the Other is such that it cannot be totalised as a whole, cannot, that is, be conceived as a self-subsistent field which would persist without the subject experiencing it. In this sense, the Other, as a unity or unifying concept does not exist (Lacan, 1977a(viii): 317). The Other is such that it is only ever Other for the subject for whom it manifests. This is clearly not to reduce the Other to a figment of the subject's imagination. It is rather to posit the impossibility of the subject's ever totalising the Other and the concomitant impossibility of the Other ever totalising the subject. Such a picture not only renders the subject ultimately responsible before the Other but also necessarily envelops others within this responsibility insofar as the Other can only be conceived as a field of social order which arises for the subject in confrontation and encounter with others. Without the mediation of others, there is no encounter with the Other.

The unique and irreversible responsibility the subject thus assumes in and through its own constitution entails a double inflection of the law. The law, as the ordering of the social, as language, social practice, convention, as civil law, constitutes the very support and context without which there would be no place or order in which the subject could assume a position. That is, the symbolic field of the Other is the necessary condition for the assumption of a subjective position. Coupled with this, the law, the Other, as the exterior, or, better, extimate, condition of the possibility of subjectivity, is that which ensures that the subject is never itself, is never, that is, adequate to its own possibility and position. The subject assumed in the place of the Other is always necessarily misplaced, incomplete, lacking. Such a condition of constitutional lack renders the subject necessarily the subject of desire. Without the condition of desire the subject would cease to be subject. The subject is then responsible not only for the assumption of the position of subjectivity which it would precariously inhabit, but is responsible for the desire which arises in it and allows the possibility of this position being impossibly inhabited. Such desire, as it arises through encounter with the other and the dislocation in the social field, cannot be divorced from the social field. This renders the relation of the subject with the desire that arises in it and arises as its very possibility paradoxical insofar as it is uniquely experienced by the subject, it is *that* subject's desire, it is *one's* desire, and, at the same time, it is the desire of the Other, the desire which could never be without the Other. The subject's desire is particular for that subject and is necessarily always somewhere else.

In such a conceptual framework, we can see that there is, structurally, no possibility of the law, of the social order, providing the accomplishment of desire. What the law can possibly provide is the facilitation of what we might, with Lacan, term the 'rut of a short and well-trodden satisfaction' (Lacan, 1992: 177). The logic here is such that any such satisfactions are never going to be *it*, never going to be, that is, the satisfaction of desire. This is not, however, to dismiss such satisfactions out of hand. It is, rather, to point towards the complexity of the relations between the subject, the law and social order, the desire which would be constitutive of the subject and the desire the subject would encounter in the other which can never, in its unicity, be reduced to a semblance of the subject's own desire. The satisfactions made available by the law are such that they will be conditioned by the law which avails them, the particular body of laws and social practices in which the subject is constituted. This is not to deny the unicity of these satisfactions, the fact that any such satisfaction will pertain to this or that subject and, as such, will vary from subject to subject. Insofar as the subject is constituted idiotically, this cannot but be the case. Whatever the apparent unity of the law, the necessity of law appearing as a universal and generalisable condition in order for it to be understood as law, it must also apply particularly to particular subjects. Moreover, the subject is defined in relation to the law whilst being irreducible to the law. This then necessitates that the subject encounter the law as something alien and particular. The satisfactions the law would condition, then, are such that they remain conditioned by the law, whilst neither being able to be reduced to the simplicity of a singular universal nor being elevated to the status of the final satisfaction of the subject's desire.

While, then, no law is capable of facilitating the ultimate satisfaction of desire and, moreover, as prohibition, law is the necessary obstacle which would allow both the maintenance of desire and the maintenance of the subjectivity which would be predicated on such desire, there does open up the possibility of law availing lesser satisfactions, satisfactions which would in turn allow the possibility of maintaining desire as necessarily unsatisfied. That is to say, such satisfactions, while necessary, are also necessarily insufficient. The interplay of desire with attainable satisfactions, the fact that such satisfactions are never *it*, gives rise to a structural excess which necessarily (re)informs those satisfactions and the value accrued to them. The formation of expectation is unstable.

There is no possibility of a position outwith any social context, there is no position available outwith social order from which this or that social order could be judged; 'there is no such thing as a metalanguage ..., no language being able to say the truth about the truth' (Lacan, 1989: 16). That is to say, the most that might be available to us would be the comparison between social orders but such that any comparison so made is made from a position within a given social order. This, again, is not to suppose that any given social order is homogenised. Any given social order necessarily contains the trace of its own excess and the proliferation of receptions it would manifest in the subjects located therein. Put simply, we are the product of our social environment without this suggesting that those produced in any social environment can be reduced to a type. The Other is not one but is rather as manifold as the subjects constituted in relation to it. At the same time, however, the subject's necessary location in the field of the Other necessitates that it will experience the proliferation of social orders as entailing distinct differences. The illusion here is that what is experienced as any one social order might ever be adequate to its own description. The question which imposes here, then, is that if no social order is capable of providing the satisfaction of the desires of its subjects and, in fact, no social order can be reduced to a singularity but rather proliferates with each subject, then what difference can adequately be marked between social orders? If no position is available but from within the multiplicity of the social order in which the subject finds itself, what value might persist with which to judge the efficacy or the rightness of any given social order? Phrased otherwise, what is there available to suggest that we are not reduced, inevitably, to a relativity wherein we are preconditioned to assume the contours and conditions of *our* social order as the measure of all possible social orders? The answer lies precisely in the excess, that which would escape the attempted delineation of the social order.

What we are left with is the certainty that desire cannot be met, that anything which assumes the place of that which would provide the satisfaction of desire is necessarily bound to failure. It is never *it*. In terms of the social, then, any system which assumes or is assumed to provide the solution is not only erroneous in such an assumption but, moreover, necessarily occludes the proliferation of competing solutions. The assumption that there quite simply are no solutions is untenable here insofar as this, in itself, would be the renunciation of desire and thus the renunciation of the possibility of subjectivity without which the social order would cease to be experienced. The only avenue available would then be the acknowledgement of the inadequacy of any solution coupled with the necessity of the search for and proliferation of completing contingent solutions.

What we are left with is the bond of the social, the impossibility of the assumption of subjectivity outwith the social field, a bond which necessitates that the assumption of subjectivity is also the assumption of responsibility wherein such responsibility would always be a limitless responsibility for the other. Such responsibility is necessarily limitless insofar as to assume to have accomplished one's responsibility towards the other would be to assume to access and secure the other's desire. As such desire is neither accessible – as we have seen, we do not know what the other desires, we cannot know what the other desires – nor accomplishable – desire accomplished, desire satiated, is desire extinguished – the responsibility one would assume before the other is necessarily without end. Coupled with this, such responsibility is also limitless in the sense that any compartmentalising and, thus, delimitation of the other's desire is, again, to claim to impossibly know what such desire would be.

What we are left with is the subject as the necessary and inconstant location of ground for the validity of the content of the law and the security of the social order within which he or she is constituted. That is to say, the possibility of ethical responsibility resides not with the system or order, whatever its make-up, but with the subject, each time uniquely; 'since the Other does not exist, all that remains to me is to assume the fault upon "I"' (Lacan, 1977a(viii): 317).

The inconstancy of the subject is such that, as we have seen, it cannot be reduced to a monad, a self-sufficient entity which would be exclusively for itself. The responsibilities we might have, as they are not and cannot be preordained, are necessarily the outcome of negotiations and challenges. Within a stable framework where the aim was apparent, where the good was an attainable goal and the considerations of the system self-evident, it would be possible to demarcate the responsibilities one ought to entertain. As no such stable framework is available, as the aim is unapparent and the good structurally and necessarily unattainable, the responsibilities and the contours of such responsibilities, for what and in what way one might be responsible, are necessarily mutable. That is, they can only be constructed and, in so being constructed, indicate their own provisional status. The demarcation of responsibilities as permanent and immutable necessarily entails a point of exclusion and thus an unjustifiable certainty of what ought and ought not to be enveloped within the scope of responsibility.

One example here would be that of rights. Insofar as rights masquerade as natural, that which would be excluded from the protection of rights would be excluded on a permanent basis. Moreover, the precise articulation and application of rights necessarily reveals the impossibility of their encompassing or achieving that which they would purport to encompass or achieve. That is to say, even when it is acknowledged that rights have no claim to a natural status, that is, that rights accrue through decisions made by a community and through the decision to conceive of ourselves as a part of a community which will decide rights, even then, the decision made must be seen to be contingent and, moreover, formed on the basis of a fragile assumption. The community which would uphold and recognise certain rights is the community which would be formed on the basis of such mutual recognition. As Arendt has noted in relation to the notion of natural equality;

> We are not born equal; we become equal as members of a group on the strength of our decision to guarantee ourselves mutually equal rights.
>
> (Arendt, 1973: 301)

Stripped of the illusion of their natural status, all rights can be seen to be not only created by but also, significantly, creative of the community who would endorse them. Clearly the rights accorded are not necessarily created by those who would be protected under the recognition of the right in question. Animal rights or children's rights are not formulated by animals and children. Rather, the point is that through the inscription of, for example, rights for animals or children a community is created of those who would ascribe to and uphold such rights, those who would be defined in terms of their duty to endorse the right(s) in question. This allows us to see that in any formulation of rights, there is necessarily a double moment of inclusion/exclusion. There is the inclusion of those who or that which would be protected, the exclusion of those who or that which would not be protected or which would not be recognised and, on the other axis, there is the inclusion of those who would be considered to be bound in duty to the recognition of the rights in question and those who or that which would be excluded or exempt from such duty. As rights are not naturally given, as rights are not transparent and beyond question and, bound to this, as rights are necessarily inscribed in a language which is never adequate to the task of their definition, all such rights are necessarily available to interpretation. That is to say, not only is the delimitation of rights and the concomitant delimitation of duty necessarily open to renegotiation but also, at each moment of its potential application, any one inscribed right and its concomitant duty must be interpreted for and coapted to the particularity of the situation or circumstance in question. Each such moment of interpretation is necessarily the decision to inscribe the point of exclusion/inclusion again.

This logic can be seen in the example of The European Convention on Human Rights, Article 1 of which reads:

> The High Contracting Parties shall secure to everyone within their jurisdiction the rights and freedoms defined in Section I of this Convention.
>
> (The European Convention on Human Rights, 1950: Article 1)

Despite the gesture of inclusivity evident here, where one might understand the term 'within their jurisdiction' to limit responsibility on the basis of the reach of legal authority rather than the exclusion of certain parties whose rights might otherwise be protected, the subsequent articles of the Convention appear to erode this opening gesture.

On a cursory reading one might suppose that those who would fall under the jurisdiction of the signatories would be the citizens of those nations and those residing within or present within the geographic borders of those nations at the moment of application of the rights in question. This point is clarified in Article 14;

> The enjoyment of the rights and freedoms set forth in this Convention shall be secured without discrimination on any ground such as sex, race, colour, language, religion, political or other opinion, national or social origin, association with a national minority, property, birth or other status.
>
> (Ibid.: Article 14)

While it is conceivable that Article 14 seeks to exemplify and thus delimit those types of discrimination which would be deemed reasonable or acceptable from those which would be deemed unreasonable or unacceptable, the status of the examples is left somewhat uncertain. Do the examples of what we might understand as unreasonable discrimination constitute an exhaustive list, an exemplary list or are they merely examples which would facilitate the conceptual space for the addition of further (examples of) unreasonable forms of discrimination? The status of this list is thrown into further uncertainty by Article 16 which stipulates that:

> Nothing in Articles 10, 11, and 14 shall be regarded as preventing the High Contracting Parties from imposing restrictions on the political activities of aliens.
>
> (Ibid.: Article 16)

Articles 10 and 11 seek to protect, respectively, the rights to freedom of expression and freedom of assembly and association.

Article 10
1. Everyone has the right to freedom of expression. This right shall include freedom to hold opinions and to receive and impart information and ideas without interference by public authority and regardless of frontiers. This article shall not prevent States from requiring the licensing of broadcasting, television or cinema enterprises.
2. The exercise of these freedoms, since it carries with it duties and responsibilities, may be subject to such formalities, conditions, restrictions or penalties as are prescribed by law and are necessary in a democratic society, in the interests of national security, territorial integrity or public safety, for the prevention of disorder or crime, for the protection of health or morals, for the protection of the reputation or the rights of others, for preventing the disclosure of information received in confidence, or for maintaining the authority and impartiality of the judiciary.

Article 11
1. Everyone has the right to freedom of peaceful assembly and to freedom of association with others, including the right to form and to join trade unions for the protection of his interests.
2. No restrictions shall be placed on the exercise of these rights other than such as are prescribed by law and are necessary in a democratic society in the interests of national security or public safety, for the prevention of disorder or crime, for the protection of

health or morals or for the protection of the rights and freedoms of others. This article shall not prevent the imposition of lawful restrictions on the exercise of these rights by members of the armed forces, of the police or of the administration of the State.

(Ibid.: Articles 10 & 11)

If Articles 10 and 11 can be understood to effectively protect the rights of 'everyone' under the jurisdiction of the High Contracting Parties, with the addition of the provisos noted in the second paragraph of each of the articles, and Article 14 can be understood to describe some examples of the types of conditions which would not warrant discrimination, then this raises a question over the status and purpose of Article 16. Not only is the exact meaning of 'alien' open to interpretation but, moreover, those who would be bracketed through any such interpretation of 'alien' are then also bracketed out of the protection supposedly safeguarded under Articles 10 and 11 and the examples of unreasonable discrimination listed in Article 14 must be reread in the light of such bracketing. That is to say, the inclusion of Article 16 appears to modify not only Article 1 but, by extension, it places under question the inclusivity implied in the list of unreasonable types of discrimination listed in Article 14, with perhaps particular emphasis on the inclusion of terms such as 'political or other opinion' and 'national or social origin'.

The point here is not that the European Convention of Human Rights constitutes an erroneous document *per se*, but rather that any such attempt at precise stipulation of rights is impossible insofar as it necessarily avails itself to a moment of interpretation particular to the circumstances of its application. The removal of Article 16 could be understood to render the signatory states unnecessarily vulnerable to, for example, terrorist factions, even given the point that the correlation terrorist-alien is extremely suspect in itself. On the other hand, however, the inclusion of Article 16 could be understood to warrant the potential exclusion of any and everyone deemed to fall under the bracket of 'alien' from the protection of the Convention.

This fragility of the convention and its avowed aims is further evident in the more extensive potential exclusion warranted under Article 15 wherein is stipulated the right of the signatory states to derogate from adherence to much of the remainder of the document under particular circumstances.

In time of war or other public emergency threatening the life of the nation any High Contracting Party may take measures derogating from its obligations under this Convention to the extent strictly required by the exigencies of the situation, provided that such measures are not inconsistent with its other obligations under international law.

(Ibid.: Article 15)

The failure of the convention to define with any adequacy what might constitute a 'public emergency threatening the life of the nation' (Ibid.) appears to leave open the possibility of suspending the very protection of rights that it is its sole purpose to guarantee. That the article stipulates that any such suspension ought to be limited in strict relation to 'the exigencies of the situation' (Ibid.), insofar as what precisely would constitute acceptable or necessary circumstances to warrant derogation from the responsibility to ensure the rights of those under the involved nation's jurisdiction is not defined, adds only fragile limitation on the possibility of derogation. Even the restrictions attached to the right to derogation as stipulated in the second paragraph of Article 15, the stipulation of those articles of the convention from which signatory states may not derogate, fail to offer firm guarantee of the rights in question insofar as these too are dependent upon interpretation.

No derogation from Article 2, except in respect of deaths resulting from lawful acts of war, or from Articles 3, 4 (paragraph 1) and 7 shall be made under this provision.

(Ibid.)

Article 2 which seeks to uphold the right to life, is supplemented in its second paragraph by conditions under which the right to life may not be upheld and is further supplemented by the clause in Article 15 specifying 'lawful acts of war' as legitimate circumstances in which the right to life may not be honoured or protected. Articles 3 and 4 (paragraph 1) which appear to be without qualification, are still susceptible to interpretation. Article 3 stipulates that,

No one shall be subjected to torture or to inhuman or degrading treatment or punishment.

(Ibid.: Article 3)

While Article 4, Paragraph 1 stipulates that;

No one shall be held in slavery or servitude.

(Ibid.: Article 4)

Clearly, what precisely constitutes 'torture', 'inhuman or degrading treatment', 'slavery' and 'servitude' is susceptible to some interpretation. To focus on Article 3, one can wonder where the line might be drawn. Does sleep deprivation or mild beating constitute acceptable treatment under this directive? When might the infliction of pain be justified and to what degree? Would what constitute acceptable treatment be relative to the possible consequences of not inflicting such treatment? For instance, would the employment of certain measures deemed unacceptable under other circumstances be considered acceptable if they are employed with the intention of extracting information which would avert what would be considered a graver outcome. What factors would be considered relevant here? The supposed status of the those who would be effected by the outcome to be averted? The estimated number of those who would be effected by the outcome to be averted? And how might one measure what would constitute necessary or acceptable means in relation to the projected outcome to be averted?

Such a moment of decision can be understood to constitute an extreme instance of subjective choice. The precise limit one would ascribe to effective and acceptable measures in any given situation is a matter which demands subjective response. This is not to suggest that the implementation of measures taken, the decision to operate at, and the very definition of, the limit of what one would consider torture or degrading treatment, becomes the sole and exclusive responsibility of the one in the situation. It is rather to suggest that the acceptance of the regulations as they stand and the acceptance of any warranted interpretation of those regulations is necessarily the responsibility of each of those who find themselves confronted by the convention. As we have seen previously, ethics entails interminable judgement.

In such a context, where a term such as 'torture' is left vague, without any precise definition, a certain danger necessarily accrues. As Žižek illustrates with regard to the climate of fear of terrorism post-September 11th 2001, the very debate as to what ought to form the proper limits of legitimate treatment of (suspected) terrorists itself imparts a certain public legitimacy to those treatments considered. Even if one does not explicitly advocate what might otherwise be considered an extreme measure, just by introducing the measures in question into the field of public, and what would be considered legitimate, debate has the effect of altering the terrain of the debate and thus the contours of what might be conceived of as torture.

> Such legitimization of torture as a topic of debate changes the background of ideological presuppositions and options much more radi-

cally than its outright advocacy: it changes the entire field, while, without this change, outright advocacy remains an idiosyncratic view.

(Žižek, 2002: 239)

It is precisely in such a case that the porosity of a document such as *The European Convention on Human Rights* opens on to the level of decision. Not only is it clearly the case that the convention does not adequately delimit what would be meant by the term 'torture', does not specify what would, under the convention, be deemed acceptable treatment but, moreover, the convention invites debate on this very point which itself allows the possibility of the erosion of the very protection the convention would otherwise claim to provide. Clearly, the point here is not that public debate concerning the limitations or definition of torture is in itself to be avoided. It is rather that the very terms with which one would enter into such a debate and the terms on which one would accept to debate such an issue are themselves open to question and demanding of a subjective response and, consequently, subjective responsibility.

To indicate some of the limits or failings of a document like the European Convention on Human Rights is not to single it out as an unavoidably suspect document, it is rather to acknowledge that any such document is unavoidably suspect. It is not as though the convention could be replaced by another document which would avoid the definitional problems this document encounters (although it could, no doubt, be improved upon). It is rather to acknowledge that any such document cannot avoid encountering its own limits (that is, that any such document could also be improved upon). Clearly, this is also not to suggest a passive acceptance of this or any other existent document on the grounds that, as any document is by definition imperfect, any inscription of rights is more or less as good as any other. Rather, it is to suggest that any such document constitutes a demand of those who would confront it to interpret it and through the process of interpretation call the existent limitations into question, assume responsibility for the particular interpretation endorsed and undertake the responsibility for the improvement of such conventions.

What this example of the Convention on Human Rights illustrates is that the symbolic order cannot contain the Real. No law, no language, no configuration of ideals is ever adequate to the particularity of its implementation. Laws, in order to be applied, necessitate interpretation. The contours and guidelines which might exist for such interpretation similarly require interpretation. The regress is infinite. The conception of any institution or institutional regulation as determinedly authorised, as 'above' interpretation, supposes the pre-existence of that body, force, idea or agency which would have authorised it, such supposition then requiring justification and authorisation. Even in the circumstance where a dictate may appear to be devoid of ambiguity, devoid of the possibility of competing interpretations – where, for example, the consensus appears absolute – the decision to apply that dictate, its supposed appropriateness, still demands justification. This is the insistence at the limitation of the symbolic which would be indicative of the encounter with the Real, that which 'resists symbolisation absolutely' (Lacan, 1988a: 66).

The insistence of such an encounter as already entailed within any social or political institution is marked not only in the occurrence of some unforeseen event – such as terrorist attacks, popular uprisings or natural catastrophes – to which, insofar as they are ill-prepared, the institutions would be inadequate. The differences between the examples here notwithstanding, such events should be understood to be indicative of the Real in the sense that they would be representations of the Real. In this sense, they can be seen to be commensurate on a social level with those representations of the Real which would insist upon the sleeping individual.

The Real may be represented by the accident, the noise, the small element of reality, which is evidence that we are not dreaming. But on the other hand, this reality is not so small, for what wakes us is the other reality hidden behind the lack of that which takes the place of representation.

(Lacan, 1977b: 60)

The insistence of the Real is not then something which might occur in the events themselves but, rather, the events, insofar as, in order to be conceived as events at all, they would require representation in the symbolic, are indicative of the Real as the force of some*thing* which would resist conceptualisation. That is to say, the insistence of the Real is inscribed in the very impossibility of the symbolic order closing the gap of the Real. It is thus that any system or body, any institution, necessarily entails its own structural weakness.

The obvious example here would be the attacks on the World Trade Centre on September 11, 2001. It is not that such attacks are in themselves instances of the Real. Insofar as they are mediated and explained, that we achieve a sense of surety about what happened, who or what was responsible, who or what was to 'blame' for the attacks, the attacks are always already mediated representations of the Real, indications, that is, of 'the other reality hidden behind the lack of that which takes the place of representation' (Ibid.). It is in reaction to this 'other reality' that no response is ever adequate. Remaining with the example of September 11, no response, be it attacks on rogue states or heightened security is ever adequate to the trauma of the encounter with the Real which would remain 'hidden' behind any representation or rationalisation of the attacks.

> The real has to be sought beyond the dream – in what the dream has enveloped, hidden from us, behind the lack of representation of which there is only one representative.
>
> (Ibid.)

The dream here, in the context of Lacan's discussion, is indicative of the (unconscious) attempt, the impetus, to provide a representation for that which cannot, in itself, be represented. That is, it is the inclination to cover over the Real with some, necessarily inadequate, signification. The same function can be seen to be operative in the example of the events of September 11 and the reactions to which they gave rise. The explanation and blame for the event, the portrayal or characterisation of certain regimes and, perhaps, by extension, ideologies, as villainous or evil, are attempts to represent and domesticate the Real which cannot in itself be represented. Such attempts are indicative of the limit point of the system wherein the relation of cause and effect exceeds the system itself;

> cause is a concept that is unanalysable – impossible to understand by reason – if indeed the rule of reason, the *Verunftsregel*, is always some *Vergleichung*, or equivalent – ... there remains essentially in the function of cause a certain *gap*.
>
> (Ibid.: 21)

This weakness, this structural inadequacy is not, in turn, something which could be embraced in and of itself. It is not that the inadequacy of the system suggests that we abandon all hope. It is rather that such inadequacy demands a response. The nihilistic abandonment of hope, the rejection of all law on the basis of the law's structural inadequacy is an impossible position. Such a position could only ever be entertained outwith the symbolic order where, clearly, no position can or could be entertained at all. In terms of the *vel* of alienation, such a choice would be the 'impossible' choice of not choosing. Rather than suggesting a self-refuting 'an-archist' position, then, the inadequacy of the system demands a response. Such a demand is a demand made of the subject. Such a response is the potential emergence of the ethical.

It is not because the subject would be some pre-existent entity or agency which could already provide the elusive authorisation or cementation, the legitimation of any system or institution. Clearly, the subject as necessarily incomplete, the subject as divided, is only ever constituted in response to this demand, in response to the lack experienced in the symbolic order, in response to S($\emptyset$), the signifier of the lack in the Other. Such a demand is a demand made of the subject precisely because the possibility of subjectivity is that which is constituted in and as the reception of this demand.

The subject, as we have seen, is itself never anything more than the division it would experience. That is, the subject is never secure or securable but, rather, is only ever possible as a pulsational emergence dislocated from any possibility of self-adequation. And yet, so dislocated, the subject emerges as the possibility of that which would experience the Other, that which would encounter the other without any such experience or encounter ever being definitive. Insofar as something is experienced, the subject is faced with the possibility of assuming itself in this transient moment. In so doing, the subject would be seizing its own possibility, constituting itself in the pure assumption of a position it cannot hold, a position which is necessarily and by definition not its own.

As pessimistic as this may sound, it is a pessimism in the face of the alternative of labouring under the impossible dream of finitude, the utopic fantasy which is necessarily inadequate to our own self-experience and our own experience of the world in which we find ourselves. Certitude in our conception of the good, certitude in the system we would have constructed to ensure our good and, then, necessarily, certitude in the demarcation and limitations of our conception of the good, precisely because such certitude is but a fantasy, precisely because such certitude is never adequate to the possibility of the good, necessarily excludes the very possibility it would purport to embrace. If we cannot know the good, then any illusory position of certainty necessarily excludes the possibility of the good emerging.

This is not, for Lacan, to suggest that we wander the world in a perpetual state of conscious doubting, as though engaged in an eternal existential crisis concerning the reality of the world in which we live. For Lacan, certainty can precisely be opposed to reality, which is always, for Lacan, 'precarious' (Lacan, 1992: 30). The 'normal subject' (Lacan, 1993: 74) is not concerned with certainty, only the psychotic is concerned with certainty. Which is precisely to mark certainty as a delusion.

> You are surrounded by all sorts of realities about which you are in no doubt, some of which are particularly threatening, but you don't take them fully seriously, for you think ... that *the worst is not always certain.*
>
> (Ibid.)

This lack of certainty which would characterise the 'normal', neurotic subject can be understood in terms of the lack in the Other or the Other experienced as lacking, the constitutional incompleteness of the symbolic order. Where the psychotic subject would be characterised by the structure of foreclosure such that it would admit of no lack in the Other (Lacan, 1990: 40), such, that is, that it would attain to a certainty, the neurotic subject, as we have seen, would precisely encounter the Other as lacking, as incapable of providing that ultimate guarantee for the symbolic order in which the subject would find itself.

The moment of subjective assumption, as we have seen, is the possibility of the ethical precisely because it is without guarantee. In the pure assumption of subjectivity, the subject so assumed necessarily assumes the weight of responsibility not only for its own constitution but also the parameters and configuration of that which it would experience. While this necessarily means that there is no preordained morality, no defined content or guide which could inform the course of action one might undertake, it is also to say that no irreparable treatment or even conception of the other is ever justifiable. If the subject is irreversibly responsible for not only the position it would itself assume but, inseparable from this, it is responsible for that which it would encounter, then any conception of the other the subject would seek to maintain is necessarily *of the subject*. That is to say, it would be the subject's conception, and would, thus, neither be adequate to nor inherent to the other. However, adjoined to this, it should be emphasised that neither is it possible to have no conception of the other one encounters. The point is rather that the conception we do assume is never *it*, never the other as such and thus always contingent, to be made again.

If the subject is responsible for its conception of the other and this conception is necessarily inadequate to the other, this is then clearly not to avail the subject of an idealism wherein the subject might absolve itself of the difficulties of any encounter by so configuring the encounter to suit his or her expectations. Reality, however 'precarious' (Lacan, 1992: 30), does persist. That is to say, the other, as incommensurate with the subject's conception of them does persist. As we have seen, in every recuperation to identification there remains an excess which refuses any such recuperation, *das Ding*. Which is also to say that the other does suffer, that torment and injustice are unavoidable possibilities. What remains is that what constitutes suffering and injustice and, moreover, what constitutes the best available, the most just, response to such suffering and injustice is never receptive to precise definition and thus the persistence of suffering and injustice cannot be avoided once and for all but must rather be encountered, defined and addressed again and again by the subject.

The subject cannot but respond to situations and circumstances without recourse to any certainty of what the correct response might be. The subject must respond to others and others' circumstances and actions without recourse to what the correct response might be. The course of non-response is not an available option insofar as no response itself constitutes a response. The subject is thus faced with an impossible dilemma but an impossible dilemma which cannot be refused. The measure by which one might decide what constitutes the lesser of two or more evils is not a certainty which can be instituted or guaranteed. It is only for the subject to configure a response, a response which might ameliorate the situation and circumstances without seeking to obliterate the potential for further amelioration.

11
The Impossibility of Ethical Examples

In discussions of ethics it is common to furnish readers with examples of what would constitute an ethical act with the examples often being drawn from myth and classical literature. Foremost amongst such examples is Sophocles' play *Antigone* and its central, titular character. Ostensibly Sophocles' drama concerns the story of Oedipus's daughter, Antigone, who refuses the order to leave her brother unburied outside the city walls. The city of Thebes, following the exile of Oedipus, was to be ruled in alternate years by Oedipus' sons Polynices and Eteocles. When Eteocles refuses to allow Polynices his turn on the throne, Polynices determines to engage in war with the city. The war results in the two brothers dying at each other's hands and, in the aftermath of the war, the throne being assumed by their uncle, Creon. Deeming Polynices an enemy of the state and Eteocles the defender of the state, Creon pronounces an edict that, while Eteocles will be honoured by a full state burial, Polynices is to be left as carrion outside the city walls. Antigone, the sister of Polynices and Eteocles, refuses this edict and determines to bury Polynices. Before his attack on the city and before the events which form *Antigone*, Polynices had asked Antigone to bury him, to guarantee him 'the honored rites of death' (Sophocles, *Oedipus At Colonus*: 366, line 1600). *Antigone*, the play, thus opens with Antigone's first determination to follow her promise to her brother, to fulfil her duty and bury him. What is striking about Antigone's stance is that she determines to do so even in the face of certain death. Creon's edict is unwavering. Anyone who attempts to cover or remove the body of the traitor shall be executed.

One possible reading of *Antigone* is that the play illustrates the conflict between two forms of law, the universal(isable) law of the city, the written, promulgated law, and, on the other hand, the singular law of the heavens, which is neither susceptible to universalisation nor interpretation. There exists an incompatibility between the law of the state, embodied in Creon's edict, and the law of the heavens, the Penates, which obliges Antigone to perform the funeral rites for her brother. One could interpret Antigone as prioritising the latter over the former, as maintaining her duty to the gods over her duty to the polis. Such an interpretation would be supported by Antigone's speech when brought before Creon and challenged for violating his decree in full knowledge of what she was doing.

> ... It wasn't Zeus, not in the least,
> who made this proclamation – not to me.
> Nor did that Justice, dwelling with the gods
> beneath the earth, ordain such laws for men.
> Nor did I think your edict had such force
> that you, a mere mortal, could override the gods,
> the great unwritten, unshakable traditions.
> They are alive, not just today or yesterday:
> they live forever, from the first of time,
> and no one knows when they first saw the light.
>
> These laws – I was not about to break them,
> not out of fear of some man's wounded pride,
> and face the retribution of the gods.
>
> (Sophocles, *Antigone*: 82, line 505)

One might argue that the dramatic tension of the play arises from the fact that there is no immediate solution to this conflict. While Antigone commits herself steadfastly to burying Polynices, to following 'the great unwritten, unshakable traditions' (Ibid.), Creon commits himself equally steadfastly to enforcing the law of the land. On the basis of such a reading, there is little to choose between the two characters. Both are in a position to appeal to a certain discourse on right or justice (Δίκη), each discourse being both irreducible to and incommensurate with the other. Without a further metadiscourse by which the discourses supported by Creon and Antigone might judged, there appears to be no means available to justify any choice between them. If there is no available means of justifying one law over the other, then, clearly, the ethicality of the characters' decisions, in such a reading, cannot lie in the possibility of their making the 'right' choice as such.

One problem that such a reading raises, however, is the status of the two laws invoked. Creon's law is not only inscribed by himself, but is done so on the basis of the authority vested in him, with appeal to prior law and in terms of what we might understand as the rule of reason. As King of Thebes, Creon is authorised to speak in the name of the people, to uphold and serve the common good. His edict would be understood, moreover, to be formed on the basis of established law; his edict that Polynices should remain unburied is the application of what Antigone herself refers to as 'the doom reserved for enemies' (Ibid.: 59, line 12) and, in Creon's eyes at least, Polynices, having raised an army against the city, would be considered such an enemy. In such an understanding, Creon's would not be a mere will for revenge but, rather, an attempt to maintain civil order and uphold the will of the populus. To honour a traitor and enemy of the city in the same way as one honours a defender of the city would be to defame the defender and, by extension, the city itself, the people of Thebes.

> His refusal to allow a sepulchre for Polynices, who is an enemy and a traitor to his country, is founded on the fact that one cannot at the same time honor those who have defended their country and those who have attacked it. From a Kantian point of view, it is a maxim that can be given as a rule of reason with a universal validity.
>
> (Lacan, 1992: 259)

This is a simple rule of difference, to honour both traitor and defender in the same way would be to extinguish the symbolic difference between them. It would be, in the language of ceremony, to say that they are the same and valued equally by the city with regard to which they would otherwise stand in different relations.

Against Creon's appeal to the authority vested in him, the support of the laws of the land and a certain rule of reason, we find Antigone's appeal to 'the gods, the great unwritten, unshakeable traditions' (Sophocles, *Antigone*: 82, lines 504–5). But, what, we might be justified in asking, are these unwritten and unshakeable traditions?

Lacan, in *The Ethics of Psychoanalysis*, argues that the divine source of the laws to which Antigone appeals cannot be understood by a contemporary audience or reader;

> we no longer have any idea what the gods are. Let us not forget that we have lived for a long time under Christian law, and in order to recall what the gods are, we have to engage in a little ethnography.

... In other words, this whole sphere is only really accessible to us from the outside, from the point of view of science and of objectification. For us Christians, who have been educated by Christianity, it doesn't belong to the text in which the question is raised. We Christians have erased the whole sphere of the gods. And we are, in fact, interested here in that which we have replaced it with as illuminated by psychoanalysis.

(Lacan, 1992: 259–60)

Lacan's point here would be that the laws of heaven invoked by Antigone would be ineffable. What we are confronted with in the play would then be the law of the polis, human law, on one side and some*thing* else on the other. In a contemporary understanding, such an opposition cannot be figured as two conflicting dialogues or interpretations of justice as this would be to impossibly recuperate the ineffable to language. It is as such that Antigone can further no argument in support of her cause, she cannot and does not attempt to justify her insistence on burying Polynices. She simply repeats her insistence.

Lacan's reference to Christianity here should remind us of his discussion of the Decalogue and Saint Paul, to, that is, the relation between law and desire. The law introduces a division which would be constitutive of desire. The immutable laws of heaven, which Antigone claims to follow, are situated beyond signification, beyond the laws of the community. As such, they are indicative of the limit point of signification and of civil law. What Sophocles, through Antigone, terms immutable laws of heaven would be another name for that which insists beyond the symbolic order. That is to say, Antigone can be understood as appealing to some*thing* in the Real. It is this aspect of Lacan's reading of *Antigone* which has perhaps encouraged a certain reading of the play as concerning Antigone's desire. Such a reading would hold the character of Antigone as exemplary of an ethics of desire, as the quintessential subject who does not cede on her desire. It is such reading that is advanced by Žižek.

For Žižek, the crucial aspect of both *Antigone* – the play – and Antigone – the character within the play – lies in what he, following Lacan (Ibid.: 282), terms her 'act' (Žižek, 2001: 165–78). The term 'act', in Lacanian theory, is differentiated from the sense of 'mere behaviour' (Lacan, 1977b: 50). What would differentiate the act from mere behaviour would be the location and persistence of desire. This is to say, the act is necessarily a subjective undertaking and it can be understood to be coterminous with the assumption of subjectivity and the responsibility entailed in such an assumption. Where behaviour might describe the response to needs, for example, the act is defined by the impetus of desire. Desire makes the subject act and, as such, the weight of responsibility for the act committed lies with the subject. Desire, as we have seen, cannot be treated as a given which would determine the subject's act without the subject's volition. The very subjectivity which would be taken to act cannot be described without the manifestation of desire which would allow its constitution. But such desire must always be particular to the subject; it is the subject's desire. The act would be the moment of subjective assumption in which the desire which is in one is manifest and thus brought into existence. The act in this sense should be understood to be coterminous with the emergence of desire; the act is desire made manifest.

As discussed in Chapter 6, and as Lacan insists immediately after his commentary on *Antigone*, the act necessarily involves a double instance of judgement. The subject, in acting, must make the judgement to act and the judgement of the act. Or, phrased otherwise, there is in the act both the judgement to act and the judgement to act in this particular way. As no rule exists to define how or when one must act, the weight of both moments of judgement must lie solely with the subject. That is, in acting, and in the moments of judgement indispensable to the concept of the act, the subject necessarily assumes the weight of responsibility for the choice to act. The act is then also contemporary with the possibility of the ethical.

For Žižek, Antigone's act at the beginning of the play is such a moment of an act in the full and properly Lacanian sense of the term. If 'the great unwritten, unshakeable traditions' (Sophocles, *Antigone*: 82, line 505) invoked by Antigone can be situated as indicative of her desire, then her act would be understood to be the manifestation and subjective assumption of this desire. There is in the act, says Lacan, always 'an element of structure, by the fact of concerning a real that is not self-evidently caught up in it' (Lacan, 1977b: 50). This would appear to correspond to the structure we encounter in Antigone. The laws of the gods 'speak' from beyond, that is, on the side of the Real. Which is, of course, to say they do not in fact speak at all. They are manifest in Antigone and given expression through her act in such a way that 'it isn't a question of recognising something which would be entirely given, ready to be coapted' (Lacan, 1988b: 229). In giving voice to the law of the gods, Antigone should be understood to have created and brought forth 'a new presence in the world' (Ibid.). She should, that is, be understood to have named her desire and, moreover, assumed herself as the cause of this desire.

The act, we can then see, is inextricably linked to the conception of the ethical as we have exposed it. It is with an emphasis on this ethical character of the act that Žižek interprets *Antigone* and, more precisely, Antigone.

For Žižek, Antigone functions as the ethical example *par excellence* insofar as she is understood to 'exemplify the unconditional fidelity to the Otherness of the Thing that disrupts the entire social edifice' (Žižek, 2001: 157). Capitalising the 'O' of 'Other' in the 'Otherness of the Thing', Žižek can be understood to be emphasising the *Thing*, *das Ding*, as it relates to the field of the symbolic. That is to say, *das Ding* as it would represent the limits of the symbolic field, *das Ding* as indicative of the insistence of the lack in the Other as it is experienced by the subject. It is as such that *das Ding* would be understood as (a name for) that which would disrupt 'the entire social edifice' (Ibid.).

The act, for Žižek, describes the moment of suspension of the symbolic, the recognition of the limits of the symbolic. In such a moment of recognition it is not that the Other would somehow be suspended to be subsequently resolved as a moment of a dialectic or integrated into a subsequent schemata. The act, for Žižek, is not a moment of *Aufhebung*. Rather, in the Žižekian act, one would assume the very location of the lack which persists in the Other;

> it is not so much that, in the act, I 'sublate'/'integrate' the Other; it is rather that, in the act, I directly 'am' the Other-Thing.
>
> (Ibid.: 160)

For Žižek, the ethical import of the act – and the act is, for Žižek, the very definition of the ethical moment – is separated from any notion of responsibility for or towards the other. His is not an ethics of responsibility but, rather, his understanding of ethics is as the momentary and, in the moment, absolute suspension of the symbolic order. The ethical act, for Žižek, is neither a response to the other nor a response to the Other.

> The (ethical) act proper is precisely *neither* a response to the compassionate plea of my neighbourly *semblant* (the stuff of sentimental humanism), *nor* a response to the unfathomable Other's call.
>
> (Ibid.: 161)

Žižek contrasts this notion of the 'ethical act' as assumption of the lack in the Other, as the assumption of the location of *das Ding*, with the Derridean notion of ethics as decision.

> The passive decision, condition of the event, is always in me, structurally, another decision in me, a rending decision as the decision of

the other. Of the absolutely other in me, of the other as the absolute that decides of me in me.

(Derrida in Žižek, 2001: 161)[6]

Žižek, rather than responding to Derrida's text here, appears to respond to Simon Critchley's commentary on it. For Critchley,

the political decision is made *ex nihilo*, and is not deduced or read off from a pre-given conception of justice or the moral law, as in Habermas, say, and yet it is not arbitrary. *It is the demand provoked by the other's decision in me that calls forth political invention, that provokes me into inventing a norm and taking a decision.* The *singularity* of the context in which the demand arises provokes an act of invention whose criterion is *universal.*

(Critchley, 1999: 277)

Žižek perceives in this passage, and by extension, in the Derridean original, '*two* levels of the decision' (Žižek, 2001: 162). It is with this bifurcation of the decision that Žižek takes issue. The decision, understood as the act, would, for Žižek, have to be such that the two moments of decision he perceives in Derrida's and Critchley's accounts would coincide. Here, Antigone is offered as the paramount example.

Is it not, rather, that her decision (to insist unconditionally on a proper funeral for her brother) is precisely an *absolute* decision in which the two dimensions of decision *overlap*?

(Ibid.)

Žižek's point here is that separating the decision into two moments, into, that is, the 'decision to decide' (Ibid.) and 'a concrete actual intervention' (Ibid.), is to render the decision or the act as non-absolute. That is, it is to render the act as less than an act. The act, for Žižek, as we have seen, is situated in the moment of suspension of the Other, what he terms directly '*being*' the '*Other-Thing*' (Ibid.: 163), the assumption by the subject of the irrecuperable rent in the social edifice. To

---

[6]The quotation as it appears in Žižek is cited as being taken from Derrida's *Adieu à Emmanuel Levinas* (p. 87) but appears to be taken from Critchley's translation as it appears in his essay 'The Other's Decision in Me (What are the Politics of Friendship?)', Critchley, 1999: 263. In English, the quotation from Derrida, with a slight difference in translation, is to be found not in *Adieu to Emmanuel Levinas* but in *Politics of Friendship*, Derrida, 1997: 68–9.

incorporate as a necessary aspect of the act its reinscription in the symbolic is, for Žižek, to miss the radicality of the act.

The question which insists here is that, in divorcing the act from any reinscription in the symbolic, is one not necessarily, from a Lacanian perspective at least, rendering the act as the impossibility of the ethical. Or, phrased otherwise, the act divorced from its reinscription is not party to a judgement which, in Lacan's understanding, would define the ethical;

> an ethics essentially consists in a judgement of our actions, with the proviso that it is only significant if the action implied by it also contains within it, or is supposed to contain, a judgement, even if it is only implicit. The presence of judgement in both sides is essential to the structure.
>
> (Lacan, 1992: 311)

Lacan's insistence upon there being two moments of judgement essential to the ethical functions to separate ethics, on the one hand, from mere behaviour and, on the other hand, from mere occurrence. What happens, in order to be understood to have happened to a subject and to be understood to have been caused to have happened by a subject, must entail a minimum inscription in the symbolic order, an inscription, that is, on the level of meaning. In order for an act to involve the responsibility which would render it ethical, this moment of inscription in meaning must be retroactively read into and assumed in the very decision to act. As we have seen in our earlier discussion of Lacan's invocation of Freud's *Wo Es war, soll Ich werden*, it is in the moment of the assumption of subjectivity that the subject retroactively reads its responsibility into its actions. The subject, in assuming itself, assumes responsibility for the act of its own emergence. The two moments of judgement on which Lacan insists as definitional of ethics cannot be reduced to a strict chronology. The two instances of judgement are, rather, indicative of two levels. The judgement to act, that it is necessary or desirable to act, necessarily entails the judgement that acting in *this* way is preferable to acting in *another* way; for example, by doing nothing. In so judging, the subject is necessarily creating a new norm, regardless of how contingent or particular such a norm may be. In judging, then, the subject must both inscribe its judgement or choice in the symbolic and assume utterly the weight of this judgement or choice. That is to say, the act, insofar as it is to be considered ethical, necessarily entails the assumption of responsibility in the field of the Other.

In this sense, Derrida's notion of 'the other's decision in me' is actually closer to Lacan's act than Žižek would have us believe (Stavrakakis, 2003). In Derrida's discussion of the decision in *Politics of Friendship* (1997) the emphasis is on the incommensurability of the decision to any traditional notion of subjective agency and the related notion of responsibility. Derrida's point is that a decision – in the classical sense of *dêcaedêre*, a cut, a break, an absolute decision, as opposed to a mere calculation which would unfurl on the basis of a prescription – is still necessarily understood in a context. This is precisely not to say that the decision is reducible to its context which would be to rejoin to the logic of a calculation. The decision must, rather, be seen as breaking from the context which would precede it and must be reinscribed in a context which would, then, be distinct from that which preceded it. It is the moment of responsibility here which would render the decision ethical and distinct from mere occurrence or behaviour. And it is the reinscription of the decision in the realm of comprehension which allows the subject to assume responsibility.

In contrast to a traditional notion of subjective agency, a subjectivity which, in Derrida's understanding, would be closed in on itself and thus incapable of responsibility, 'a subject to whom nothing can happen, not even the singular event for which he believes to have taken and kept the initiative' (Derrida, 1997: 68), Derrida posits the notion of the decision as signifying 'in me the other who decides and rends' (Ibid.).

> The passive decision, condition of the event, is always in me, structurally, another event, a rending decision as the decision of the other. Of the absolute other in me, the other as the absolute that decides on me in me. Absolutely singular in principle, according to its most traditional concept, the decision is not only always exceptional, *it makes an exception for/of me*. In me. I decide, I make up my mind in all sovereignty – this would mean: the other than myself, the me as other and other than myself, *he makes or I make* an exception of the same. This normal exception, the supposed norm of all decision, exonerates from no responsibility. Responsible for myself before the other, I am first of all and also *responsible for the other before the other*.
>
> (Ibid.: 68–9)

We might understand Derrida here as indicating that there is that in the subject which is irrecuperable to any sense of self-identity, that which would escape the monadology of the ego; the subject, that is, as inadequate to itself. The decision reduced to a moment of self-sufficiency of the subject would not be a decision in the traditional sense at all but would, rather, be contained as a moment of calculation, inextricable from the 'calculable permanence [which would] make every decision an accident which leaves the subject unchanged and indifferent' (Ibid.: 68). It is in contrast to this that the notion of the other's decision in me figures as the impossibility of self-identity, the rupture in the subject which can neither be contained nor recuperated. It is precisely from such a notion that Derrida adduces the possibility of responsibility.

Responsibility cannot remain responsibility when it is immersed in the pre-given. If subjectivity is closed upon itself, then responsibility cannot lie with the subject. The weight of the occurrence would rather remain with that system or field of understanding of which the calculation would be a moment. It is in response to the other, to 'the other in me', that responsibility becomes a possibility precisely because such a response cannot be contained within a pre-given system of knowledge.

> To give in the name of, to give to the name of, the other is what frees responsibility from knowledge – that is, what brings responsibility unto itself, if there ever is such a thing.
>
> (Ibid.: 69)

This is not, for Derrida, to separate responsibility in any absolute sense from knowledge, it is not to say that responsibility has nothing to do with knowledge. It is, rather, to point to the fact that, in the decision, as an ethical possibility, responsibility is impossible if the decision is reduced without remainder to knowledge.

> one *must* certainly *know, one must know it,* knowledge is necessary if one is to assume responsibility, but the decisive or deciding moment of responsibility supposes a leap by which an act takes off, ceasing in that instant to follow the consequence of what is – that is, of that which can be determined by science or consciousness – and thereby *frees itself* (this is what is called freedom), by the act of its act, of what is therefore heterogeneous to it, that is, knowledge.
> *In sum, a decision is unconscious.*
>
> (Ibid.)

Knowledge, for Derrida, is an indispensable prerequisite for the decision and, subsequently, for the assumption of responsibility but the decision cannot itself be reduced to knowledge without this rendering it 'less' than decisive, rendering it, that is, in the realm of pure calculation. On the other hand, without knowledge, there remains no possibility of responsibility insofar as responsibility would entail a context, a conception of that for and towards which one would be responsible and how. Responsibility thus figures and can only arise between the closed automaticity of the system of knowledge and the 'meaninglessness' which would be beyond any systemisation. Without exceeding knowledge, the decision is but a part of knowledge and thus not of the subject. Without returning to knowledge, the decision has no sense; it is purely arbitrary.

Is not this notion of the decision commensurate with the notion of the ethical in Lacan, with the notion of the ethical act as that which can appeal to no guarantor in the Other, as that which, by definition, takes place at the limits of the symbolic order, as that which cannot be reduced to the law and, yet, at the same time, must be inscribed in the symbolic order? Is not this commensurate with the notion of the ethical as a pulsational moment which emerges from, but must also assume a place in, the symbolic?

Contra Žižek's notion of the act which must be located absolutely beyond the symbolic order, both Derrida's decision and Lacan's act are such that, in order to be understood as ethical, they must entail a moment of (re)inscription in the order of the comprehensible, or, for Derrida, knowledge, and for Lacan, the symbolic. That is to say, in insisting on the exclusivity of what he terms identification with the 'Other-Thing' as the defining moment of the act, Žižek might be understood to precisely occlude the ethical potential from the act. Returning to Antigone, if, in Žižek's terms, her act is possible because of 'the *direct* identification of her particular/determinate decision with the Other's (Thing's) injunction/call' (Žižek, 2001: 163), then it is difficult to see in what sense such an act might be considered ethical.

It is, however, for Žižek, precisely this exclusivity, the radical suspension of the Other without recourse to a further moment of reinscription, which *does* render the act ethical. Antigone figures here as the paramount example of the act as a moment of absolute suspension. Antigone, for Žižek, 'does not merely relate to the Other-Thing, she – for a brief, passing moment of, precisely, decision – directly *is* the Thing, thus excluding herself from the community regulated by the intermediate agency of symbolic regulations' (Ibid.). It is in so excluding herself from the community, in situating herself beyond the regulations of the symbolic order, that Antigone can be understood, for Žižek, to have engaged in a proper act, precisely because the act, for

Žižek, is not simply 'beyond the reality principle' in the sense that it would be the engagement of a performative reconfiguration of reality, of, that is, the symbolic. Rather, the act is that which would '*change the very co-ordinates of the "reality principle"*' (Ibid.: 167). This is not to suggest that, for Žižek, the act entails a magical performance of the impossible. Žižek's point concerns the very structuration of what would be considered (im)possible in the first place. The radical character of the act lies in the fact that it would be that which alters the very contours of what would be considered possible. Or, in moral terms, it would not be that which would challenge the received notion of the good but rather it would be that which would fundamentally redefine what might be considered as good.

In this context, Žižek conceives of Antigone as an example of (ethical) civil disobedience. This is not to resort to the reading of *Antigone* as the story of a conflict between two notions of justice or two instances of the law. In Žižek's reading there is the law on the one hand – the sociopolitical world of Creon's city – and there is the suspension of this law or 'reality' on the other. That is to say, Žižek recognises Lacan's point that the 'unwritten, unshakeable traditions' (Sophocles: 82, line 505) invoked by Antigone should not be understood to constitute an alternative conception of justice or competing sense of law so much as that which would insist in her beyond the law. Antigone, in Žižek's reading, does not 'decide to disobey the positive law out of respect for a more fundamental law' (Žižek, 2001: 167), rather she 'defies the predominant notion of the Good' (Ibid.: 168).

Žižek explains this point in terms of the Platonic distinction between truth and doxa. Where for Plato, we might understand that doxa is insubstantial opinion, while the truth is universal, eternal and immutable, in Žižek's understanding, our conception of this distinction is reversed. That is, doxa would reflect how things 'really are' (Ibid.) in the sense that we would derive our notion of the Good or even our understanding of the world and the manner in which 'it works' from consensus, tradition or even opinion polls. Opposed to this, it would be the act which would intervene as the purely subjective and unique 'truth'. A 'truth' which is clearly, then, not 'true' in the Platonic sense of corresponding to some perpetual higher order but is rather 'true' in the sense of the moment of a pure creation which would 'expose' the conventions of knowledge to be inadequate and force their reconfiguration. For Žižek, the act would be such a truth insofar as the act would be that which would resist and refuse recuperation to the pre-existent symbolic matrix. Where something like a speech act would, by definition, rely 'for its performative power on the pre-established set of symbolic rules and/or norms' (Žižek, 1999: 263), the Žižekian act would signal a break with any pre-established or given order. This, for Žižek, would be 'the whole point of Lacan's reading of *Antigone*' (Ibid.). In his reading, Žižek emphasises Antigone's willingness to risk her 'entire social existence' (Ibid.), her defiance of the 'social-symbolic power of the City embodied in the ruler (Creon)' (Ibid.). Through so doing, Antigone could be understood to have entered the realm of 'symbolic death' (Ibid.), that is to say, she can be understood to have situated herself outside the symbolic space of what was, previously, her society. For Žižek, such a moment of self-expulsion is tantamount to a 'suspension of the big Other' (Ibid.), a radical break with and from the symbolic order.

In order to emphasise and clarify this radical character of the act, the fact that the act should be radically divorced from the symbolic, that it should be envisaged as irrecuperable to the symbolic, Žižek contrasts it with what he terms the performative 'staging' of revolt, or 'performative reconfiguration' (Ibid.: 264) of the symbolic order. Such performative reconfiguration would be exemplified in the position taken by Judith Butler in *The Psychic Life of Power* (1997) where she discusses the possibilities of subjective 'resistance to given forms of social reality' (Butler, 1997: 97). In *The Ticklish Subject* (1999) Žižek responds to Butler's advocation of forms of resistance which would successfully reconfigure and thus, contingently at least, offer the potential of ameliorating one's social condition(s), warning against the illusion of assuming to have successfully challenged from within that which is always already in a position to recuperate any such challenge. The distinction here, for Žižek, is that between a reconfiguration which would maintain the terms of the symbolic and a reconfiguration which would transform the very contours of the symbolic and, thus, transform the terms in which the reconfiguration might be understood;

> one should maintain the crucial distinction between a mere 'performative reconfiguration', a subversive displacement which remains *within* the hegemonic field and, as it were, conducts an internal guerrilla war of turning the terms of the hegemonic field against itself, *and* the much more radical *act* of a thorough reconfiguration of the entire field which redefines the very conditions of socially sustained performativity.
>
> (Žižek, 1999: 264)

Žižek's point can perhaps be illustrated in the common-place notion of reverse discrimination where the very points of discrimination are precisely upheld in the process of their supposed politically correct reversal. Some negative aspects of discrimination against 'the disabled', for example, may be addressed through the implementation of quotas for the employment of a certain percentage of 'disabled' workers but such regulation cannot but uphold the demarcation of certain people as 'disabled' and potentially stigmatised *and* maintain the significance of factors otherwise deemed 'irrelevant' to the criteria of employment or ability to 'do the job'. A position like Butler's entails, for Žižek, both an overestimation of the effectivity of 'performative reconfiguration' and an underestimation of the potential for the more thoroughgoing revolt which would be exemplified in the character and act of Antigone. For Žižek, it seems, it is this thoroughgoing rupturing status of the act with regard to the symbolic, the impossibility of situating the act in or recuperating the act to the symbolic which renders it ethical.

What, however, are we to make of Žižek's insistence on the act as irrecuperable to the symbolic? In the distinction that he puts forward between performative reconfiguration and absolute reconfiguration, one might be justified in asking how the latter might be possible. Clearly here Žižek is not suggesting that everything of the symbolic is razed. He is not suggesting, for example, that the Greek spoken in Thebes would cease to be spoken after Antigone's act. He appears, rather, to be suggesting that the meaning of the symbolic or social edifice is unavoidably altered. Emphasising the moral aspect, as Žižek does, this would mean, for example, not that the term 'good' could no longer be applied but rather that what would be understood by the term 'good' would have been altered. That is, the contours of the symbolic would have changed such that the relations between terms within the symbolic would have been altered. But is this the same as saying that the symbolic would have undergone a thorough revision? Or, to phrase the question slightly differently, how might one judge whether the change in the symbolic has been thorough enough to count in Žižek's schema as *thorough*? This brings us to a significant point concerning the symbolic which Žižek appears to glide over.

The symbolic order is necessarily experienced by the subject as Other, as an Other of which there is available no objective and totalising conception. That is to say, the symbolic as Other figures only insofar as it figures in relation to the subject who would encounter it. The symbolic order is a structural condition which, as it manifests for and in relation to the subject, can only be seen to exist insofar as it exists for that subject. Conjoined with this, the symbolic would be the field in which the subject would assume its constitution and, thus, from which it would retroactively posit its emergence. While, then, the symbolic and the subject obviously cannot be reduced to (aspects of) one another, neither can they, in this context, be separated from one another.

The conception of the act as a reconfiguration of the symbolic would then have to figure as a subjective undertaking. In terms of Antigone's act, the act would not only be Antigone's in the sense that she performs it but it would be hers in the sense that it is performed in relation to the symbolic order as it manifests for her. This would be to acknowledge that the act can only be experienced by the subject. But even in order for the subject to be understood to have experienced the act or to have experienced itself as acting this would necessitate the act's (re)inscription in the symbolic. The act, as coterminous with the assumption of subjectivity, is necessarily pulsational. One cannot (permanently) occupy the act.

We should perhaps remember here Lacan's claim from *Television* that 'Suicide is the only act which can succeed without misfiring' (Lacan, 1990: 43). Suicide would be such an act precisely because it is not, from the subjective perspective, reinscribed in the symbolic. There is in suicide no continuation, no possibility of recuperation by or to the symbolic, but also, quite clearly, there is no possibility of subjectivity either. That suicide is the only act which can succeed without misfiring is not to advocate suicide. It is, rather, to recognise the impossibility of other acts not misfiring. Suicide is the only act which would not entail a recuperation to the symbolic by the subject who would have committed it.

The point remains, however – even acknowledging this subjective relation to the Other – that any act at all, in Žižek's understanding of it, might figure as ethical even if this means that it only figures as ethical for the particular subject who has acted. Which is precisely to say that there is available no means to differentiate the ethical from the unethical. Does this mean that situating the act in exclusive relation to the symbolic cannot but render the ethics which might otherwise pertain to the act as purely arbitrary.

Invoking Kant, Žižek represents the 'proper ethical act' as 'doubly formal: not only does it obey the universal form of law, but this universal form is also its sole motive' (Žižek, 2001: 170). Moreover, the proper ethical act is inherently transgressive. It is not merely a matter of allegiance to a universal duty without pathological motives but it is an allegiance to a form of action which will redefine the very form of the prior conception of what would constitute the good, the norm, the symbolic order. Žižek's '*moral* law does not follow the Good – it generates a new shape of what counts as "Good"' (Ibid.). The proper ethical act is then, for Žižek, not so much defined by its irrational nature but is that which would institute a new conception or criteria for what counts as rational at all. Nothing which precedes an act is adequate to the task of judging the act.

What Žižek's description of the act omits is the crucial point that even that which would 'appear' to conform to the existent law might be an act. The act does not need to be 'transgressive' in the sense Žižek applies the term, which is to say that, because the existent norms are, or the existent system is, always already without adequate foundation, the act is always already, by definition, excessive with regard to the law. That is to say, the existent system cannot somehow be bracketed off such that only that which would appear to be transgressive of the system (providing that it is also enacted without pathological motives) is admissible as an ethical act. As the existent system itself is without adequate ground, that it can neither account for its own founding moment nor achieve any totality, even apparent adherence to the law, apparent maintenance of the system can be ethical as such adherence would still require the subject's assumption of, and as, the cause or justification of that existent practice or norm. It is in this sense, as we have seen before, that not only can the ethical not be reduced to the law, but neither can it be reduced to an aberration of the law.

As Žižek himself makes clear, the act is radically distinguished from 'a simple criminal violation' (Ibid.). This, not because the act is necessarily a violation without pathological intent or because the act is a violation in the name of a competing conception of right or justice but precisely because the act entails the assumption of cause by the subject without illusory appeal to some other foundation for action. It is in this sense that the act would be properly described as a suspension of the Other. The act is located at the limits of the authority of the Other, the act is the point of subjective intervention without appeal to anOther authority.

This is a point that can perhaps be deduced from Žižek's comments on the impossibility of coincidence between one's particular act or insistence, the fidelity to this or that cause, and the insistence of *das Ding*. This point in Žižek is somewhat obfuscated by his insistence on conflating the Other with the Thing. It is perhaps possible to clarify this point by allowing these two terms the specificity with which Lacan applies them. The Other, as we have seen, can be understood as coterminous with the symbolic order insofar as it manifests as a subjective experience. The Other, that is, is the symbolic order as it is, and with the specificity with which it is, encountered by the subject. *Das Ding* is that which cannot be recuperated to either the symbolic order or to the imaginary order. It is that of the Real which would insist at the limits of subjective experience. It is, in the context of the *Nebenmensch*, that of the other which cannot be accommodated to a point of recognition, that in the other which can neither form an aspect of identity nor be reduced to a point of signification. It is also, then, that in and of the subject which can neither be reduced to imaginary identification nor recuperated to a system of signification. What Žižek characterises as the insistence of 'the Other-Thing' (Ibid.: 165) would be more accurately described as that which cannot be recuperated to a whole, that in any encounter with the other and the Other which it is simultaneously impossible to recuperate to an understanding and is indicative of their lack. The call of the Other would thus be something like the *Che vuoi?* Where *Che vuoi?* might be understood, in this context, to be indicative of *das Ding*, insofar as *das Ding* would be that which might answer the question, which might satisfy the Other, insofar as *das Ding* would be a name for that which the Other is experienced as lacking.

It is clear then that, as Žižek appears to acknowledge, there is no possible correlation between the (particular) insistence of the subject in the act and the call of the Other. Similarly, there is no possible correlation between the (particular) insistence of the subject and *das Ding*. If there were, then this would be to say that, in the case of the former, the Other is no longer lacking and, in the case of the latter, the subject is no longer lacking. It is, again, in this sense that we can understand Lacan's comment that '[s]uicide is the only act which can succeed without misfiring' (Lacan, 1990: 43). It is not here that suicide would somehow be the only truly authentic ethical act. It is rather that it would be the only act which could be capable of not misfiring precisely because it is the only act which can be undertaken without the possibility or necessity of it being reinscribed in the symbolic. Suicide is the only act available to the subject which cannot result in a persistence of lack. Post-suicide, there is no subject to lack. And just as there is no subject, neither is there an Other for the subject; there is, that is, no symbolic order in which the act could be (re)inscribed.

The act should then be understood as the subject's always inadequate response to the Other (and the other). The act is the moment of production of some*thing* in response to the other and the Other, precisely in the sense that that some*thing* is not *the Thing*, is not adequate to *das Ding*. The act would be the moment of subjective assumption, the moment of the subject's causing its desire to come forth. But that desire is never something which would be 'entirely given' (Lacan,

1988b: 229). It is something which must be brought into the world anew. Insofar as the subject's act is to be understood, it must be reinscribed in the symbolic and, in being so inscribed, it necessarily alters the symbolic. It is in this sense that, as Žižek correctly notes, the act is a *creatio ex nihilo*. It is in the act that 'the subject creates, brings forth, a new presence in the world' (Ibid.). It must however by emphasised that it, the act, is commensurate with the moment of subjective assumption. That is, that the act is the act for the subject.

It is precisely for this reason that Antigone's act does not constitute the *exemplary* instance of the *ethical act*. Antigone, that is, cannot, and does not in Lacan's reading, function as an ethical example. The central significance of *Antigone*, the play, for Lacan, lies in the repeated motif of the limit. Importantly, the limit cannot be reduced to the simple limit 'between' the symbolic and the Real. It is also the limit of the imaginary.

The act is only an act for the subject who would have constituted itself in the act. The act is the subjective moment of assumption and is, thus, only experienced as such by the subject. This is not to argue that Antigone is a non-ethical example. It is rather to emphasise that the very concept of an ethical example is non-sensical. The ethical consists in the moment of assumption of and as the cause of one's existence as subject. It is availed of no exterior support or justification.

Lacan's reading of Antigone is not, then, concerned with the ethical status of her choice or her act. Lacan is rather concerned with *Antigone* as artefact, as a dramatic work, and with the work's relation to the spectator. Within the context of the play, Antigone, the character, functions as a spectacle. It is her splendour, not her act which has ethical significance. This, not because her splendour is in itself ethical but, rather, because the spectacle of Antigone forces a potentially ethical reaction from the audience.

One manner in which we might begin to appreciate Lacan's discussion of *Antigone* is in the relation between the imaginary, symbolic and Real. What one might term the conventional reading of *Antigone*, a reading which would interpret the play as staging the confrontation between two competing conceptions of justice, such as that presented by Hegel in *The Phenomenology of Mind* (Hegel, 1967: 484–99), is what we might characterise as a reading which prioritises the symbolic. Žižek's reading, which acknowledges the Lacanian point that the 'unshakeable traditions' (Sophocles: 82, line 505) might not refer to another conception of justice, is no less such a symbolic reading. In his interpretation, the act is defined exclusively in relation to the symbolic and thus Antigone's revolt is, for Žižek, a revolt against the symbolic. Against such exclusive prioritising of the symbolic, Lacan's own reading places considerable emphasis on the realm of the imaginary. This is not to suggest that Lacan's reading rebounds to another extreme. The point is, rather, that the three realms can never be fully disentangled, without engendering psychosis.

For Lacan, the significance of *Antigone* lies precisely in its ability to convey the limit point which would mark the intersection of the realms of the symbolic, the imaginary and the Real. It is crucial to acknowledge here that this limit point does entail but cannot be reduced to the limit of the symbolic. To so reduce the limit point to the gap where the symbolic opens onto the Real, to, that is, occlude the imaginary, results in those notions of the play as a contest or opposition between different approaches to the law or convention, whether this be in the sense of two competing conceptions of justice (Hegel) or between two competing approaches to the law, that is to say, between fidelity to the law and transgression of the law (Žižek). While such approaches are not without significant insights, it is only in reinstating the imaginary dimension that we can really begin to appreciate the ethical significance of the play. Those readings which would emphasise exclusively the rent in the symbolic cannot but render the play a discourse on law to the exclusion of the ethical. As such, the so-called ethical example of Antigone cannot but falter. Where there is no ethics, where ethics is foreclosed, there can be no example of the ethical. It is only in reintroducing the imaginary dimension that the ethical import of the play can be brought to light. It will, however, be brought to light in a manner which directly occludes the possibility of commandeering it as an example. That is to say, through Lacan's reading of *Antigone* we can begin to appreciate that the ethical avails itself of no examples.

As we have seen previously, the figure of the *Nebenmensch* entails for Lacan the correlation of the symbolic, the imaginary and the Real. The encounter with the other, that is, can be reduced to neither the dimension of the symbolic nor the imaginary but, rather, insofar as it entails both, it indicates the limit point where they would open onto the Real. That is to say, there is imaginary identification and there is symbolic comprehension, there is an overlap wherein imaginary identification would partake of a minimum of symbolic ordering and, beyond this, some*thing* insists which would refuse any such recuperation. This would be the limit point of what Lacan terms *das Ding*. For Lacan, '[i]t is around this image of the limit that the whole play turns' (Lacan, 1992: 268). The image of the limit is dispersed so thoroughly through the play that it, quite literally, cannot be contained. It cannot, that is, be recuperated to a straightforward symbolisation. The play, in this sense, demonstrates the insistence of the limit without itself becoming a self-contained discourse on the limit.

That the figure of Antigone might be held up as the focal point here is not to say that the limit is, exclusively, Antigone's. The motif and functioning of the limit is evident too in the other characters, the action and the setting of the play. The notion of the limit central to the play is, as Lacan stresses, not only articulated 'throughout the text of *Antigone*, in the mouths of all of the characters and of Tiresias' (Ibid.: 248), the seer or prophet who can be understood to signify the limit which would open onto the future, but also 'in the action itself' (Ibid.). One example of the functioning of the limit in the play would be the sentence passed on Antigone; that she is to be entombed alive. The sentence unfolds a complex array of instances of the limit. Not only is the sentence itself to place Antigone in the realm between life and death. She is to be placed in a chamber reserved for the dead while still alive, she is to be made to experience that which would be the reserve of the dead before she is dead. But, in addition, the passing of the sentence itself already situates her in a living relation to death such that her anticipation of certain death must be borne while she still lives. Hers is a 'situation or fate of a life that is about to turn into certain death, a death lived by anticipation, a death that crosses over into the sphere of life, a life that moves into the realm of death' (Ibid.).

What does make the character of Antigone stand out in the play is her beauty or, more precisely, her function as the beautiful, as that which would exceed the limits described in the play, the limits both of comprehension and of imagination. What makes the character of Antigone exceptional within the play is that she is presented as that which would be situated, impossibly, on the other side of the limit, in the realm of the Real. It is in this sense that Antigone comes to figure as or is raised to the status of *das Ding*. This is to say, in Lacan's terms, that Antigone is presented as 'inhuman' (Ibid.: 263). This is not, how-ever, to situate her as something monstrous or abhorrent. When the chorus describes her as ὠμός, a term Lacan translates as 'something uncivilized, something raw' (Ibid.), it, the chorus, is still intent on recuperation. To describe her as ὠμός would still be to situate her, to recuperate her to an idea. It would be to insist on situating her in terms of the symbolic. It is precisely insofar as Antigone cannot be situated, cannot be recuperated to a fixed idea, that she functions for Lacan as the beautiful. It is important here to grasp that the notion of 'beauty' is not meant to refer to any convention, any delimited conception of (what would count as) physical or idealised beauty (Ibid.: 297). Beauty cannot be captured in an image as such. Beauty is rather a function and to speak then of Antigone's beauty is to relate something of her function. That is to say, what is important in the character of Antigone is how she functions in relation to desire. Not, that is, how Antigone functions in relation to her desire but rather how Antigone, as beauty, functions in relation to the desire of the one who watches her, in relation, that is, to the desire of the spectator.

Significant here, then, is the relation between beauty and desire, a relation which Lacan describes as 'strange and ambiguous' (Ibid.: 238).

> On the one hand, it seems that the horizon of desire may be eliminated from the register of the beautiful. Yet, on the other hand, it has been no less apparent … that the beautiful has the effect, I would say, of suspending, lowering, disarming desire. The appearance of beauty intimidates and stops desire.
>
> That is not to say that on certain occasions beauty cannot be joined to desire, but in a mysterious way, and in a form that I can do no better than refer to by the term that bears within it the structure of the crossing of some invisible line, i.e. outrage. Moreover, it seems that it is in the nature of the beautiful to remain, as they say, insensitive to outrage, and that is by no means one of the least significant elements of its structure.
>
> (Ibid.)

The function of the beautiful here is extrapolated in terms of the work of art and it is as a work of art that both *Antigone*, as dramatic art work, and Antigone, as an artistic creation within that art work, would be understood to function in relation to desire. This mysterious relation between beauty and desire cannot be reduced to the idea that beauty would simply be that at which desire would aim. Rather, in relation to the object which would be constituted as an object of beauty, desire is split such that it is this very splitting which would constitute the object as beautiful. That would be to say, the object might only be understood as beautiful as an effect of the desire which would manifest in relation to it while, at the same time, as so constituted as beautiful, the object would necessarily also affect that desire. There is, here, no discernable and monolinear relation of cause and effect.

In its status as limit point, the beautiful is that which would split desire, or in the terminology of later Lacan, that which would render the separation and, at the point of separation, the conjunction of desire and the drive. Desire as we have seen, is that which defines the subject in relation to lack. Desire, as such, cannot attain satisfaction. The drive, on the contrary, is that which maintains satisfaction through continuously circulating its object. The beautiful is that which would encompass both such points, thus, simultaneously reflecting the drive and allowing it to continue on its route and drawing desire on. There is, thus, in the object of beauty both a moment of transfixion and a moment of satisfaction. If the object of beauty were capable of entirely satisfying desire it would be destructive of the subject but if it were incapable of providing satisfaction, it would lose its attraction. It is this conjunction of seemingly incommensurate characteristics which sets the beautiful apart.

Desire is thus not 'completely extinguished by the apprehension of beauty' (Ibid.: 249) but it is drawn on into that realm in which it could not subsist.

> It [beauty] seems to split desire as it continues on its way, for one cannot say that it is completely extinguished by the apprehension of beauty. It continues on its way, but now more than elsewhere, it has a sense of being taken in, and this is manifested by the splendor and magnificence of the zone that draws it on. On the other hand, since its excitement is not refracted but reflected, rejected, it knows it to be most real. But there is no longer any object.
>
> (Ibid.: 248–9)

Desire, as we have seen, has no object in the proper sense of the term. It is, in the terms of later Lacan, the drive which would take for itself, or which would be constituted in relation to, an object. The beautiful is unique in that it would allow for the conjunction of these two terms or, as Lacan has it in the context of *Seminar VII*, for the splitting of desire into that which will retain an object and that for which 'there is no longer any object' (Ibid.: 249).

It is as an example of the beautiful that Lacan reads *Antigone* and, particularly, within the play, Antigone. It is as such that, with Lacan, we find something in the text 'other than a lesson on morality' (Ibid.). This is not to claim that *Antigone* has, for Lacan, no ethical import. It is, after all, in the context of his seminar on the ethics of psychoanalysis that he spends considerable time discussing the play. It is rather to stress that the ethical import of the play lies not in the moralising arguments it might be understood to put forward, whether these be in the sense of a discourse between competing conceptions of the just or (moral) good or in the sense of an advocation of a position of transgression. While, as we have seen, both these positions are, of course, possible, neither addresses the question of ethics. They remain, rather, on the side of (questions of) the law. The ethical, as we have seen, is by definition a subjective moment, the moment of subjective assumption in response to the lack encountered in the Other and the other. The ethical, that is, is the moment of assumption of that point which refuses recuperation to an image or to a rule, that point where the symbolic and the imaginary break down or break open upon the Real. In terms of the moral law, the ethical is the point at which the subject assumes upon itself the impossible place of that which would guarantee the law. In terms of the imaginary, ethics is the response to that in the other which refuses recuperation to a coherent image of identification. To render *Antigone* or Antigone as an ethical example, or as *the* ethical example *par excellence*, is to assume to generalise that which is by definition beyond generalisation. That is to say, to confer upon Antigone the status of example would be to make of Antigone and her act a rule which might be followed; *thou shalt transgress the symbolic*. But such an example is clearly not an ethical example at all (de Kesel, 2002). The ethical moment would necessarily resist any such generalisation and return in the form of the necessity of the subject assuming upon itself the impetus to follow (or reject) the example. This is clearly, also, not to set *Antigone* apart. It is not especially that *Antigone* or Antigone's act cannot function as an ethical example. It is rather that the ethical cannot be exemplified without recuperating it to a law. Which is to say, precisely, without rendering it other than ethical.

What Antigone can function as is an example of the beautiful. But even here, it should be stressed that the example is not definitive. As Lacan stresses in a number of places, other examples can be found and the example should be one's own; '[i]f you don't find this example convincing, find others' (Lacan, 1992: 297). That is to say, Antigone functions as an example of the beautiful only insofar as she functions as the beautiful for the (particular) spectator. Insofar as she does function so, she and the play of which she is an element can be understood to situate the spectator in relation to their desire and *this* is what is significant in terms of ethics.

As beautiful, as that which would simultaneously reflect and lure our desire, Antigone would demand a response. This demand would be the subject's confrontation with the desire that is in it. That is to say, in its location at and as the limit point of the Real, as that at which desire would impossibly aim, the beautiful can be understood to be that which would ask of the subject, 'Have you acted in conformity with the desire that is in you?' (Ibid.: 314). As, that is, that which can simultaneously support and lure desire, that which allows the subject to confront *das Ding* without destroying it, the beautiful would be that which would allow the subject to confront the desire that is in it and thus begin to name this desire, to bring it into the world. That is to say, it is precisely insofar as the beautiful allows the possibility of encountering the limit of the Real without subsuming the subject in the Real and thus rendering the subject impossible, that it allows the subject the possibility of both confronting its desire and inscribing its desire in the symbolic.

It is in this sense that the beautiful would entail a cathartic function. The beautiful would allow the possibility of the purification of desire, not in the sense of allowing the subject to attain and occupy pure desire but in the sense of allowing the subject to experience its desire stripped of the trappings of the symbolic and imaginary orders and, significantly, to return to the symbolic and imaginary orders, bringing with it 'a new presence' (Lacan, 1988b: 229), something which cannot simply be accommodated as though it had always already been there.

We can see, then, that the ethical significance of *Antigone* lies not in Antigone's act in the sense that her act would function as the quintessential ethical example but, rather, the ethical significance of the play lies in the manner in which it would relate to the desire of the spectator.

The extent to which we can discuss Antigone's act at all is the extent to which it has been or is being (re)inscribed in the symbolic. This should alert us to the ambiguity of the act insofar as it can become a topic for discussion. Antigone's act, in the proper Lacanian sense, is *her* act. It is only available for her. What impacts of Antigone's act on others is either/both a moment of emergence of the Real and/or a symbolic recuperation depending on the moment of logical time from which it is perceived. That is to say, we might discern separate moments in Antigone's so-called act. There would be the moment of incomprehension, wherein the act disrupts and cannot be explained. There would also be the moment of comprehension, wherein the act is slotted into a framework of explanation – e.g. Antigone promotes an alternative discourse on what is just or, with Žižek, that Antigone constitutes the revolutionary stance *par excellence* precisely because she promotes no discourse on justice at all but is understood to have introduced a moment of radical disruption for the social weave of Thebes. Neither of these perspectives, however, can be adequate to the act as it is assumed by Antigone, if it is in fact an act at all. Given that she is never more than a fictional character, one might be justified in pointing out that 'she' cannot assume anything. The pertinent ethical question in *Antigone* is how we, the audience, the spectator, the reader, respond to and beyond the play. The only true act in *Antigone* is precisely not *in Antigone*, it is *in response to Antigone*.

12
Eating the Book

We have seen, then, that the notion of ethics which can be drawn from Lacan is such that the ethical can be reduced neither to an example nor to a prior prescription. It is such that what constitutes ethics or the ethical must reside always with the singular subject in question. Phrased otherwise, ethics, for Lacan, is reducible neither to a model which might be glorified, inflated or simply transposed beyond the particular context in which it might have occurred, nor to an abstraction and inscription which bears no, or no longer bears, any unique relation to any one context. The ethical cannot even be taken to reside in the particular context viewed as an empirical or objective event. The ethical can only ever come to be as that which is assumed by the subject and, thus, only ever *is* for that subject.

This manner of interpreting Lacan, and this manner of conceiving of the ethical, does appear to run the risk of opening itself to accusations of *anything goes*. If ethics cannot be ascribed beyond the unicity of the particular subject in question, then is not anything at all describable as ethical? It is simply a matter of what each subject perceives or chooses to perceive as ethical. To entertain such an accusation is, however, to impossibly abstract Lacan's conception of ethics from his conception of the subject as divided, barred or incomplete. The necessity of this division points to the fact that the subject only arises as a possibility within the realm of language, within the realm of the social, and is thus, while clearly irreducible to, also inseparable from the social order in which it emerges. In terms of ethics, then, this means that the ethical, as it is assumed uniquely by the particular subject, is still inevitably bound to the social order, the symbolic and consequently to others. The ethical cannot be ascribed beyond the unicity of the particular subject who would act, but neither can it be divorced from the insistence of the other implied in the social field.

Such an understanding of Lacan's ethics runs counter to the conception of Lacanian ethics as an 'ethics of the Real'. Towards the end of *The Ethics of Psychoanalysis*, Lacan invokes the famous notion of ceding on or giving way in relation to desire. Lacan's point here is often summarised as the imperative 'ne pas céder sur son désire' (e.g. Žižek, 1997: 239, and Zupančič, 2000: 238), a phrase Lacan himself does not actually employ. This has commonly been taken as the encapsulation of Lacan's stance on ethics, as his ethical imperative; do not give way on or do not give up on your desire. As desire would be taken to point to the Real, that is, as desire is such that it cannot, by definition, find its satisfaction within the symbolic, then the conception of ethics being advanced here must be one which prioritises the Real, which situates the Real as the proper realm of the ethical. What is not so clear here is what this would mean. The symbolic order is the place of the signifier, the place of language and thus can be understood as the place of rules, of systems, of codes, insofar as language itself is the fundamental instance of a coded, rule-based system and insofar as rules, systems and codes require some form of language in order to be articulated. To emphasise the Real in ethics, to describe ethics as *of the Real*, implies moving beyond signification, implies an ethics which resists comprehension, an ethics about which we could, quite literally, not know anything nor have anything to say.

In some regards, it is easy to see the attraction of an ethics of the Real. It pushes away from the symbolic, from the sense of domination by instituted norms and mores. But at the same time, it cannot help but float free in a realm of non-sense, a realm not only beyond good and evil, but a realm, by definition, beyond the ethical. Ethics may not be reducible to prior knowledge and preformed codes of practice, but what, to put it in a nutshell, is the sense of an ethics of which we can know nothing? This, however, is, arguably, for Lacan, to touch precisely upon the point. The ethical, for Lacan, emerges in response to a lack of knowing, but does not itself dispense with all knowledge. We can, *stricto sensu*, know nothing of the ethical but, at the same time, in order to function as a concept at all, the ethical must bear a relation to knowledge. It is in this gap between knowing and not knowing, between known and unknown, between knowledge and the impossibility of knowledge, that the possibility of the ethical emerges.

As we saw in Chapter 6, Lacan argues that ethics must contain within it two instances of judgement; judgement of the action under consideration and a judgement *in* the action under consideration. For Lacan, 'the presence of judgement on both sides is essential to the structure'

(Lacan, 1992: 311). The first of these judgements, the judgement of the action, entails a consideration of 'the relationship between action and the desire that inhabits it' (Ibid.: 313). That is, ethics can be understood as consisting in the judgement of an action insofar as that action embodies both a desire and the, at least implied, judgement of that desire. The clearest formulation of this latter judgement would be the question 'have you acted in conformity with the desire that is in you?' (Ibid.: 314). This is not, however, to impose from the outset the ethical response to the question. The important thing here is the consideration or work demanded by the question. The answer which unfolds in response will be unique for each subject.

Traditional morality, for Lacan, is the morality of power, the morality of the master. It is a morality which constrains and seeks to maintain order, safeguarding against the locus of 'the unthinkable' where 'the signifiers are unleashed' (Ibid.: 314), uncoupled from signification, where meaning is not a possibility. This morality of power has at root always the same agenda; to maintain the services of goods, to keep the social working and, thus, to sublate desire.

> As far as desires are concerned, come back later. Make them wait.
>
> (Lacan, 1992: 315)

The attempted sublation of desire is, however, not the negation of desire. Where there is the subject, there is desire. The very attempt to fortify ourselves against the unthinkable, the very desire to defer desire, cannot but attest to desire. The subject, for Lacan, is the subject of desire. It is only in relation to the signifier that the subject can come to be at all but, in so emerging, the subject is necessarily split. This inescapable 'break, splitting or ambivalence is produced in him at the point where the tension of desire is located' (Ibid.: 317). Traditional ethics, such as Aristotle's, which seek to maintain order and the service of goods, which keep the social functioning, utilise and rely upon an objective notion of guilt, insofar as there is a measure by which it can be judged whether one has acted correctly or not. For Lacan, while such ethics may function very well, and he is clear to point out that he is not dismissing them as such (Ibid.: 315), they necessarily occlude the subjective position which is inescapably a position entailing, and even defined by, desire. This is the meaning of the so-called maxim concerning ceding on one's desire.

For Lacan, the point is that, whatever the system, be it political, social or moral, there is still necessarily the subject of this system or for whom this system applies and, thus, there is always necessarily desire. However guilty someone may be judged by this or that system, the guilt which is felt by the subject is determined in relation not to a prior norm but in relation to desire; 'what a subject really feels guilty about when he manifests guilt at bottom always has to do with ... the extent to which he has given ground relative to his desire' (Ibid.: 319).

Far from being an ethical directive then, Lacan's use of the notion of giving ground relative to desire is concerned with subjective feelings of guilt. This, in itself, is scarcely an ethical proclamation. Rather, it can be understood as a meta-ethical or even socio-political comment. Traditional ethics concern themselves with the maintenance of order and the service of goods and tend to sublate desire to the greater good, however formulated. Desire, however, cannot be extinguished or dispensed with. Consequently, while the regime of traditional ethics continues to function, promoting the service of goods, the subject continues to desire in another field. Insofar as the subject is subjected to and subordinate to the service of goods, the maintenance of the social order, he or she is liable to give ground relative to his or her desire and consequently to feel guilty. Or to put it another way, it is this giving ground which explains why the subject experiences such feelings of guilt.

The point here for Lacan is not, then, an ethical or moral directive, a maxim which states that one *must* not cede on one's desire. The ethical point is to assume the position of responsibility with regard to the choice of whether to give ground with regard to this or that desire and, crucially, to assume responsibility for having given ground when one does. The service of goods by which Lacan characterises traditional ethics, is one wherein desire is subjected to an accounting. That is to say, one deliberates or calculates when to follow one's desire and when to cede on it. To pursue one's desire, however, carries a cost; it is 'not a path one can take without paying a price' (Ibid.: 323). Key to this position relative to desire is that, in choosing to cede, it is a subjective choice to have ceded.

> One knows what it costs to go forward in a given direction, and if one doesn't go that way, one knows why. (Ibid.)

Crucial here is an appreciation of the nature of desire. To interpret ceding on one's desire as renouncing this or that desired object is to miss the point. What is being referred to as ceded or not is desire itself, not the particular and contingent object of desire. Lacan clearly defines desire here as 'the metonymy of our being' (Ibid.: 322), referring to the fact that we are desiring subjects or we are only subjects insofar as we desire. It is, arguably, in locating this desire which goes so far in defining us that Lacan indicates what can be understood as the centrality of the Real to questions of ethics.

> The channel in which desire is located is not simply that of the modulation of the signifying chain, but that which flows beneath it as well; that is, properly speaking, what we are as well as what we are not, our being and our non-being – that which is signified in an act passes from one signifier of the chain to another beneath all significations. (Ibid.)

The path of desire, the channel in which it is located, cannot be reduced to the language in and through which we live. It is, however, inseparable from language. Desire and, more specifically, the direction of desire, is not simply a function or facet of the symbolic order but neither is it conceivable outwith the symbolic order. There is in any significant act, in any act which would be understood to be meaningful or to have meaning, that which necessarily escapes signification. This would also, then, be to say that there is necessarily something in the subject which escapes signification. As Lacan put it in his remarks made at the 1960 Bonneval Colloquium, four months after the close of the seventh seminar, the subject 'is what the signifier represents, and the latter cannot represent anything except to another signifier' (Lacan, 1995: 265). In this process of signification, the subject is that which 'disappears beneath the signifier that he becomes' (Ibid.). It is, possibly, references such as this to the beneath of the signifying chain which allows the interpretation of Lacan's ethics as *of the Real*. If ethics concerns the maintenance of desire and desire follows a path beyond signification, beyond the confines of the symbolic order, as desire is what defines the subject, is the metonymy of our being, then the path of desire is also, by definition, a path the subject follows in not ceding on its desire. This would lead the subject into the Real, as that which lies beyond the symbolic. The Real emerges as the site of the ethical beyond signification.

Such an understanding necessarily misses two points. When Lacan refers to the channel in which desire is located, he points out not only that it entails that which 'flows beneath' the signifying chain, but also that it implies 'the modulation of the signifying chain' itself (Lacan, 1992: 322). That is to say, it is not possible to reduce desire or, by extension, to reduce the ethical to the Real without distorting what is at play here. To occlude the modulation of the signifying chain from the realm of the ethical is to determine the ethical as strictly meaningless, obscure and forever beyond reach. This is not, clearly, to recourse to the other extreme where we would seek to encapsulate ethics in precise formulations to be applied at all times and all situations. The point is that without retaining a relation with knowledge, with the social, with the symbolic, what would be termed the ethical is utterly devoid of meaning. This links to the second point which is easily missed in the notion of an *ethics of the Real*; the ethical as Lacan sees it is not concerned with maintaining desire. The ethical is concerned with recognising desire for what it is and with the assumption of responsibility for and as the cause of the desire that is in one. Which is also then to say that ethics for Lacan must relate to a knowledge of desire. This relation is exposed in Lacan's discussion of sublimation and the notion of eating the book.

The concept and function of sublimation may be more conventionally situated in discussions of aesthetics than ethics, however, Lacan seeks to conjoin an aspect of aesthetics and ethics insofar as he considers the former as revealing a crucial phase of the latter (Ibid.: 159). Sublimation is thus rendered as 'one of the phases of the function of the ethics' (Ibid.) and not as it is more commonly understood as a super-egoistic defence mechanism. In its commonplace interpretation, the Freudian concept of sublimation is generally understood as entailing 'the substitution of a culturally valorized object for one that is immediately gratifying sexually' (Copjec, 2002: 39). That is, sublimation is a defence mechanism which keeps the subject on the social straight and narrow. The libidinal energies which would, in terms of *Ichziele*, seek satisfaction in sexual release, are channelled elsewhere. The classic illustration of the rechannelling or substitution would be the great artists;

> [Sublimation] enables excessively strong excitations arising from particular sources of sexuality to find an outlet and use in other fields, so that a not inconsiderable increase in psychical efficiency results from a disposition which in itself is perilous. Here we have one of the origins of artistic activity.
>
> (Freud, 1953b: 163)

For Freud, the very possibility of sublimation only arises due to the 'very incapacity of the sexual instincts to yield complete satisfaction' (Freud, 1953c: 259). It is, at the same time, the function of sublimation which allows the emergence of the super-ego as a force of conscience and morality, in that it is through the libidinal cathexes of the Oedipus complex being 'abandoned, desexualised and in part sublimated' (Freud, 1953d: 341) that the nucleus of the super-ego is formed. The very characteristics of the super-ego, then, for Freud, would be tied to the process or function of sublimation which can then be seen to facilitate a 'victory of the race over the individual' (Ibid.). That is, sublimation is here characterised as one phase of the functioning of what Lacan has characterised as traditional ethics, in that it has the function of carrying out the command, 'As far as desires are concerned, come back later. Make them wait' (Lacan, 1992: 315).

Lacan seeks to clarify this standard interpretation or understanding of sublimation. As he rather pithily puts it;

> Sublimation is not, in fact, what the foolish crowd thinks; and it does not on all occasions necessarily follow the path of the sublime. The change of object doesn't necessarily make the sexual object disappear.
>
> (Ibid.: 161)

In terms of our understanding of ethics, and the manners in which it relates to desire, the central issue here is the meaning of 'the change of object'. Lacan's point is that it is in fact the changing of the object itself which would define sublimation, not the object to which the aim is 'diverted';

> sublimation is the satisfaction of the drive with a change of object, that is, without repression. This definition is a profounder one, but it would also open up an even knottier problematic, if it weren't for the fact that my teaching allows you to spot where the rabbit is hidden.
>
> In effect, the rabbit to be conjured from the hat is already found in the instinct. This rabbit is not a new object; it is a change of object in itself.
>
> (Ibid.: 293)

This does not mean, as Copjec has interpreted it, that sublimation is defined in the mutation of the object, in the alteration of that object which was already aimed at, the 'fact' that the 'object of the drive is never identical to itself' (Copjec, 2002: 39). It is rather to emphasise the very process of change which occurs with regard to the object.

> It is change as such. I emphasise the following: the properly metonymic relation between one signifier and another that we call desire is not

a new object or a previous object, but the change of object in itself.

(Lacan, 1992: 293)

It is the changing of the object, the process or *act* of change, which is significant here. Desire arises as the metonymic relation between one signifier and another which would be to say, again, that the subject, which is by definition the subject of desire, is what the signifier represents to another signifier (Lacan, 1995: 265). This is not to suggest that desire is the process of metamorphosing the object – which would be the interpretation implied in Copjec's reading – but rather that, in the process of moving from one object to another, we find desire in its purity. That is to say, in changing, desire undergoes catharsis. It is sublimated or, in the Latin root, *sublimationem*, purified. Desire does not find its proper object in the new object. It is not that desire was somehow aimed incorrectly, an error to be rectified in the location of the 'correct' object. It is rather that, in undergoing change, desire is experienced in its proper sense as the moment of change. Such would be the moment of traversing the fantasy, of the subject's locating themselves as the cause of their desire in place of *objet petit a*. Sublimation, in Lacan's understanding of the term, does not, then, mean that the object must be changed or mutated. It means, rather, that desire can only be experienced when the object is no longer confused as or with the true source of satisfaction, when, that is, the object is no longer assumed to be the cause of desire.

In experiencing or recognising desire *qua* desire, beyond the misrecognition of this or that object as the object of desire, the subject would not simply be recognising that which was there all along but neither would they be venturing headlong into the desert of the Real. The process or act of recognising desire, the sublimation of desire, is a creative process. In *Seminar II*, in the context of discussing the resistance of the analysts and the mistake of interpreting desire as the desire for this or that object, and thus leading the subject to believe that what they desire is a particular sexual object, Lacan clearly spells out the creative, nominative aspect of recognising desire;

> what's important is to teach the subject to name, to articulate, to bring this desire into existence, this desire which, quite literally, is on the side of existence which is why it insists. If desire doesn't dare to speak its name, it's because the subject hasn't yet caused this name to come forth.
>
> That the subject should come to recognise and to name his desire, that is the efficacious action of analysis. But it isn't a question of

recognising something which would be entirely given, ready to be coapted. In naming it, the subject creates, brings forth, a new presence in the world.

(Lacan, 1988b: 228–9)

This creative aspect of recognising desire allows us to better appreciate the relationship between desire and language, between desire and the symbolic order. It is not that desire is *of the Real* and can be simply made to fit in the symbolic. Desire can only be recognised by being named, which is to say that it can only be recognised under the condition that the subject work on it and that it can only be recognised within the symbolic order. This creative work of bringing desire forth is conterminous with the act of sublimation. It is also, then, conterminous with the emergence of subjectivity and with the responsibility which would describe the possibility of the ethical. In recognising and naming desire, the subject relies upon the symbolic matrix. In so doing, the subject, and the desire which is the condition of its possibility, emerges as that which one signifier represents to another and, at the same time, in an aphanisic movement, the subject fades again beneath the signifying chain. The notion of eating the book is introduced here to illustrate this emergence of the subject and, consequently, to clarify the significance of the symbolic order, and thus of knowledge, to Lacan's conception of ethics.

> Think of the shift from a verb to what in grammar is called its complement or, in a more philosophical grammar, its determinative. Think of the most radical of verbs in the development of the phases of the drive, the verb 'to eat'. There is 'eating'. That is how the verb, the action, appears head-first in many languages, before there is any determination as to who is involved. Thus one sees here the secondary character of the subject, since we don't even have the subject, the something that is there to be eaten.
>   There is eating – the eating of what? Of the book.

(Lacan, 1992: 293–4)

Grammatically, a complement is that which would be added to the verb to form a complete predicate. Thus, a simple sentence, would comprise of;

(grammatical) subject + verb + complement

Or, following the example used by Lacan, we would have;

you [the implicit subject] + *eat* [the verb] + *the book* [the complement].

Lacan's point here appears to be that without the complement, there is no subject. Without that which would be desired, there is no subject. As we have seen previously, desire is the condition of subjectivity. Between the verb and the complement, the subject arises.

In the example 'eat the book' we have on the one hand an illustration of the emergence of subjectivity between the two signifiers, the subject as that which is represented by one signifier to another, between 'eating' and 'the book'. On the other hand, as Lacan marks this example as paramount, we have an indication of the functioning of the drive here. The verb 'to eat' is 'the most radical of verbs in the development of the phases of the drive' (Ibid.: 294).

The reference here to eating, to the oral drive, should alert us to the notion of incorporation and remind us of the consumption of the primal father in the myth of the primal horde. It is, according to Freud, through the act of devouring him that the band of brothers accomplish their identification with the father and it is through this process that the law and social ordering is inaugurated (Freud, 1950: 141–2). Incorporation entails the process of identification wherein it is possible for the subject to emerge in the field of the Other, in the symbolic order.

That a book 'isn't really made to be eaten' (Lacan, 1992: 322) serves to emphasise once again the proper definition of sublimation; that it is not primarily concerned with the change in object but rather with the change in aim. Entailed in this understanding of sublimation is 'a passage from not-knowing to knowing' (Ibid.: 293). The book here should be understood to be synonymous with or indicative of the processes of signification, the field of knowledge. In emphasising the consumption of the book, Lacan would be indicating that the subject would be that into which the book would be incorporated. But, as the subject would be that which would only arise as a possibility on the basis cf the signifying chain which would produce it, the subject is also that which would be produced through this process. The subject, that into which the book would be incorporated, is also that which would be constituted in the process of this very incorporation. This is the instance of *Wo Es war, soll Ich warden*; Where it was, there must I come into being. The change in aim, the catharsis or sublimation of desire, is the assumption by the subject of itself in the place of the cause of the desire which is in it, the subject's situating of itself as the cause of its own desire. The constitution of the subject as that which would 'eat' is also the aphanisis of the subject as that which will have 'eaten'.

> When I ate the book, I didn't thereby become book any more than the book became flesh. The book became *me* so to speak.
>
> (Lacan, 1992/1986: 322)

In eating the book, the subject enters the symbolic realm. It is neither that the signifiers become 'flesh' here, that the symbolic order is somehow subsumed into the subject, as though the subject were a pre-given entity, nor is it that the subject constituted in the process becomes a mere part of the signifying order. It is rather that the book becomes *me* ('*me* devient' (Lacan, 1986: 371)), that is, in process of consumption, in the passage from *being* to *meaning*, the subject arises, constituting itself in and with the field of knowledge that would be its. In the terms of the *vel of alienation,* this would be to say that the signifying order does not consume the realm of being any more than the realm of being consumes the signifying order but, rather, that in the process of sublimation, in the process of subjective assumption, the two converge in the constitution of the subject which cannot exist outwith either but can neither be reduced to either. Such a process also necessarily entails the renunciation of a certain *jouissance,* of the mythical wholeness which will be taken to have been prior to one's emergence in the field of the symbolic.

> But in order for this operation to take place – and it takes place everyday – I definitely have to pay a price. Freud weighs this difference in a corner of *Civilization and Its Discontents.* Sublimate as much as you like; you have to pay for it with something. And this something is called *jouissance.* I have to pay for that mystical operation with a pound of flesh.
>
> (Lacan, 1992/1986: 322)

In terms of morality, then, it makes no sense to consider the originary or innate goodness of humanity or of this or that particular individual. But neither does it make sense to consider the innate goodness of this or that *book,* that is to say, this or that form of knowledge or prescription. The book which will be incorporated is never *it,* is never adequate. The ethical moment is purely subjective and, as Lacan stresses, one will have to pay for it. It is not already, and cannot already, be formulated in the symbolic order as one would encounter it but, rather, it entails the separation from and return to and, thus, change in and in relation to, the symbolic.

Prescription, the realm of knowledge, can provide the service of goods, can provide, that is, particular satisfactions which would conform to its contours. What it cannot do is account for and thus provide for that which would exceed its own limitations; desire, the desire of the subject. Whatever the prescription, whatever the strategy, whatever the concrete implemented and instituted form of the good, this or that particular body of law, it is always and necessarily inadequate to the moment of subjective emergence, to the subject's assumption of responsibility as the cause of its own emergence and desire.

> Of him who ate the book and the mystery within it, one can, in effect, ask the question: 'Is he good, is he bad?' That question now seems unimportant. The important thing is not knowing whether man is good or bad in the beginning; the important thing is what will transpire once the book has been eaten.
>
> (Ibid.: 325)

This is therefore to say that ethics cannot be reduced to a certain knowledge. To so reduce ethics would be to seek a guarantee where no guarantee can be attained. The systems of thought, the socio-political systems and the laws they would institute can neither satisfy, capture or dispel desire. Desire may be sublimated in the Freudian sense of being diverted into other socially acceptable pursuits, but such a process or function only serves to lose touch with desire;

> the desire of man, which has been felt, anesthetized, put to sleep by moralists, domesticated by educators, betrayed by the academies, has quite simply taken refuge or been repressed in that most subtle and blindest of passions, as the story of Oedipus shows, the passion for knowledge.
>
> (Ibid.: 324)

This is, at the same time, not to divorce ethics from knowledge. It is rather to indicate the endlessness of the process and the necessity for involvement in this ever continuing process. Knowledge itself cannot (successfully) pretend to completion or totalisation. Knowledge is necessarily open, even when it purports to be closed and completed, insofar as it cannot account for its own limitations or the insistence of that which lies beyond its limits. It is this essential breach in the system which can be understood as the possibility of the subject's arising and which can, in turn, be understood as the possibility of the ethical as the subject's assumption of responsibility for its own constitution, its response to the infinite which escapes the confines of, and insists at the limits of, the system in and with which it finds itself. As outwith any system of thought or body of knowledge, outwith the symbolic order, there is no possibility of the subject being at all, any such encounter with the infinite beyond the system necessarily requires a return to the system, a return in the terms of the system without this suggesting that the system itself remains unaffected. In this movement of encounter and return, we can situate the ethical as an aphanisic moment, a moment of assumption, but a moment which cannot be occupied as such, a moment which must, rather, be repeated, but repeated each time anew. The moment here requires both the possibility of perpetually inadequate knowledge and the possibility of the perpetual encroachment of the incomprehensible. It requires both the symbolic and the Real, with the emphasis strongly on the conjunction.

It is, then, in the sublimation of desire – in the process of recognising and changing the aim of desire, in giving meaning to desire – that an ethical position, however fleeting, becomes possible. Desire is neither reducible to nor maintainable outwith the order of the symbolic, the rules and language in which it could be given meaning, a meaning which in turn would never be adequate to it. Desire is not 'entirely given' (Lacan, 1988b: 229), its articulation is not and cannot be predetermined, insofar as it is not reducible to the available language in which it would be articulated. Desire is not 'ready to be coapted' (Ibid.), not ready to be fit seamlessly into the symbolic order. And yet, the only possibility of its articulation is in the terms, in the context, of the symbolic order. In so articulating its desire, the subject is, thus, by necessity, reconfiguring the terms of the symbolic order, reconfiguring its relation to and within the symbolic order. The subject is giving meaning to, developing a knowledge of, a desire which, up until then, strictly had no meaning, was meaningless. To situate ethics as of the Real would be to seek to occupy and celebrate this meaninglessness, would be to refuse knowledge while at the same time purporting access to knowledge of such a refusal. Ethics can neither be of the Real, of the symbolic nor of the imaginary but can only be of the conjunction between these, can only be, that is, *of the subject*.

References

Aquinas, St. T. (1988) *On Politics and Ethics*, trans. ed. P. Sigmund. London: W.W. Norton and Company, Inc.

Arendt, H. (1973) *The Origins of Totalitarianism*. New York: Harvest.

Aristotle (1996) *The Nicomachean Ethics*, trans. S. Watt. Ware: Wordsworth.

Badiou, A. (1998) *Petit manuel d'inésthétique*. Paris: Seuil, quoted in Hallward, P. (2003) *Badiou: A Subject to Truth*. Minneapolis: University of Minnesota Press.

Badiou, A. (2001) *Ethics: An Essay on the Understanding of Evil*, trans. P. Hallward. London: Verso.

Bernheimer, C. and Kahane, C. (eds) (1985) *In Dora's Case: Freud· Hysteria· Feminism*. London: Virago.

Boothby, R. (2001) *Freud as Philosopher: Metapsychology After Lacan*. London: Routledge.

Butler, J. (1997) *The Psychic Life of Power*. Stanford: Stanford University Press.

Copjec, J. (2002) *Imagine There's No Woman: Ethics and Sublimation*. Cambridge: MIT Press.

Critchley, S. (1999) *Ethics-Politics-Subjectivity*. London: Verso.

de Kesel, M. (2002) 'Is Not Antigone a Proto-Totalitarian Figure?: On Slavoj Žižek's Interpretation of Antigone', paper at Globalization … and Beyond Conference, Rotterdam, June 2002, unpublished ms.

Derrida, J. (1992) 'Force of Law: The Mystical Foundation of Authority', trans. M. Quaintance, in Cornell, D., Rosenfeld, M. and Carlson, D.G. (eds) (1992) *Deconstruction and the Possibilities of Justice*. London: Routledge, pp. 3–67.

Derrida, J. (1997) *Politics of Friendship*, trans. G. Collins. London: Verso.

Descartes, R. (1993) *Meditations on First Philosophy*, trans. D.A. Cress. Indianapolis: Hackett.

Evans, D. (1996) *An Introductory Dictionary of Lacanian Psychoanalysis*. London: Routledge.

Fink, B. (1995) *The Lacanian Subject: Between Language and Jouissance*. Princeton: Princeton University Press.

Freud, S. (1950) *Totem and Taboo*, trans. J. Strachey. London: Ark.

Freud, S. (1953a) *On Sexuality*, trans. J. Strachey. London: Penguin.

Freud, S. (1953b) 'Three Essays on the Theory of Sexuality', in Freud, S. (1953) *On Sexuality*, trans. J. Strachey. London: Penguin, pp. 33–170.

Freud, S. (1953c) 'On the Universal Tendency to Debasement in the Sphere of Love', in Freud, S. (1953) *On Sexuality*, trans. J. Strachey. London: Penguin, pp. 243–60.

Freud, S. (1953d) 'Some Psychical Consequences of the Anatomical Distinction Between the Sexes', in Freud, S. (1953) *On Sexuality*, trans. J. Strachey. London: Penguin, pp. 323–44.

Freud, S. (1966) *A Project for a Scientific Psychology* in *The Complete Works of Sigmund Freud, Vol.1: Pre-Psychoanalytical Publications and Unpublished Drafts*, trans. J. Strachey. London: Hogarth.

Freud, S. (1973) *New Introductory Lectures on Psychoanalysis*, trans. J. Strachey. London: Penguin.

Freud, S. (1977) 'Fragment of an Analysis of a Case of Hysteria', in Freud, S. (1977) *Case Histories I*, trans. J. Strachey. London: Penguin.

Freud, S. (2001a) *Beyond the Pleasure Principle, Group Psychology and Other Works*, trans. J. Strachey. London: Vintage.

Freud, S. (2001b) 'On Narcissism: An Introduction', in *The Standard Edition of the Complete Psychological Works of Sigmund Freud Vol. XIV*, trans. J. Strachey. London: Vintage, Hogarth Press.

Freud, S. (2002) *Civilization and Its Discontents*, trans. D. McLintock. London: Penguin.

Glynos, J. (2000) 'Sex and the Limits of Discourse', in Howarth, D., Norval, A.J. and Stavrakakis, Y. (eds) (2000) *Discourse Theory and Political Analysis: Identities, Hegemonies and Social Change*. Manchester: Manchester University Press, pp. 205–18.

Hegel, G.W.F. (1967) *The Phenomenology of Mind*, trans. J.B. Baillie. New York: Harper and Row.

Hume, D. (2002) *Enquiries Concerning Human Understanding and Concerning the Principles of Morals* (3rd Edition). Oxford: Clarendon Press.

Husserl, E. (1991) *Cartesian Meditations: An Introduction to Phenomenology*, trans. D. Cairns. London: Kluwer Academic Publishers.

Johnston, A. (2001) 'The Vicious Circle of the Super-Ego: The Pathological Trap of Guilt and the Beginning of Ethics', in *Psychoanalytic Studies*, Vol.3, Nos.3/4, 2001, pp. 411–65.

Kafka, F. (1992/1914) 'Before the Law', trans. W. and E. Muir, in *Kafka: The Complete Short Stories*. London: Minerva.

Kant, I. (1965/1787) *Critique of Pure Reason*, trans. N. Kemp Smith. New York: St. Martin's Press.

Kant, I. (1993) *Grounding for the Metaphysics of Morals*, trans. J.W. Ellington. Indianapolis: Hackett.

Kant, I. (1997) *Critique of Practical Reason*, trans. M. Gregor. Cambridge: Cambridge University Press.

Kierkegaard, S. (1995/1847) *Works of Love*, trans. H.V. and E.H. Hong. Princeton: Princeton University Press.

Lacan, J. (1977a) *Écrits: A Selection*, trans. A. Sheridan. London: Routledge.

Lacan, J. (1977a(i)) 'Aggressivity in Psychoanalysis', in Lacan, J. (1977) *Écrits: A Selection*, trans. A. Sheridan. London: Routledge, pp. 8–29.

Lacan, J. (1977a(ii)) 'The Mirror Stage as Formative of the Function of the I as Revealed in Psychoanalytic Experience', in Lacan, J. (1977) *Écrits: A Selection*, trans. A. Sheridan. London: Routledge, pp. 1–7.

Lacan, J. (1977a(iii)) 'Function and Field of Speech and Language', in Lacan, J. (1977) *Écrits: A Selection*, trans. A. Sheridan. London: Routledge, pp. 30–113.

Lacan, J. (1977a(iv)) 'The Freudian Thing, or the Meaning of the Return to Freud in Psychoanalysis', in Lacan, J. (1977) *Écrits: A Selection*, trans. A. Sheridan. London: Routledge, pp. 114–45.

Lacan, J. (1977a(v)) 'The Agency of the Letter in the Unconscious or Reason Since Freud', in Lacan, J. (1977) *Écrits: A Selection*, trans. A. Sheridan. London: Routledge, pp. 146–78.

Lacan, J. (1977a(vi)) 'The Signification of the Phallus', in Lacan, J. (1977) *Écrits: A Selection*, trans. A. Sheridan. London: Routledge, pp. 281–91.

Lacan, J. (1977a(vii)) 'On a Question Preliminary to Any Possible Treatment of Psychosis', in Lacan, J. (1977) *Écrits: A Selection*, trans. A. Sheridan. London: Routledge, pp. 179–225.

Lacan, J. (1977a(viii)) 'Subversion of the Subject and Dialectic of Desire', in Lacan, J. (1977) *Écrits: A Selection*, trans. A. Sheridan. London: Routledge, pp. 292–325.

Lacan, J. (1977a(ix)) 'The Direction of the Treatment and the Principles of Its Power', in Lacan, J. (1977) *Écrits: A Selection*, trans. A. Sheridan. London: Routledge, pp. 226–80.

Lacan, J. (1977b) *The Four Fundamental Concepts of Psychoanalysis*, trans. A. Sheridan. London: Penguin.

Lacan, J. (1982) 'Intervention on Transference', trans. J. Rose, in Mitchell, J. and Rose, J. (eds) (1982) *Feminine Sexuality: Jacques Lacan and the École Freudienne*. London: Macmillan, pp. 61–73.

Lacan, J. (1986) *Le Séminaire de Jacques Lacan, Livre VII: L'Éthique de la psychanalyse, 1959–1960*, ed. Jacques-Alain Miller. Paris: Éditions du Seuil.

Lacan, J. (1988a) *Freud's Paper on Technique: The Seminar of Jacques Lacan, Book I, 1953–1954*, trans. J. Forrester. New York: Norton.

Lacan, J. (1988b) *The Ego in Freud's Theory and in the Technique of Psychoanalysis: The Seminar of Jacques Lacan, Book II, 1954–1955*, trans. S. Tomaselli. New York: Norton.

Lacan, J. (1989) 'Science and Truth', trans. B. Fink, in *Newsletter of the Freudian Field 3*, pp. 4–29.

Lacan, J. (1990) *Television*, trans. D. Hollier, R. Krauss and A. Michelson. New York: Norton.

Lacan, J. (1992) *The Ethics of Psychoanalysis: The Seminar of Jacques Lacan, Book VII, 1959–1960*, trans. D. Porter. London: Routledge.

Lacan, J. (1993) *The Psychoses: The Seminar of Jacques Lacan, Book III, 1955–1956*, trans. R. Grigg. London: Routledge.

Lacan, J. (1995) 'Position of the Unconscious', trans. B. Fink, in Feldstein, R., Fink, B. and Jaanus, M. (eds) (1995) *Reading Seminar XI, Lacan's Four Fundamental Concepts of Psychoanalysis*. New York: SUNY Press, pp. 259–82.

Lacan, J. (1998) *Encore – On Feminine Sexuality, The Limits of Love and Knowledge: The Seminar of Jacques Lacan, Book XX, 1972–1973*, trans. B. Fink. New York: Norton.

Levinas, E. (1969) *Totality and Infinity*, trans. A. Lingis. Pittsburgh: Duquesne University Press.

Miller, J.A. (1987) 'Les responses du réel', in *Aspects du malaise dans la civilization*. Paris: Navarin Editeur.

Miller, J.-A. (1994) 'Extimité', in Bracher, M., Alcorn, M.W. Jr., Corthell, R.J. and Massardier-Kenney, F. (eds) (1994) *Lacanian Theory of Discourse: Subject, Structure and Society*. New York: NYUP, pp. 74–87.

Mitchell, J. and Rose, J. (eds) (1982) *Feminine Sexuality: Jacques Lacan and the École Freudienne*, trans. J. Rose. London: Macmillan.

Neill, C. (2005) 'The Locus of Judgment in Lacan's Ethics', *The Journal of Lacanian Studies*, Vol.3, Number 1.

Neill, C. (2006) 'An Idiotic Act: On the Non-example of Antigone', *The Letter*, Issue 34.

Neill, C. (2006) 'Choang-tsu's Butterfly: Objects and the Subjective Function of Fantasy', *Objects: Material, Psychic, Aesthetic*, a special issue of *Gramma: Journal of Theory and Criticism*, Vol.14.

Nietzsche, F. (2001/1886) *Beyond Good and Evil*, trans. J. Norman. Cambridge: Cambridge University Press.

Plato (1992) *Republic*, trans. G.M.A. Grube, rev. C.D.C. Reeve. Indianapolis: Hackett.

Plato (1994) *Symposium*, trans. R. Waterfield. Oxford: Oxford University Press.

Rimbaud, A. (1963) *Oeuvres complètes*. Paris: Gallimard.

Sophocles (1984) *The Three Theban Plays: Antigone, Oedipus The King, Oedipus at Colonus*, trans. R. Fagles. London: Penguin.

Stavrakakis, Y. (1999) *Lacan and the Political*. London: Routledge.

Stavrakakis, Y. (2003) 'The Lure of Antigone: Aporias of an Ethics of the Political', *Umbr(a)*, in press.

Žižek, S. (1989) *The Sublime Object of Ideology*. London: Verso.

Žižek, S. (1997) *The Plague of Fantasies*. London: Verso.

Žižek, S. (1999) *The Ticklish Subject: The Absent Centre of Political Ontology*. London: Verso.

Žižek, S. (2001) *Did Somebody Say Totalitarianism?* London: Verso.

Žižek, S. (2002) 'Afterword', in Žižek, S. (ed.) (2002) *Revolution at the Gates: Selected Writings of Lenin from 1917*. London: Verso

Zupančič, A. (2000) *Ethics of The Real: Kant, Lacan*. London: Verso.

The European Convention on Human Rights and Its Five Protocols (1950) www.hri. org/docs/ECHR50.html#Convention (accessed 14.01.03).

The Holy Bible, Authorised King James Version (1956). Glasgow: Collins.

The Hebrew Bible (1922). Cambridge: The British and Foreign Bible Society.

The New English Bible (1970). Oxford: Oxford University Press, Cambridge University Press.

Index